The Economics
of Soviet Bloc Trade
and Finance

About the Book and Author

Reflecting Professor Holzman's recent important work, this book deals with major issues relating to both East-West and intrabloc trade. Professor Holzman explores the transition in Soviet bloc economies over the past fifteen years from balanced hard-currency trade to large deficits with the West and the consequent development of a huge hard-currency debt. He compares the causes and treatments of deficits in planned economies with those in market economies and explores the dramatic differences in foreign trade behavior exhibited by Eastern and Western nations and the difficulties that arise when these conflicting systems interact in world markets. He also assesses the impact of Western economic warfare on the Soviet Union and makes recommendations for future U.S. trade policy.

The author next turns to the issue of intrabloc trade. In its early years the USSR economically exploited the smaller East European nations, but many argue that the Soviet Union now subsidizes trade with its partners in the Council for Mutual Economic Assistance in exchange for political, military, and ideological support—an argument that Professor Holzman strongly challenges. He also contends that CMEA, when viewed as a preferential trade group or customs union, has been markedly unsuccessful. On another level, Professor Holzman assesses the causes and possible cures for the serious, chronic problems related to currency inconvertibility, rigid bilateralism, and inability to use exchange rates as tools of economic adjustment.

In an international economy growing ever more interdependent, the issues raised in these previously uncollected essays will continue to gain in importance as East and West meet in trade.

Franklyn D. Holzman is professor of economics at Tufts University and a research associate at the Russian Research Center, Harvard University.

The Economics of Soviet Bloc Trade and Finance

Franklyn D. Holzman

Westview Press / Boulder and London

Copyright © 1987 by Westview Press, Inc., except for Chapter 1, which is in the public domain

Published in 1987 in the United States of America by Westview Press, Inc.; Frederick A. Praeger, Publisher; 5500 Central Avenue, Boulder, Colorado 80301

Library of Congress Cataloging-in-Publication Data
Holzman, Franklyn D.
    The economics of Soviet bloc trade and finance.
    Includes index.
    1. Europe, Eastern—Commerce. 2. Finance—Europe,
Eastern. 3. Balance of payments—Europe, Eastern.
I. Title.
HF3496.5.H62   1987   382'.0947   86-32598
ISBN 0-8133-7274-7

Printed and bound in the United States of America

The paper used in this publication meets the requirements of the American National Standard for Permanence of Paper for Printed Library Materials Z39.48-1984.

10   9   8   7   6   5   4   3   2   1

To Mathilda

Contents

Acknowledgments

In writing the articles reprinted in this volume, I benefited from the suggestions of many of my colleagues. Their help was acknowledged in the original articles at the time of publication and, with gratitude, is acknowledged again. I am further indebted to Tom Wolf for suggestions regarding the Introduction. Pat Callahan and Rosie Condon good-humoredly bore the burdens of typing and other logistical problems connected with preparing the manuscript, for which I am very grateful. Finally, my wife, Mathilda, a former economist, often helped me think through issues. In addition, she willingly accepted the reduction in quality of life usually entailed by the creation of a spouse's book. To her the book is lovingly dedicated.

Franklyn D. Holzman

Introduction

The USSR, the first Communist nation and destined to be the first centrally planned economy (CPE), came into being in 1917. In the years just after World War II, the number of European Communist nations with planned economies increased to eight—and since then still other nations around the world have adopted similar economic systems. The existence of these nations has provided a field day for academics, especially political scientists and economists. The nations represent, in effect, a new field on which we can apply our theories, concepts, and techniques. The situation is analogous to the opportunity provided to an anthropologist who finds a "lost" tribe with an unknown language and culture; an archeologist who stumbles on and begins to excavate a lost city; or a geologist with first access to the rocks brought back from the moon.

Planned economies are very different from market economies (MEs), and understanding the principles by which planned economies operate has required considerable study by western economists. The international economic relations of countries with planned economies are especially interesting. Imagine nations whose currencies are totally inconvertible; who have no use for tariffs; who conduct trade virtually without reference to exchange rates; and who, when they trade with one another, bilaterally balance their accounts! How could an economist with some training in international economics resist studying nations with such eccentric foreign trade behavior?

My first work, however, was not on Soviet bloc foreign trade but rather on international economic theory and inflation theory as applied to western market economies. I probably would have been interested in studying the Soviet economy, but the question never arose. My interest in the USSR was kindled during World War II, at which time, through no choice of my own, I was assigned by the U.S. Air Force to a joint U.S.-Soviet airbase in the Ukraine, where I remained for more than a year—until the war ended. The opportunity to study the Soviet economy came when, in 1949, I was offered a fellowship by the newly established Russian Research Center at Harvard University to write my doctoral dissertation. I chose to write on Soviet finance rather than on trade because the problems of the former appeared much more interesting (e.g., a CPE with control over prices experiencing open inflation in the 1930s!) and because current data on finance were available whereas there were almost no current data on Soviet trade; moreover, the idiosyncratic features of Soviet trade (noted above) had not yet become visible. By the late 1950s I had become bored with Soviet finance and had returned to work on western trade and inflation problems when, under Nikita Khrushchev, the Soviets began to publish handbooks of statistical data including the annual foreign trade returns. Furthermore, partly as a result of the rapid expansion of Soviet bloc trade, interesting economic problems had begun to surface.

So, in about 1958, I began to research Soviet bloc trade and finance. Over the next decade and a half, I wrote numerous articles and a book (*International Trade Under Communism*). In 1974, seventeen of those articles were republished in book form by Harvard University Press; to provide a framework for the essays, I included a substantial introduction that was based on a survey of most of the major postwar writings in the field. Since that volume was published, there have been many new developments in both East-West and intrabloc trade and finance. These new developments, along with much unfinished work on earlier problems and ideas, have led to an outpouring of books and articles by both eastern and western economists as well as to the articles collected in this volume. While I hope that the remarks that follow will provide background and framework for understanding the articles included here and will also illuminate both their virtues and limitations, they should not be taken to be a comprehensive review of the literature.

Balance of Payments Problems and Adjustment Mechanisms

Very little was written on balance of payments problems and economic adjustment mechanisms of the nations belonging to the Council for Mutual Economic Assistance (the CMEA or Comecon nations) before 1970, undoubtedly due largely to the fact that before 1970 CMEA nations did not seem to have balance of payments problems. By and large, they paid their way in trade with the West, generating small deficits and very modest external debts. Moreover, virtually all intra-CMEA trade was bilaterally balanced, a situation compelled by the extreme inconvertibility of CMEA currencies (see Chapters 4 and 8). Obviously, the "balance" in intrabloc trade reflected, and still reflects, not economic adjustment but the use of direct government controls over trade flows. The smallness of the hard currency deficits of the CMEA nations before 1970 likewise was brought about by repression of import purchases and did not reflect the excess demand that undoubtedly existed for western products (and credits). That this was the case is evidenced by the sharp increases in hard currency imports and external debt with the advent of détente. Clearly, the volume of East-West trade is heavily dependent on the political climate.

Many explanations have been proposed to explain balance of payments problems of market economies, and it is useful to look at some of those explanations for purposes of comparison. In market economies, changes in imports and exports are functions of rates of change in gross national product (GNP) levels and in prices of tradables; thus, it is often possible to attribute deficits in particular nations to relatively high rates of inflation or rapid rates of economic growth. In theory, of course, balance of payments equilibrium could be maintained, despite rapid growth and/or inflation, under a flexible exchange rate regime. Conversely, under fixed exchange rates, a major cause of persistent deficits has been the maintenance by governments of overvalued currencies. Moreover, in recent years, the United States has had an overvalued exchange rate and huge trade deficits despite a fairly flexible exchange rate regime. This has been the result of large net capital inflows caused by much higher interest rates in the United States than in other major trading nations. Balance of payments problems are also caused by so-called structural changes. Nations that exhaust their supplies of major natural resource exports may have balance of payments problems until they are able to adjust; such a situation may also exist when newly developed substitutes capture part of the market held by old products (e.g., synthetic fibers vs. silk and cotton). Similar to structural causes are difficulties caused by price shocks. Over the past fifteen years, the huge increase in the price of oil caused serious payments problems among oil importers, while the sharp drop in the price of oil over the past few years has caused serious problems among those oil exporting nations that had restructured their economies to be dependent upon the new, much higher level of foreign exchange earnings.

The centrally planned economies suffer balance of payments problems for many of the same reasons. Romania's balance of payments has been hurt by the gradual exhaustion of its oil resources and loss of exportable oil surpluses. Hungary and several other Eastern European nations faced serious payments problems after oil prices rose in 1973 and 1979, and the USSR faced rapidly shrinking foreign exchange earnings in the early 1980s with the fall in oil prices—oil revenues at that time accounted for 60 percent of its hard currency receipts. Another example:

CPE imports are also a function of changes in the growth of GNP, although not necessarily to the same extent as in MEs. A rise in GNP will lead to an increase in imports of essential intermediate products required as inputs. It need not, however, lead to an increase in imported consumers' goods, since in CPEs all imports are under government control. Although an increase in GNP does tend to lead to some increase in CPE imports, a relative (to world prices) increase in CPE domestic prices, if such occurred, would not lead to a fall in exports and rise in imports, and hence to a worsening balance of payments, as is the case with MEs. The CPEs, with their irrational domestic prices, inconvertible currencies, and nonfunctioning exchange rates, conduct foreign trade at world prices quite unrelated to domestic prices (Chapter 8).

There are several factors that lead to the hard currency payments deficits systemic to the CPEs, as discussed in Chapter 1. For example, the absence of functional exchange rates leads CPEs to underestimate the cost of imports and, therefore, to over-import. The situation is analogous to that of an ME with an overvalued exchange rate. Fortunately, an ME can eliminate the problem by devaluation; unfortunately, a CPE cannot.

The persistence of excess demand plays an important role in the balance of payments problems of CPEs, adversely affecting payments both directly and indirectly. In Chapter 1, excess demand is attributed to overfull employment planning. While this is true of the Soviet Union and was true of all the CMEA nations in the early postwar period when Stalinist methods of planning were closely copied, in more recent years some of these nations have avoided setting such ambitious goals. Nevertheless, excess demand still characterizes many CPEs, generated, for the most part, in the industrial sector by plant managers who have been motivated to secure the resources needed to increase investment above planned amounts (see Hewett [1981] on Hungary and Montias [1981] on Poland). This practice has produced the same effects on external payments as overfull employment planning.

One important cause of the serious deficits in the late 1970s in many of the CMEA nations is not discussed in Chapter 1. It was also neglected by East European planners, by U.S. bankers who loaned money to Eastern European enterprises, and possibly by Western European bankers as well. Until the Eastern European debt crisis developed in the late 1970s, it was considered sound policy for Eastern Europe to borrow money from foreign banks and governments as long as the funds were invested "productively."[1] This faith was badly misplaced, as has been widely known since the publication some forty years ago of a classic article by J. J. Polak (1943). Polak demonstrated that for a nation to be able to service its foreign debt, it must invest in activities that will generate the necessary foreign exchange—that is, invest in activities that substitute for imports and/or increase exports. In the case of CPEs, of course, a further constraint is that import-substitution and export-promotion must be directed at hard currency, not intra-CMEA markets, because the latter are balanced by direct controls. Although every CMEA nation put some investments into import-substitution and export-promotion, they did not pursue these policies with the necessary intensity, at least not until some nations were in a near-crisis situation (Snell, 1974, pp. 688–689; Crawford and Haberstroh, 1974, p. 38; Chapter 2 below). Moreover, in some cases, investment based on imports required increased hard currency imports of inputs on a continuing basis.

As noted above, the CMEA nations incurred very little hard currency debt before 1970. In 1971, the gross debt of the USSR was $1.8 billion and that of Eastern Europe, $6.1 billion. When their hard currency financial assets are taken into account, their net debts were $0.6 billion and $4.9 billion, respectively (CIA, *Handbook*, 1985, pp. 48, 73). However, Soviet gross debt rose to $10.5 billion in 1975 and $17.8 billion in 1980. The comparable Eastern European figures were $23.2 and $66.1 billion. The 1980 figures are near the peak, and for all nations but Poland the 1984 debt was either about the same or a little less than that in 1980. Stabilization of this debt in the early 1980s was due not to an increase in exports but to a decline in imports, which represented, among other things, serious belt-tightening. Between 1980 and 1983, Eastern European exports actually declined by $1.5 billion, whereas imports declined by $10 billion. The decline in imports was encouraged, of course, by the growing reluctance in the early 1980s of the western industrial nations to lend money as freely as before, especially after Poland and Romania were forced to reschedule their debt service payments and Hungary came very close to having to do the same.

As the current account deficits and resulting outstanding foreign debts of the CMEA nations rose during the 1970s, questions were raised as to whether the debts were serious and whether they should be evaluated by the same criteria as those of capitalist nations. In Chapter 2, written in 1976, this and related questions are considered. At the time, most western analysts were quite optimistic about the creditworthiness of the CPEs, an optimism reflected in the continued expansion, until 1980, of substantial medium- and long-term credits from western bankers. The CPEs had always paid their bills, and they did so on time. Further, western analysts felt that the Soviet Union would always come to the aid of a socialist nation faced with default, the so-called umbrella theory. This theory was subsequently refuted by Soviet unwillingness or inability to guarantee the debt services of North Korea, Romania, and, especially, Poland. A novelty of the approach used in Chapter 2 was the treatment of the debt problems of CPEs as "transfer" problems and the use of the "absorption" approach for their evaluation. In transfer problem terms, the CPEs (and all other nations with large external debts) are viewed as facing two distinct problems. First, in order to service or repay debt they must divert additional resources from current domestic use. This turns out, algebraically, to be a smaller problem for CPEs than for capitalist nations simply because hard currency trade is only a small part of the total trade of CPE nations. Second, they must use these resources to generate a hard currency export surplus by either reducing imports or expanding exports. This aspect of the problem was evaluated in terms of elasticity analysis and found to be much more stubborn, implying potentially large secondary burdens of transfer. Surprisingly, the analysis also demonstrated that the fact that CPEs cannot devalue their currencies has second-best effects that reduce the secondary burden of transfer. By selectively lowering export prices as a substitute for devaluation CPEs reap the gains of a discriminating monopolist.

In the introductory section of Chapter 2, the reader is warned that the basic aim of the discussion is methodological and that many of the empirical estimates and judgments are "casual." This turned out to be a proper warning. The data presented in Table 1 are now dated, and many are misleading. In particular, the data refer to the mid-1970s and provide no hints of the rapid rise in debt that followed over the next five years.[2] Analytically, perhaps the major omissions were the failure to anticipate the degree of ineptness with which many of the CPEs, especially Poland, would manage their external economic relations with the West and the rapidity with which their hard currency payments balances would deteriorate.

Since Chapter 2 was originally published, much has been written on creditworthiness and the hard currency debt problems of the CMEA nations. Balance of payments models and projections have been made for the Soviet Union (Grossman and Solberg, 1983); for Poland, Hungary, and Romania (Crane, 1985); and for all CMEA nations (Zloch, forthcoming). Following the pioneering work of Avramovic (1964), Grossman and Solberg (1983) and Crane (1985) attempted to estimate the degree of "compressibility" of imports in the Soviet Union and Eastern Europe, respectively; their models also assess the impact on the domestic economies of efforts to meet debt service obligations and to improve current account balances. Some indication of Eastern Europe's ability (necessity) to "compress" imports is conveyed by the one-third cut in hard currency imports implemented there between 1980 and 1983. Numerous recent articles on Eastern Europe's balance of payments problems appear in

Joint Economic Committee volumes (1981, 1986). One of the best studies of Soviet payments problems is that by Portes (1983).

Portes also wrote an important, pioneering paper (1980) in which he developed a detailed macroeconomic model of a traditional CPE. The focus of this model is the interrelationship between internal and external balance. Portes used the model to explore the choices facing the planners, given their goals, when external disturbances lead to internal and/or external imbalances. Portes' paper is discussed in Chapter 3; his model is compared with the analogous Swan and Mundell models of market economies. The extent to which various policy variables chosen by Portes reflect reality is also considered.

The volume in which Portes' paper was first published (Neuberger and Tyson, 1980) is largely devoted to the adjustment mechanisms of CPEs to international economic disturbances. Especially noteworthy are Wolf's paper, which explores the adjustment mechanisms of small, partially decentralized planned economies (so-called modified CPEs, or MCPEs) such as Hungary;[3] an overview paper by Neuberger and Tyson; and a taxonomic paper by Tyson and Kenen. Although all of the remaining papers in the Neuberger and Tyson volume are interesting, one cannot avoid mentioning Treml's paper because it seriously challenges the conventional wisdom that Soviet trade participation is extremely low. The validity, interpretation, and policy implications of Treml's estimates are still being debated (see, e.g., Vanous, 1982).

Many other articles and a few books have appeared on the subject of internal-external adjustment—some theoretical, others econometric. Brada'a article (1982) is a good example of the former; SOVMOD (Green and Higgins, 1977), of the latter.[4]

Foreign Trade Behavior and Commercial Policies

The basic idea of Chapter 4, which deals with the foreign trade behavior of CPEs, came to me in Geneva in the summer of 1963 while I was serving as a consultant to the UN Economic Commission for Europe in preparation for the first United Nations Conference on Trade and Development (UNCTAD). My assignment was to devise ways of facilitating East-West trade, concentrating, in particular, on the obstacles presented by eastern practices. As a first step, it seemed reasonable to try to understand why CPE foreign trade behavior differs from that of market economies—why, for example, tariffs either are not used or have no effect; currencies are incurably inconvertible; exchange rates are not functional; trade participation ratios are low; exported manufactured products are of poor quality; and so forth. It quickly became clear that foreign trade of CPEs should be viewed as an extension of their domestic economies and that most foreign trade behavior could be deduced by (1) looking at the major features of a centrally planned economy, which relies heavily on direct controls to implement plans, and (2) taking into account nationalism and each nation's interest in maximizing its sovereignty. I first published these ideas in 1966; Chapter 4 is an improved and updated version. It is possible, incidentally, to use the same model to deduce much of the foreign trade behavior of market economies.[5]

In a major empirical and methodological paper, Hewett (1980) also examined the impact of central planning on foreign trade. In addition to analyzing the impact on the level and country composition of trade (two aspects discussed in Chapter 4), he also dealt with the impact on the commodity composition of trade. In all instances, he summarized and criticized the empirical literature on the subject. In the case of the commodity composition of trade, he examined the interesting work of van Brabant (1973), who not only analyzed the impact of "system" on commodity composition of trade, but also did seminal research on "structural bilateralism." (The latter refers to the fact that the CPEs, with the exception of the USSR, bilaterally balance trade separately among so-called soft and hard goods[6] in addition to bilaterally balancing trade total with one another.)

The major foreign economic policy issue that the western industrial nations have faced in their relations with the eastern bloc involves export controls, the subject of Chapter 5. There are several reasons why export controls dwarf other East-West commercial policy issues in importance. First, given the political tensions and the arms race between East and West since the end of World War II, export controls over military and military-related goods were inevitable and bound to be prominent. Second, because the western industrial nations have been more advanced in technology than the eastern nations, and because gains from importing technology are believed by many to be greater than the gains from other types of imports, there has been considerable sentiment, in the United States at least, to restrict export of products embodying advanced technology to the eastern nations to prevent them from reaping unduly large gains from trade. Such gains were even proscribed (in the U.S. Trade Act of 1962)[7] on the grounds that economic strength translates into potential military power.

Concern with relative gains from trade has always played a much greater role in U.S. policymaking toward the Soviet Union than toward other nations. In general, nations assume that world prices represent appropriate terms of trade and do not stop to ask if country B is gaining more from a transaction than they are[8]—any more than a retailer worries whether the consumer surplus experienced by a particular customer is too large and whether that customer should be charged more than other customers or not be allowed to make the purchase. Of course, relative to almost all other nations, the Soviet Union stands to gain little from trade; its vast size and wide variety of resources make it relatively self-sufficient. In contrast, think of the plight of Japan if it could not import petroleum. And what would happen to the British metallurgical and cotton textile industries if the British were unable to import iron ore and cotton? Of if Great Britain could not import food, think of the drop that would occur in its per capita GNP as, of necessity, agriculture crowded out many other industries! In comparison, the losses to the USSR (and the United States) from not being able to trade are very modest. Not only are the gains per dollar of trade smaller for these two nations, their trade participation ratios (X/Y or M/Y) are also relatively low.[9]

Aside from the moral issue, gains from trade are important because they provide a clue to the susceptibility of a country to linkage and leverage and to economic warfare. The greater the gains from trade, the more effectively foreign trade can be employed as either "carrot" or "stick." There was, for example, enough carrot in the U.S.-USSR Commercial Agreement of 1972 in the form of most-favored-nation (MFN) status and the promise of huge U.S. investments in Siberian oil and gas that the Soviets were willing to agree to a lend-lease debt settlement and to an increase in Jewish emigration, on an informal basis, to about 50,000 persons a year. There was not enough carrot left, however, to keep the Soviets from canceling the agreement after (1) the Jackson-Vanik Amendment to the U.S. Trade Act of 1974 formalized into law the Soviet obligation to allow liberal emigration and (2) the Jackson-Vanik and Stevenson amendments sharply cut back the scale of possible U.S. investment, not to mention investment in Soviet energy projects.

With the exception of grain exports, U.S. nonmilitary export controls have focused on machinery and equipment, especially machinery and equipment that is high-technology and/or military related. It is believed by many that Soviet economic gains from importing products embodying advanced western technology are very large—large enough to make a "difference," although, admittedly, much depends on how "difference" is defined. Let us look at some data for 1980, the year in which western machinery and equipment exports to the USSR reached a peak of some $6 billion, roughly 3 billion rubles.[10] In 1980, Soviet investment in machinery and equipment (including inventories) amounted to 50.2 billion rubles (Ts SU SSSR, *Narkhoz*, 1980, p. 334), of which imports constituted only 6 percent. The impact of imports on the economy is better judged in relation to the total capital stock of machinery and equipment than to just the current investment. Since the value of capital stock exceeded annual investment by more than tenfold, the percentage of imports to capital stock of machinery and equipment must have been only about 0.5 percent. This figure should be discounted additionally for the fact that most Soviet imports of machinery and equipment from the West are run-of-the-mill products like their own and only a very small percentage—probably no more than one-fifth—can be classified as "high technology" (Young, 1978). A final discount should be made to allow for the fact that the performance of the Soviet economy as a whole depends on investment and capital stock in other sectors than machinery and equipment and on other factors of production, especially labor. One can only conclude that even if the productivity of imported machinery and equipment from the West were many times greater than that of domestically produced products, the aggregate impact of these imports on growth of GNP would necessarily be very small. Further, the more recent literature comparing the productivity of Soviet domestically produced equipment with western imported equipment surprisingly finds little evidence to favor the latter (Hanson, 1981, Chapter 9).[11]

This should not be taken to imply that the Soviets do not stand to gain from trade, because they undoubtedly do. But clearly, the gains from trade in the recent past have not been momentous. One important piece of evidence is that while both total trade with the West and imports of western machinery and equipment rose sharply after 1970, the growth of Soviet GNP declined sharply. It is possible that rising trade with the West slowed the decline in Soviet growth. My own feeling is that the imported equipment hardly made a "difference": the forces that reduced the Soviet growth rate were far too powerful to be offset by foreign trade in a relatively self-sufficient nation like the USSR.

It is interesting to note, however, that during the Soviet Union's First Five-Year Plan (1928–1932), a rapid rise in Soviet growth coincided with a rapid increase in imports of producers' goods.[12] There are several explanations for the difference in experience. First, the imports of producers' goods during the First Five-Year Plan were much more intensive than in recent years, amounting to almost 15 percent of total gross investment in comparison with a maximum in recent years of about 6 percent of gross investment in machinery and equipment, or 2 percent of total investment. Second, while Soviet machinery and equipment capital stock in 1980 was approximately 10–12 times the level of annual investment, it must have been much smaller in 1928–1932, and imports, therefore, must have had a much bigger impact. In effect, imported machinery during the First Five-Year Plan often was installed where no machinery had previously existed. Third, and related to the previous point, the technological gap in 1928–1932 was much greater than it is today—say fifty years in comparison with ten to fifteen years at present—and the potential gains were therefore much greater. The citation of these important sources of growth attributable to imports might lead one to believe that without such imports, the Soviet economy would have stagnated during the First Five-Year Plan. Not at all. Although imports were very important, even more important in my opinion was the fact that the potential gains from extensive growth were never higher in the Soviet Union than they were when the planners put vast idle and inefficiently employed factors of production to work productively during the early 1930s.[13]

Despite the low Soviet dependence on foreign trade, the United States has conducted economic warfare against that country on numerous occasions since the end of World War II. In effect, U.S. foreign economic policies toward the USSR have kept in step with its political relationships. By the late 1930s, the Soviet trade participation ratio had declined to less than .01, practically pure autarky and not leaving much room for economic warfare. Nevertheless, in the immediate postwar period, characterized by cold war political relationships between East and West, the United States took the initiative in trying to keep East-West trade (as well as trade with the People's Republic of China) at a very low level. These policies were relaxed during the détente period and resumed after the Soviet invasion of Afghanistan.

U.S. trade policies toward the USSR and Eastern Europe need serious reconsideration at this point in time (Wolf, 1982). The possibility of improvement in U.S./USSR political relations appears to have increased sharply when Mikhail Gorbachev assumed leadership. Trade policies may need to be updated to keep in step. Moreover, for reasons suggested above, U.S. trade policies have not been very successful in achieving their stated purpose of hurting the Soviets economically and militarily. Not only does the United States lack the economic leverage, it also has never had adequate cooperation either from its allies in Western Europe or from nonaligned nations. The latter, for example, happily supplied the USSR with the grain that President Jimmy Carter's 1980 embargo was designed to deny. U.S. allies have resisted cooperating more fully with the United States for at least two reasons. First, they do not perceive the Soviet threat as serious and as imminent as the United States does. In this connection, they view their own territories and not that of the United States as the primary battleground in the event of military conflict. Second, most of the NATO nations have a much larger economic stake in East-West trade both in terms of markets for their industries and as sources of needed raw materials. This is particularly true of West Germany.

The most recent instance of major policy conflict between the United States and Western Europe involved Western European assistance to the USSR in the development of gas pipelines from the Urengoi Basin in the Soviet Union to various nations in Western Europe that are eventually to consume the Soviet gas. The United States opposed this project because (1) the exports of natural gas might eventually net the USSR huge hard currency earnings and (2) it was thought that some Western European nations might become so dependent on Soviet gas that they would be vulnerable to a Soviet cutoff of supply should a diplomatic crisis arise or hostilities develop. The U.S. case was not helped by the fact that upon taking office in 1980, President Ronald Reagan canceled the U.S. grain embargo for domestic political reasons. Agriculture is probably the only U.S. sector that is as dependent on trade with the USSR as many Western European industries.

U.S. concern that Western Europe might be weakened militarily by becoming too dependent on Soviet natural gas reflects a belief in what might be called the effectiveness of a long-run strategy of economic warfare. However, the United States has practiced a short-run strategy in its economic warfare policy toward the Soviet Union. That is, the United States has never tried to lure the Soviet Union into an economic dependency but has, in contrast, tried to deny it anything of great value, thereby forcing it to become independent or to seek dependency from other and less desirable sources. The low level of Soviet dependency on the United States is, thus, partly a result of U.S. postwar policy; and the low level of dependency combined with lack of cooperation from Western Europe has doomed U.S. economic warfare against the USSR to impotency. It might well be, however, that the USSR is too self-sufficient, partly as a matter of resources and partly as a result of conscious policies, ever to be very vulnerable to economic warfare. If this is the case, U.S. short-run economic warfare is reduced to being simply an expression of displeasure.[14]

One final point on economic warfare should be mentioned. Although the United States has implemented economic warfare measures in its relations with the USSR and Eastern Europe, the Soviet Union has not responded in kind. This is, of course, because the Soviet Union has virtually no economic leverage to apply against the United States. The Soviet Union, however, has demonstrated that it is not loathe to apply restrictive trade and financial measures in appropriate situations in which it possesses leverage. The most notorious cases were the sanctions it applied to three members of its own bloc: Yugoslavia, Albania, and the People's Republic of China (Holzman, 1976, Chapter 3; Freedman, 1970).

The previous discussion highlights the fact that export controls are a form of trade obstruction that is usually used to hurt other nations by denying them military, military-related, and strategic products or civilian products of great economic value. Most other types of trade controls are primarily designed not to hurt other nations—although they may do so incidentally—but rather are either straight-out protectionist measures or are measures designed to protect industries that are being subjected to unfair competition. Tariffs and (import) quotas are largely protectionist,[15] as are voluntary export restraints (VERs); anti-dumping and anti–market disruption laws, on the other hand, are designed to protect industries against unfair trade practices, although enterprises often attempt to have them invoked for protectionist purposes.

Anti-dumping laws, as applied to centrally planned economies, are the subject of Chapter 6, which deals incidentally with the Polish golf-cart case because the various issues regarding how to apply the anti-dumping laws to CPEs came to a head in connection with the successful Polish invasion of the U.S. golf-cart market. The anti-dumping regulations were amended in 1978 to apply better to CPEs, and these amended regulations were first applied in the Polish golf-cart case. I was fortunate to have attended a conference on the case called by the U.S. Departments of State and Treasury in July 1978 and a follow-up conference in Poland in June 1980, and later to have been a consultant to the law firm defending Pezetel against the dumping charges.[16] (Pezetel is the Polish foreign trade organization [FTO] that exported the golf carts.)

The anti-dumping regulations are of special interest because these regulations, as written for market economies, cannot be readily applied to CPEs due to the systemic differences in how the two types of economies operate. "Dumping" means exporting a product to another country at below the cost or price at which the exporter sells the product in its own country. Dumping is viewed as unfair competition. In order to determine whether dumping is actually taking place, it is necessary to know the cost or domestic price in the exporter's country and the functioning exchange rate by which to translate the cost or price into the importing nation's currency. The procedure breaks down in the case of CPEs because their costs and prices are "irrational," being administered rather than market-determined, and their exchange rates, also administered, do not reflect the relationships between domestic and external prices. Chapter 6 describes and evaluates attempts to bridge the systemic gap so that the anti-dumping laws can be applied to CPEs. These attempts have not been too successful in my opinion.

An alternative method of protecting domestic enterprises and industries from "injury" is through invoking various so-called escape clauses. The first U.S. legislation to deal specifically with Communist (actually Soviet) exports on a market disruption basis was the U.S.-USSR Commercial Agreement of 1972, in which it was agreed that if either country had industries threatened by market disruption, the offending exports would be limited, if this appeared necessary. This is, in effect, a VER (voluntary export restraint) and was adopted apparently because of the difficulties with applying, at that time, the anti-dumping laws. A similar article is contained in the U.S.-Romanian Trade Agreement of 1975. The U.S. Trade Act of 1974 contains a later version of the market disruption clauses and includes, among other things, a special article (No. 406) applying to the CPEs. This article applies stricter standards against the exports of Communist countries than does Article 201 against market economies. The first case brought under Article 406 (in December 1977) dealt with imports of work gloves from the People's Republic of China. This was followed by a case dealing with exports of clothespins by the PRC and Romania.

For the CPEs, it is probably easier if aggrieved U.S. firms choose to employ Article 406 than if they employ the anti-dumping procedure. Systemic gap problems cloud the results of the anti-dumping procedures to such an extent that the procedure cannot be considered a reliable defense. Moreover, the dumping procedures usually take a long time to implement, which is costly to all concerned. There are no systemic gap problems with market disruption nor are the procedures as time consuming; for these reasons, Article 406 is probably a simpler approach to use in the case of CPE exports. If it is so used, there would not seem to be a particularly good reason why the CPEs should be subjected to stricter standards than the market economies.

As noted earlier, most controls over imports are not used for political purposes but are meant to protect domestic industries or to prevent unfair competition by foreign exporters. The discriminatory U.S. quotas placed on South African exports are an exception; other exceptions are the complete import (and export) embargoes placed on Cuban and, for many years, Chinese exports. Still another exception has been the refusal of the U.S. government since the Trade Agreements Extension Act of 1951 to grant MFN status to the Soviet Union and the other Communist nations. At present, the major legal reason for not granting MFN to these nations is their denial of human rights particularly, their not allowing freer emigration,[17] a prerequisite included in the U.S. Trade Act of 1974. While MFN status entitles a second nation to a level of commercial privileges equal to those extended to any third nations, the most important privilege usually relates to tariff levels. Not having MFN means that exports (primarily of manufactures goods) to the U.S. face the almost prohibitive Smoot-Hawley tariffs dating back to 1930, tariffs that average probably 5 times the present level. Those Communist nations without MFN strongly resent being so discriminated against by the United States. This is discrimination, of course, since among all nations with poor human rights records, only Communist nations are denied MFN.

The unique aspect of U.S. policy regarding the granting of MFN to Communist nations is that during peacetime, the United States is the only country in the world to deny MFN on noneconomic grounds—on the basis of not approving of another nation's internal policies. There are many who feel that such denial of MFN is totally inappropriate. As Theodore Sorenson, formerly a high official in the Kennedy administration, put it:

> Part of the problem arises from confusion over the term "most-favored-nation." Congressional debate has frequently labeled the extension of this status a "concession," a "subsidy," a "favor," a "preference," or a "privilege." In fact, it is none of these. On the contrary, it is a recognition of normal, equal status, in effect a determination that *no* nation or nations will be favored. It simply assures the recipient that its goods will enter the United States at the same low tariff rates applicable to comparable goods of our other trading partners who make available equal status to us. It is a common worldwide approach. (Sorenson, 1974, p. 276)

This is certainly a strong argument. Not only do all nations grant MFN to each other, but the principle has been enshrined as a basic one by both the General Agreement on Tariffs and Trade (GATT) and UNCTAD. In response, it might be argued that human rights have also been enshrined as a fundamental principle in many world forums, including the United Nations and the Helsinki Conference on Security and Cooperation in Europe (CSCE). Yet it is clear that the Soviet Union has ignored its obligations on human rights as a founding member of the UN and as a major signator of the Helsinki Final Act. No one would deny that in the field of human affairs, human rights are more important than conformity with MFN. By this token, one might justify U.S. denial of MFN to the USSR (and other nations), although one might at the same time (1) deplore the fact the Communist nations are singled out among nations with poor human rights records and (2) worry that the U.S. failure to uphold GATT's "rules of the game" could lead to further breakdown in the world's trading order.

Before leaving tariffs and MFN, it is worth noting that denial of MFN has cost the Soviet Union relatively little—much less than it costs most of the other CPEs—because the USSR exports to the United States mostly raw materials and other products that are either not subject to tariffs or are subject to tariffs that are very low. Raffel et al. (1977) estimated that in 1975, extension of MFN to the USSR would have increased Soviet exports to the United States by only 7.5 percent. However, that figure may, for the following reasons, understate somewhat the effect of MFN. First, estimates such as this one examine the impact of tariff removal on goods that are already being exported to the United States, yet many products that are not exported might be marketed with MFN. Second, and related to the previous point, it is costly for a nation like the USSR to mount an export drive in the very competitive U.S. manufactured goods markets, and a nation is unlikely to do so on a large scale without some of the economic and political preconditions for at least partial success. MFN provides the economic precondition, namely lower tariffs. It would also provide some of the political preconditions, in the present context, standing as a symbol of better relations and goodwill (Marer and Neuberger, 1974). Despite these caveats, it appears unlikely that the Soviets have much chance, in the foreseeable future, of significantly penetrating the U.S. market, a feat that has eluded Russia for over one hundred years.

Chapter 7 deals very briefly with the extent to which trade with Communist nations might have a "deliberalizing" impact on western trade because of monopolistic and monopsonistic power, use of countertrade, and so forth. More on this topic can be found in many sources, among the best of which are two articles by Wolf (1982b, 1982c).

Convertibility and Exchange Rates

The centrally planned economies have fairly primitive financial systems, considering their levels of development. This is to be expected of nations in which most industry is nationalized and in which the role of money in the economy is attenuated in many sectors by the dominance of direct controls wielded by the state. The narrow choice of financial services and limited range of financial instruments available are striking and are the counterpart, in the real economy, of the relatively narrow range and variety of consumers' goods available to the population. In both sectors—the financial and the real economy—the planners do not respond flexibly and quickly as does the capitalist market to every transient whim or change in taste and to every opportunity to make a profit. As a result, capitalism undoubtedly spawns too much variety, central planning too little.

The financial system of the Soviet Union, for example, consists basically of a state budget, a state central bank (Gosbank), and a savings bank system. The Gosbank lends money to state enterprises, keeps their accounts, and transfers payments between them by adjusting the accounts.

The Gosbank also issues cash money, which is the medium of exchange in transactions involving the population. That's about it. There are no stocks or bonds, stock markets or bond markets, checking accounts or credit cards. There is no wide variety of savings institutions or of institutions that finance industry, and enterprises cannot grant one another credits. There is no wide continuum of interest rates—just two. The role of money and monetary institutions is so slight in these nations that domestic monetary policy is virtually nonexistent.

If domestic monetary policy is almost nonexistent, international monetary policy is even more so. Its scope is severely limited by official exchange rates that serve no real economic function but are simply units of account with values that usually neither relate domestic and foreign prices nor reflect the forces of supply and demand. One result of these circumstances is that the domestic currencies of the CMEA countries are just that—domestic currencies; they are usually forbidden to be used in foreign trade transactions or to be taken outside of national borders. Under these circumstances, the domestic currencies of the CMEA nations obviously are inconvertible. Analysis of the inconvertibility of the CMEA national currencies and of the CMEA common international currency, the transferable ruble (TR), are the main subjects of Chapter 8.

Inconvertibility and its consequences, especially rigid bilateralism in intra-CMEA trade, are not conditions that are accepted either gracefully or passively in the Eastern nations. Their efforts to achieve convertibility are chronicled in Chapters 4 and 10. The first attempt was quite dramatic, involving the creation in 1964 of the International Bank for Economic Cooperation (IBEC) with its new international currency, the TR. In a paper I published in 1966 (one of two earlier papers upon which Chapter 4 is based), I predicted that neither IBEC nor its TR would free intra-CMEA trade from bilateralism. This was not a very risky prediction, and it was borne out by events. Another attempt was made to move toward convertibility in the CMEA Comprehensive Program of 1971–1975, in which was planned that after a short period of time, each CMEA nation would settle 10 percent of its trade imbalances with other CMEA nations in hard currency and that the percentage of hard currency settlement was to increase periodically. This also was doomed to failure. At an East-West international monetary conference in Greece in October 1974, I became aware of an impending development: an attempt to make the TR "externally convertible" to western nations, banks, and traders (but not convertible within CMEA). This was basically an attempt to secure cheaper credit and was proposed by Janos Fekete and Z. Federowicz, the leading international banking experts of Hungary and Poland, respectively. A replay of the debate in Greece occurred in July 1976 at the International Economic Association Meeting in Dresden.

At the Dresden meeting, devoted to East-West international economic issues, Federowicz and I presented papers that addressed the question of convertibility. Federowicz argued that considerable progress was being made toward convertibility of CMEA currencies, especially of the transferable ruble, and that it would not be long before full convertibility would be achieved. I demonstrated, in a paper included here as Chapter 8, why neither internal nor external convertibility were feasible for CPEs either at that time or *ever*. Not very long after the Dresden meeting, CMEA declared the TR to be externally convertible. The attempt quickly failed, for reasons discussed in Chapter 8.

At the time I wrote that chapter, I had never come across an Eastern bloc writer who seemed to understand the impossibility of achieving convertibility under central planning. In 1979, in Budapest, I picked up a copy of the late Sandor Ausch's *Theory and Practice of CMEA Cooperation,* published in English in Hungary in 1972 and undoubtedly earlier in Hungarian. Chapters 9 and 10 of Ausch's book show a full understanding of the issues relating to convertibility, both under capitalist market and central planning conditions. Since Ausch was a well-known economist in Hungary, it is difficult to understand why so many eastern economists had remained so unenlightened. In recent years, however, more and more eastern economists have demonstrated in writing a more sophisticated awareness of convertibility problems. This is particularly true of Hungarian economists and is probably partly due to the fact that they live in an economy that has been moving toward less plan and more markets and in which convertibility of the forint may one day be a real possibility.

Two final points: First, although a true international monetary policy may not be feasible under central planning with direct controls, one should not think that Janos Fekete, Z. Federowicz, and their counterparts in other CMEA countries do not engage in international financial operations—for they do. They are extremely busy managing their portfolios of foreign assets; borrowing money; and servicing, repaying, and in some instances rescheduling their foreign debts. However, the values of their exchange rates are irrelevant to those activities, since all transactions are in hard currencies.

And, second, some of the conditions that are responsible for inconvertibility, namely irrational domestic prices and administered exchange rates, also render it very difficult to make meaningful international economic comparisons. In a noteworthy attempt to surmount these problems, the World Bank, some years back, launched a substantial study by a number of academic experts and under the overall direction of Paul Marer. A summary volume of the results of that study was recently published (Marer, 1985).

Intrabloc Trade

A major development in world political life since World War II has been the simultaneous existence of NATO and the Organization for European Economic Cooperation (OEEC) on the one hand and the Warsaw Treaty Organization (WTO) on the other. Under the domination of the USSR, the Eastern nations formed the CMEA as an economic counterpart organization to the OEEC. Part of the impetus for forming CMEA came from the cold war economic policies that most of the NATO nations applied to trade with Eastern Europe, especially the USSR. The eastern nations were, in effect, partly driven into each others' arms. They were also being pulled together by the Soviet Union, which, at least until the troubles in East Germany in 1953 and in Hungary and Poland in 1956, exploited the smaller nations in its trade with them.

The enormity of the trade shifts involved in the formation of what Joseph Stalin called "two parallel world markets" (Stalin, 1952, p. 30) is evidenced by the increase in the percentage of Soviet imports from Eastern Europe between the late 1930s and 1953—an increase from 5 percent to 61 percent (Holzman, 1976, p. 70). In subsequent years, intra-CMEA trade continued to grow, though not percentagewise. The motives behind this expansion were partly economic and partly political. The USSR looked upon close trade relations as a way of cementing the bonds of the bloc nations. While intra-CMEA trade has continued to expand until the present, in the 1960s and 1970s East-West trade grew more rapidly, partly because of the thaw in the political climate—i.e., détente—but also because nations found that expansion of trade with the West offered more profitable opportunities than did further intrabloc trade. Availing themselves of these opportunities became more urgent to CMEA nations as their economic growth rates declined and the need to shift from extensive to intensive growth became apparent. Clearly, intensive growth could be more efficiently pursued by increasing imports of more advanced western technology and of products embodying those technologies. The mindless enthusiasm with which some of the CMEA nations (especially Poland, Hungary, and Romania) pursued this policy was partly responsible for the serious international hard currency debt problems mentioned earlier.

Trade with the West would have been relatively much more profitable than intrabloc trade during the first twenty years after World War II as well. When the nations of CMEA redirected their trade away from the West and toward each other, they experienced both gains and losses, but the losses undoubtedly outweighed the gains. The nature of such gains and losses is analyzed by economists typically in terms of customs union theory. CMEA is not a classical market-variety customs union in which member nations reduce or eliminate tariff and other trade barriers to each others' exports. Rather, not needing tariffs, they simply *decide* to import more from each other and to import less from nonmembers. Nevertheless, customs union theory is still applicable as an analytical tool. The gains from forming a customs union are called trade creation and result when, with trade barriers reduced, nations buy more from one another at the expense of higher priced domestic products. The losses, called trade diversion, result when, with trade barriers reduced, the members import more from each other but at the expense of products from cheaper and more efficient nonmember nations. It has been shown (see Chapter 9) that becoming a member of CMEA mostly involved losses for the Eastern European nations, since most of their trade with each other was diverted from previously cheaper sources. It is further argued that Eastern European nations experienced additional losses from having joined CMEA, above and beyond those from trade diversion. These losses were due to "trade destruction" and are not likely to have been found in any of the world's customs unions except for CMEA, particularly in its earlier years.[18]

One goal of CMEA desired by the USSR was an increase in intra-CMEA commodity trade, which, though it would achieve small economic gains (or losses relative to trade with the West), would increase the political cohesion of the bloc. Efforts were also made to increase what might be called "economic integration" along several other lines. One of the most important was the effort to deepen the division of labor and specialization among the CMEA nations by careful planning not only of trade, but of investments as well. To this end, an attempt was made by Khrushchev to upgrade CMEA, as reflected in two formal documents, a charter and a statement on goals and methods entitled "Basic Principles of International Socialist Division of Labor." These documents stressed the need for coordination and cooperation in economic, technical, and scientific areas and for *multilateral* coordination of the national economic plans. All nations were to be *equal* in CMEA, and no nation had to be bound by others' desires or decisions. That is to say, the implementation of projects or plans had to be unanimous— majority rule was not enough. In effect, CMEA did not have supranational power; therefore, neither did the USSR—a fact that had considerable practical consequences. Between 1962 and 1964, a battle ensued over supranationality versus national sovereignty, with the Soviet Union and Romania the major adversaries. In more concrete terms, the battle was over the fact that the USSR envisioned Romania and Bulgaria eschewing industrial development to become raw material suppliers to the rest of CMEA. Romania, in particular, refused to accept this role and finally prevailed (Montias, 1967). As a result of this battle, all CMEA projects not unanimously supported by CMEA members had to be undertaken outside of the CMEA framework.

Despite this monkey wrench in its mechanism, CMEA launched two huge five-year plans for economic growth and integration, the "Comprehensive Programme" for 1971–1975 and the "Coordinated Plan of Multilateral Integrated Measures" for 1976–1980. These programs set forth extensive and detailed plans for cooperation, integration, specialization, joint research, steps toward convertibility, and the like, but the results appear to have been meager (Hewett, 1977b). In general terms, the obstacles confronting CMEA integration can be summarized as follows. Although a fairly substantial degree of integration can be achieved either through free-market mechanisms or, where barriers to trade and investment exist (e.g., tariffs), through reduction of those barriers, the CPEs have very inadequate market mechanisms for facilitating international trade and investment. Lacking adequate market mechanisms, and given the antipathy to integration that seems inherent in the CPE model (e.g., an unwillingness to let foreigners outcompete domestic enterprises, to allow foreign ownership, to allow bankruptcy, to pay a reasonable price for capital, or to allow migration), substantial integration undoubtedly required the establishment, voluntarily or by force, of supranational power in economic matters. It seems, as noted earlier, that the USSR did not have power to institute supranationality when the issue was contested in the early 1960s nor were all of the smaller nations willing to cede sovereignty on these matters to CMEA (read USSR).[19]

Much has been written about CMEA's development and problems. The pioneering study is Michael Kaser's *Comecon* (1965). Two early studies that concentrate on the obstacles to integration are those by Neuberger (1964), which employs a customs union model, and Montias (1969). Another excellent source on integration is a volume edited by Marer and Montias (1980); the introduction by the editors is especially useful. Marie Lavigne (1975), in a fascinating article, describes how irrational prices in CMEA nations seriously complicate attempts at multinational enterprises. At this point, it is worth noting that irrational prices and accompanying inconvertibility complicate integration through joint ventures and joint investment as much as, if not more than, they complicate intra-CMEA trade relations.

An issue of major interest to western scholars has been the distribution of gains from intra-CMEA trade between the USSR and its Eastern European trade partners.[20] As is fairly well known, during the first ten years after World War II the USSR took a lion's share of those gains. That the USSR had been an exploiter was evidenced by, among other things, the large rebates it gave to compensate (after the

Hungarian and Polish uprisings in 1956) for the very low prices it had been paying for Polish coal and Romanian oil. These rebates, and other similar measures taken, led many to assume that the gains were probably more equally distributed in the later 1950s. When, in 1958, the Soviet Union published its first detailed foreign trade returns (for 1956 and 1957) in about twenty years, the possibility of testing this assumption appeared to be at hand. As soon as I received the volume, I calculated and compared the average unit values (prices) at which the Soviets traded with Eastern and Western Europe, respectively. I found that the Soviets were generally selling to the West at lower prices, and buying from the West at higher prices, than to and from Eastern Europe. This appeared to signal discrimination (exploitation) against the bloc.

Upon reflection, it occurred to me that these estimates could not be taken at face value. They assumed that Soviet-West prices were a fair standard against which discrimination should be judged. At least two other factors needed to be taken into account. First, it was well known that the Soviet Union and Eastern Europe were being discriminated against by Western Europe in trade. Second, the Soviet bloc nations were fairly insulated at that time from world markets, and according to economic theory, one could deduce that they might trade with one another at different sets of relative prices than western nations. I predicted that if these latter two factors were important, then performing the same calculations with the trade statistics of another CMEA nation would show that nation discriminating against other CMEA countries, including the Soviet Union. In other words, the Soviet exports to Western Europe might be at lower prices than to CMEA not because the USSR was discriminating against CMEA but because Western Europe was discriminating against the Soviet Union, and similarly with imports. While I waited to get data from another CMEA nation to test this hypothesis, Horst Mendershausen published two articles (1959, 1960) based on the Soviet trade returns, seeking to demonstrate Soviet discrimination. These papers, appearing to substantiate the conventional wisdom regarding Soviet discrimination against Eastern Europe, received wide publicity. A few years after Mendershausen's articles were published, I finally obtained Bulgarian and Polish trade returns; they showed (Holzman, 1962, 1965) that Bulgaria and Poland appeared to discriminate against the USSR, thereby refuting Mendershausen's proof.

By the mid-1960s, the conventional wisdom on Soviet/Eastern Europe gains from trade had changed, and indeed, the Soviets were often heard to complain that they weren't getting a fair deal in their trade with Eastern Europe. Moreover, Carl McMillan (1973) and Ed Hewett (1977a), using input-output tables, independently estimated that not only were the Soviets not getting a fair share of the gains from trade with Eastern Europe, they were actually experiencing net losses from that trade—and would be better off without bloc trade. Although questions have been raised regarding the validity of these estimates, no one any longer doubts that Eastern Europe has been getting its fair share of the gains from its trade with the USSR. These gains must be weighed, however, against the long-term losses incurred from having to concentrate trade in the CMEA.

Western analyses along these lines culminated in 1983 with the publication of a major monograph by Michael Marrese and Jan Vanous entitled *Soviet Subsidization of Trade with Eastern Europe*. Even as Mendershausen estimated Eastern Europe's losses from Soviet exploitation, so Marrese and Vanous estimated its gains from Soviet subsidization. The estimates are much more careful and detailed than those of previous studies. While some have questioned the magnitude of the estimates (e.g., Marer, 1984), others (Brada, 1985; Desai, 1985; Holzman, Chapters 10 and 11 below) have quarreled with the interpretation. Marrese and Vanous argued that the subsidies are actually implicit payments by the Soviet Union to Eastern Europe for noneconomic services rendered. Such services include availability of military bases, allegiance in international forums, ideological support, and so forth. I have attempted to show that much of Marrese and Vanous's data are inconsistent with this interpretation, and Brada, Desai, and I all argue that a customs union interpretation provides a better explanation of the so-called subsidies. I also argue that one can test which hypothesis is correct, as in the Mendershausen case, by using the trade data of one of the Eastern European nations.

Final Remarks

The essays in this volume address what I believe to be some of the more important aspects of current research on Soviet bloc trade and finance. These introductory remarks were designed to provide a framework that would make the essays more meaningful to readers not familiar with the field. Moreover, references have been made to many major contributions by other scholars to each of the topics covered so that anyone wishing to pursue a subject further would have available references to relevant publications.

Notes

1. To digress for a moment, a western banker need not, in fact, have cared whether his funds were invested productively. Unlike loans to capitalist enterprises in foreign countries, loans to CPE enterprises are repaid as long as the *nation*

is solvent, even if the investment turns out to be unsuccessful. That is to say, loans to CPE enterprises are guaranteed by the country—there is no project risk, only country risk. And almost everyone believed, until the Polish and Romanian crises of a few years ago, that in lending to CMEA nations there were no country risks. At the very worst, the USSR would give aid to any nation unable to service its hard currency debt. This, of course, did not turn out to be true.

2. For up-to-date figures, see CIA, *Handbook,* published annually; also see Joint Economic Committee (1986, pp. 147–258).

3. Wolf has written a number of papers on this subject, including Wolf (1980); Wolf (1985a); and his latest, Wolf (1985b), a valuable survey article.

4. On SOVMOD, see Portes' critical review article (1979).

5. It is also worth noting that most of the analysis in Chapter 1 deals with "system-induced foreign trade behavior"—in this case, how the system of central planning causes balance of payments disequilibria.

6. The rationale behind this bizarre practice is presented in Chapter 11.

7. The Export Administration Act of 1969 shifted U.S. policy toward encouragement of East-West trade and eliminated this proscription.

8. A major exception was the concern expressed by Raul Prebisch and others that the less developed countries (LDCs) did not get a fair share of the gains in their trade with the developed nations.

9. One of the best papers on Soviet gains from trade is Wolf (1979).

10. This assumes that the appropriate machinery and equipment conversion ratio in 1980 was 1 ruble = \$2. Estimates of the conversion ratio vary widely, but even if the 1 ruble = \$2 rate were off by 100 percent, my argument would not be invalidated.

11. There was an extensive debate over this question in the late 1970s, which first surfaced in published form in a paper by Green and Levine (1977) (there were several earlier unpublished, but widely circulated, papers), in which imported machinery was estimated to have had 14 times higher marginal productivity than domestic machinery, and more or less ended with a paper by Weitzman (1979), which concluded that the evidence does not permit a judgment regarding the relative value to the Soviet economy of domestic and imported capital. The debate is summarized in Hanson (1981).

12. These goods were mostly, but not totally, machinery and equipment.

13. Actually, most of the labor productivity gains from the imports of machinery and equipment in the First Five-Year Plan were not realized until the Second Five-Year Plan because the Soviet economy was incapable of absorbing rapidly so much new technology.

14. The literature on export controls and related subjects is much too large to be listed. A few recent, selected books are Hufbauer and Schott (1983); Parrott (1985); and Bertsch and McIntyre (1983).

15. One exception is the recent U.S. embargo (October 1986) on imports of many products (e.g., gold, uranium, diamonds) from the Union of South Africa, designed to punish that nation for its apartheid policies.

16. The proceedings of the two conferences were published in Wallace et al. (1979) and Wallace and Flores (1982), respectively. See also Marer and Tabaczynski (1981).

17. The U.S. denial of MFN to Poland in 1981 was related to the crushing of Solidarity and arrest of its leaders. See Chapter 4 for further discussion of MFN.

18. Minor exceptions would occur where the relatively low tariff nations forming a customs union are required to raise their tariffs to the union's new common tariff level to nonmembers.

19. For an up-to-date and more nuanced statement on CMEA integration, see Lavigne (1983).

20. For an excellent survey, see Marer (1974).

References

Avramovic, Dragoslav. *Economic Growth and External Debt*. Baltimore: Johns Hopkins, 1964.

Bertsch, Gary K., and John R. McIntyre. *National Security and Technology Transfer: The Strategic Dimensions of East-West Trade*. Boulder, Colo.: Westview Press, 1983.

Brada, Josef C. "Real and Monetary Approaches to Foreign Trade Adjustment Mechanisms in Centrally Planned Economies." *European Economic Review* 19 (1982): 229–244.

———. "Soviet Subsidization of Eastern Europe: The Primacy of Economics over Politics." *Journal of Comparative Economics* 9 (March 1985): 80–92.

CIA. *Handbook of Economic Statistics*. Washington, D.C.: Directorate of Intelligence, various years.

Crane, Keith. *The Creditworthiness of Eastern Europe in the 1980s*. RAND (R-3201-USDP). Santa Monica, Calif.: RAND Corporation, January 1985, 181 pp.

Crawford, J., and J. Haberstroh. "Survey of Economic Policy Issues in Eastern Europe: Technology, Trade, and the Consumer." In *Reorientation and Commercial Relations of the Economies of Eastern Europe*. Washington, D.C.: Joint Economic Committee, U.S. Congress, 1974.

Desai, Padma. "Is the Soviet Union Subsidizing Eastern Europe?" *European Economic Review* 29 (1985): 107–116.

Freedman, Robert. *Economic Warfare in the Communist Bloc*. New York: Praeger, 1970.

Gardner, H. Stephen. "East-West Economic Relations: The Policy Implications of Recent Scholarship." *International Economic Perspectives* 10 (4), edited by Thomas A. Wolf (no date).

Green, Donald W., and Christopher I. Higgins. *SOVMOD I: A Macroeconometric Model of the Soviet Union*. New York: Academic Press, 1977.

Green, Donald W., and H. S. Levine. "Macroeconometric Evidence of the Value of Machinery Imports to the Soviet Union." In *Soviet Science and Technology,* edited by J. R. Thomas and U. Kruse-Vaucienne. Washington, D.C.: National Science Foundation, 1977.

Grossman, Gregory, and Ronald L. Solberg. *The Soviet Union's Hard-Currency Balance of Payments and Creditworthiness in 1985*. RAND (R-2956-USDP). Santa Monica, Calif.: RAND Corporation, April 1983, 90 pp.

Hanson, Phillip. *Trade and Technology in Soviet-Western Relations*. New York: Columbia University Press, 1981.

Hewett, Ed. "Prices and Resources Allocation in Intra-CMEA Trade." In *The Socialist Price Mechanism*, edited by A. Abouchar. Durham, N.C.: Duke University Press, 1977a.

———. "Recent Developments in East-West European Economic Relations and Their Implications for U.S.–East European Economic Relations." In *East European Economies Post-Helsinki*. Washington, D.C.: Joint Economic Committee, U.S. Congress, 1977b.

———. "Foreign Trade Outcomes in Eastern and Western Economies." In *East European Integration and East-West Trade*, edited by Paul Marer and J. Michael Montias. Bloomington: Indiana University Press, 1980.

———. "The Hungarian Economy: Lessons of the 1970's and Prospects for the 1980's." In *East European Economic Assessment*, Part 1. Washington, D.C.: Joint Economic Committee, U.S. Congress, 1981, pp. 483–524.

Holzman, Franklyn D. "Soviet Foreign Trade Pricing and the Question of Discrimination: A 'Customs Union' Approach." *Review of Economics and Statistics* 44 (May 1962): 134–147.

———. "More on Soviet Bloc Discrimination." *Soviet Studies* 17 (July 1965): 44–65.

———. "Foreign Trade Behavior of Centrally Planned Economies." In *Industrialization in Two Systems: Essays in Honor of Alexander Gerschenkron*, edited by Henry Rosovsky. New York: John Wiley and Sons, 1966.

———. *International Trade Under Communism: Politics and Economics*. New York: Basic Books, 1976.

Hufbauer, Gary C., and Jeffrey J. Schott. *Economic Sanctions in Support of Foreign Policy Goals*. Washington, D.C.: Institute for International Economics, October 1983.

Joint Economic Committee (JEC), Congress of the United States. *East European Economic Assessment*, Parts 1 and 2. Washington, D.C., 1981.

———. *East European Economies: Slow Growth in the 1980's*, Vols. 2 and 3. Washington, D.C., 1986.

Kaser, Michael. *Comecon: Integration Problems of the Planned Economies*. London: Oxford University Press, 1965.

Lavigne, Marie. "Problems of Multi-national Socialist Enterprise." *ACES Bulletin* 17 (Summer 1975): 33–62.

———. "The Soviet Union Inside Comecon." *Soviet Studies* 35 (April 1983): 135–153.

McMillan, C. H. "Factor Proportions and the Structure of Soviet Foreign Trade." *ACES Bulletin* 15 (Spring 1973): 57–82.

Marer, Paul. "Soviet Economic Policy in Eastern Europe." In *Reorientation and Commercial Relations of the Economies of Eastern Europe*. Washington, D.C.: Joint Economic Committee, U.S. Congress, 1974.

_____. "The Political Economy of Soviet Relations with Eastern Europe." In *Soviet Policy in Eastern Europe*, edited by Sarah Terry. New Haven, Conn.: Yale University Press, 1984.

_____. *Dollar GNPs of the U.S.S.R. and Eastern Europe*. Baltimore, Md.: World Bank, 1985.

Marer, Paul, and J. M. Montias, eds. *East European Integration and East-West Trade*. Bloomington: Indiana University Press, 1980.

Marer, Paul, and Egon Neuberger. "Commercial Relations Between the United States and Eastern Europe: Options and Prospects." In *Reorientation and Commercial Relations of the Economies of Eastern Europe*. Washington, D.C.: Joint Economic Committee, U.S. Congress, 1974.

Marer, Paul, and Eugeniusz Tabaczynski, eds. *Polish-US Industrial Cooperation in the 1980's*. Bloomington: Indiana University Press, 1981 (see Paul Marer's chapter, "Import Protectionism in the US and Poland's Manufactures Exports," pp. 228–250).

Marrese, Michael, and Jan Vanous. *Soviet Subsidization of Trade with Eastern Europe*. Berkeley: University of California Institute of International Studies, 1983.

Mendershausen, Horst. "Terms of Trade Between the Soviet Union and Smaller Communist Countries, 1955–57." *Review of Economics and Statistics* 41 (May 1959): 106–118; and "The Terms of Soviet-Satellite Trade: A Broadened Analysis." *Review of Economics and Statistics* 42 (May 1960): 152–163.

Montias, John Michael. "Poland: Roots of the Economic Crisis." *ACES Bulletin* 24 (Fall 1982): 1–20.

_____. *Economic Development in Communist Rumania*. Cambridge: MIT Press, 1967.

_____. "Obstacles to Integration." *Studies in Comparative Communism* 2 (July/October 1969): 38–60.

Neuberger, Egon. "International Division of Labor in CMEA." *American Economic Review* 54 (May 1964): 506–515.

Neuberger, Egon, and Laura Tyson, eds. *The Impact of International Economic Disturbances on the Soviet Union and Eastern Europe: Transmission and Response*. New York: Pergamon Press, 1980.

Neuberger, Egon, and Laura Tyson. "The Transmission of International Economic Disturbances: An Overview." In Neuberger and Tyson (1980), pp. 3–19.

Parrott, Bruce, ed. *Trade, Technology, and Soviet-American Relations*. Bloomington: Indiana University Press, 1985.

Polak, J. J. "Balance of Payments Problems of Countries Reconstructing with the Help of Foreign Loans." *Quarterly Journal of Economics* 57 (February 1943): 208–240.

Portes, Richard. "SOVMOD: A Macroeconometric Model of the Soviet Union." *Economic Journal* 89 (September 1979): 669–674.

_____. "Internal and External Balances in a Centrally Balanced Economy." In Neuberger and Tyson (1980), pp. 93–118.

———. "Background Paper." In *Deficits and Detente*. New York: The Twentieth Century Fund, 1983, pp. 13–92.

Raffel, Helen, Marc Rubin, and Robert Teal. "The MFN Impact on U.S. Imports from Eastern Europe." In *East European Economics Post-Helsinki*. Washington, D.C.: Joint Economic Committee, U.S. Congress, 1977.

Snell, E. "Eastern Europe Trade and Payments with the Industrial West." In *Reorientation and Commercial Relations of the Economies of Eastern Europe*. Washington, D.C.: Joint Economic Committee, U.S. Congress, 1974.

Sorenson, Theodore. "Most-Favored Nation and Less Favorite Nations." *Foreign Affairs* 52 (January 1974): 273–286.

Stalin, J. V. *Economic Problems of Socialism*. Peking: Foreign Languages Press, 1972 (reprint of 1952 Soviet edition in English).

Treml, Vladimir G. "Foreign Trade and the Soviet Economy: Changing Parameters and Interrelations." In Neuberger and Tyson (1980), pp. 184–211.

Ts SU SSSR. *Narodnoe khoziaistvo SSSR v. 1980 godu: statisticheskii sbornik*. Moscow: Finances and Statistics, 1980.

Tyson, Laura, and Peter Kenen. "The International Transmission of Disturbances: A Framework for Comparative Analysis." In Neuberger and Tyson (1980), pp. 33–62.

van Brabant, Jozef M.P. *Bilateralism and Structural Bilateralism in Intra-CMEA Trade*. Rotterdam: Rotterdam University Press, 1973.

Vanous, Jan. "Dependence of Soviet Economy on Foreign Trade." In *Centrally Planned Economies: Current Analysis*, edited by Jan Vanous. Washington, D.C.: Wharton Econometric Forecasting Associates, 1982.

Wallace, Donald and David A. Flores. *Interface Two: Conference Proceedings on the Legal Framework of East-West Trade*. Washington, D.C.: Georgetown Institute for International Trade and Foreign Trade Law, 1982.

Wallace, Donald, et al., eds. *Interface One*. Washington, D.C.: Georgetown Institute for International and Foreign Trade Law, 1979.

Weitzman, M. L. "Technology Transfer to the U.S.S.R.: An Econometric Analysis." *Journal of Comparative Economics* 3 (June 1979): 167–177.

Wolf, Thomas A. "Distribution of Economic Costs and Benefits in the U.S.-Soviet Trade." In *Time of Change*, Vol. 2. Washington, D.C.: Joint Economic Committee, U.S. Congress, 1979, pp. 327–341.

———. "External Inflation, the Balance of Trade and Resource Allocation in Small Centrally Planned Economies." In Neuberger and Tyson (1980), pp. 63–92.

———. "On the Adjustment of Centrally Planned Economies to External Economic Disturbances." In *East European Integration and East-West Trade*, edited by P. Marer and J. M. Montias. Bloomington: Indiana University Press, 1980.

———. "Choosing a US Strategy Towards the Soviet Union." In *Soviet Economy in the 1980s*. Washington, D.C.: Joint Economic Committee, U.S. Congress, 1982a, pp. 400–418.

———. "Soviet Market Power and Pricing Behavior in Western Export Markets." *Soviet Studies* 24 (October 1982): 529–546 (1982b).

_____ . "Optimal Foreign Trade for the Price-Insensitive Soviet-Type Economy." *Journal of Comparative Economics* 6 (March 1982): 37–54 (1982c).

_____ . "East-West Trade: Economic Interests, Systemic Interaction and Political Rivalry." *ACES Bulletin* 25 (Summer 1983): 23–60.

_____ . "Economic Stabilization in Planned Economies: Toward an Analytical Framework." International Monetary Fund *Staff Papers,* Vol. 32, No. 1, 1985a, pp. 78–131.

_____ . "Exchange Rate Systems and Adjustment in Planned Economies." In International Monetary Fund *Staff Papers,* Vol. 32, No. 2, 1985b, pp. 211–247.

Young, John P. "Quantification of Western Exports of High Technology Products to the Communist Countries." Washington, D.C.: Office of East-West Policy and Planning, Department of Commerce, 1978, unpublished.

Zloch, Iliana. *The Debt Problems of Eastern Europe*. Cambridge University Press, forthcoming.

Part One
BALANCE-OF-PAYMENTS PROBLEMS AND ADJUSTMENT MECHANISMS

1

Some Theories of the Hard Currency Shortages of Centrally Planned Economies

Summary

Centrally planned economies have experienced persistent balance of payments pressures in western markets. These have been expressed partly as deficits and rising debt, but have been partly repressed. To some extent these pressures have resulted from systemic factors inherent in central planning. In terms of the theory of comparative advantage, one might say that the CPE's have a comparative disadvantage in selling. Among other things, central planning leads the CPE's to overestimate the salability of their manufactured products which, for systemic reasons, tend to be of relatively low quality. The term "quality" here stands as a proxy for all nonprice dimensions of products, such as: Servicing, packaging, style, level of technology, availability of spare parts, et cetera. A second systemic disadvantage is "inability to devalue" in order to get into balance of payments equilibrium. A third is the endemic practice of "taut" planning which automatically generates external excess demand. Finally, CPE balances of payments have proved very vulnerable to cyclical fluctuations of demand from the West. Since 1974, this has been the major factor behind the rising hard currency debt.

I. Introduction

Since East-West trade began to expand in earnest about a decade ago, a major concern of governments, business men, and economists in the West (as well as in the East) has been the fact that the socialist

Reprinted from *Soviet Economy in a Time of Change*, vol. 2, Joint Economic Committee, U.S. Congress (Washington, D.C.: U.S. Government Printing Office, 1979), pp. 297–316.

nations (Eastern Europe and the U.S.S.R.) appear to want to import more from the West than they can pay for with current exports plus reserves and credits. Of course, they often manage to keep their payments within these bounds by the exercise of rigid trade controls but this barely disguises their obvious excess demands reflected, in part, in constant requests for credits and in rapidly increasing debt service/export ratios.[1] At the moment, there seems to be no solution to this problem in sight. I would like to argue here that the hard currency payments difficulties faced by the socialist nations are, in fact, likely to continue for a long period of time. This is because they are due to certain systemic features of the Stalinist model of central planning as presently practiced in Eastern Europe and the U.S.S.R. and are unlikely to disappear in the absence of rather drastic reforms in planning methods.[2] Such reforms, I feel, are unlikely to be implemented in the near future.

The discussion will begin with a brief outline of three well-known features of the Stalinist central planning model which are relevant to the foreign trade problem. This will be followed in section III by the impact of planning on the quality and competitiveness of Communist bloc products and implications are drawn in the framework of comparative advantage theory. Beginning with section IV, an attempt is made to demonstrate why central planning with direct controls leads to persistent deficits (or repressed deficits) with the West. It will be argued that the planners suffer from three illusions, each of which leads them to make ex ante foreign trade plans which cannot be fulfilled and which result in unplanned deficits and/or repressed demands. These illusions are termed: A "salability" illusion (related to the discussion in section III), a "terms of trade" illusion, and a "macro-balance" illusion.[3] The "terms of trade" illusion results from the inability of Socialist nations to use devaluation to improve their balance of payments.

II. Some Major Features of
Central Planning Under Communism[4]

Virtually all industrial enterprises in the Communist bloc are owned by the state and operated by managers appointed by the government. The planners set output, sales, and profit targets as well as prices for most enterprises, determine delivery dates, and tell each enterprise from whom it is to buy a large part of its nonlabor inputs and to whom it is to ship its products. Since there is, in effect, no real market through which supply and demand can seek an adjustment, this particular chore which is accomplished anonymously by "invisible hands" in the West, must be handled explicitly by state planning organs. This is a laborious process which requires the establishment, for literally thousands of products (in the U.S.S.R.), of "material balances" in which all sources of a commodity are listed on one side and uses or shipments on the other. If the supply and demand for a product do not balance, or balance is upset by some unpredicted event, substantial difficulties are encountered because of the complexity of interindustry relationships. Suppose, for example, that the steel balance shows a 1 million ton deficit, and a decision is made to increase steel output by this amount. The steel industry will have to be allocated more coal, limestone, machinery, labor and so forth—upsetting the balances for each of these latter commodities. Further, in order to produce more coal, limestone, and machinery, it is necessary to have more steel (and machinery, labor, etc.) than the original million extra tons desired; this requires still more coal, limestone, and machinery; and so forth in a many-staged regress. Alternatively, if it had been decided to solve the balance problem by cutting back on shipments of steel (rather than increasing steel output), similar adjustments would have to be made as various enterprises found themselves with less steel than anticipated, were forced to cut back shipments to other enterprises, and so on.

In practice, central planning has always been overfull employment planning. As some scholars have put it, the plans are "taut" envisioning higher levels of economic activity than can possibly be sustained given the available resources, including labor. Enterprises are given targets which cannot all be fulfilled despite the fact that each manager has strong bonus-type incentives to reach his individual target. The result is that there are always more demands for goods than goods available, sellers' markets are pervasive, inventories are inadequate and badly distributed because of hoarding, planners' balancing problems are aggravated, and there is repressed inflation—more money than goods.

Partly as a consequence of central planning with direct controls, prices in the CPE's (centrally planned economies) have always been disequilibrium prices which would not equate demand and supply if the economy were "freed" and which do not bear rational relationships to each other. Prices do not, of course, have to equate supply and demand since this is accomplished directly by the planners through their method of "balances." There are other factors behind price irrationality. Until recently, enterprise accounts have not included proper charges for rent, interest, and profits—only labor has been adequately accounted for. Furthermore, many enterprises have received subsidies selling their products below labor cost; others, mainly those in the consumer goods industries, have had very large excise taxes levied on their products. The overall picture is one of great confusion with each bloc nation having its own individual set of irrational prices, incomparable with its neighbors'.

This is frankly admitted as the following statement by three Polish economists testifies:

> . . . Because of the autonomous system of domestic prices in each country, an automatic and purely internal character of the monetary system and arbitrary official rates of exchange which do not reflect relative values of currencies, it is impossible to compare prices and costs of production of particular commodities in different countries.[5]

III. Bloc Competitiveness and Comparative Advantage Theory

The static comparative advantage model tells us that every nation can produce some products *relatively* more cheaply than other nations and presumably these are the products which are likely to be exported. To be useful in interpreting the real world, of course, the model has to be modified for actual conditions such as costs of transport, tariffs, and so forth. In the case of the centrally planned economies (CPE's) modification is necessary for a unique reason: namely, their relative inability to "sell" products to the West except for relatively homogeneous raw materials. This inability to "sell the product" is expressed in the difficulties in adapting to the special requirements of western buyers and to the generally low quality of most industrial products. In the words of Imre Vajda, until his death Hungary's leading expert on East-West trade, the lack of competitiveness of CMEA's exports is attributable to lack of innovation and to deficiencies in "performance, reliability, . . . appearance, packing, delivery and credit terms, assembling facilities, after-sale services, advertising, . . . selling itself . . ., *primarily factors other than price* . . ." (Vajda, p. 53, my italics).

These deficiencies are all rooted in central planning as it has been practiced over the past two decades. For most enterprises, sales of goods in domestic markets depend on direct allocation of products via the plan rather than on "salesmanship". Products are really "distributed" rather than "sold". Management incentive to do a good job is further weakened by overfull employment planning and the perennial sellers' markets which this has generated. Buyers are generally so glad to get the deliveries planned for them that they are unlikely to complain if product quality is not up to specification. In effect, the usual beneficial effects of competition under capitalism are not experienced in internal Socialist markets. Nor does competition play a significant role in intrabloc foreign trade. Trade flows between pairs of socialist nations are determined in large bilateral bargaining sessions. Not only does each enterprise export into a protected predetermined market but, in fact, there is usually no contact between the producing enterprise of the exporting nation and the consuming (using) enterprise or person in the importing nation. The major form of contact is between exporting and importing state-trading enterprises in the two nations and, under these circumstances, the feedback from consumer to producer is either absent or very weak.

The net result of distribution via plan, perennial sellers' markets, and insulation of a seller from buyer in foreign trade is low quality and a reduced ability to sell manufactured products in competitive Western markets.[6] To have a comparative disadvantage in "selling" is much more of a handicap than having a comparative disadvantage in the production of certain products because it cuts across a wide range of products (below).

A second factor which adds to the comparative disadvantages of the Socialist nations is their relative weakness in innovation and technological change. This weakness has been documented many times (Wasowski, 1970) and was a major impetus for economic reforms, mostly unsuccessful, undertaken in the late 1960's and still in process. Many institutional factors can be adduced which explain these problems in innovation. One of the major factors is the same lack of competition due to distribution by plan and sellers' markets that was responsible for "inability to sell" discussed above. Further, enterprise incentive systems inadequately reward managers for introducing new technology in comparison with the rewards for just fulfilling output and distribution targets. Since introducing new products and new techniques upsets traditional supply channels and disturbs established production routines, managers view innovation as inherently risky. Another impediment: While R. & D. expenditures in the Socialist nations are relatively large, the tie between producing enterprises and R. & D. establishments is not the intimate one that exists in Western industry and in a significant sense the productivity of these establishments appears to be quite low, and so forth.

In the days of the so-called permanent dollar shortage, it was argued by some that U.S. superior ability to generate and apply new technology was a major cause of our balance of payments strength. It was argued, in effect, that an equilibrium based on traditional static comparative advantage was constantly upset by the destabilizing dynamic influence of U.S. innovations. The wheel was turned full circle by Raymond Vernon's product cycle theory in which it was argued that innovators quickly lose their markets to lower cost (usually lower wage) imitators and after a short time are forced to import the products they formerly exported—and from the same nations (Vernon, 1966). Balance between innovator and imitator is maintained when the innovators substitute a new product for the old.

Now, not only are the Socialist nations poor innovators, but, for the same basic reasons, they are also poor imitators. What this suggests then is that insofar as technology, innovation, and imitation are important factors in the determination of world trade flows, and that they are important is now fairly well established (see, for example, Vernon, ed. 1970), the Socialist nations tend to be in a constant moving disequilibrium with the West.

The comparative disadvantages suffered by the CPE's would not be as serious as they are were it not for the fact that manufactured products comprise such a large and increasing part of world trade. Between 1938 and 1969, their share in world trade rose from 39 to 64 percent in constant 1963 prices, and from 46 to 64 percent in current prices. Commodities in the SITC categories 5 through 8 (manufactured goods) constituted, in 1969, 74.5 percent of the exports of the developed market economies.[7] To be limited in ability to export products to the West which are the major fare of world trade is a serious limitation, indeed. The Soviet bloc nations do produce respectable amounts of industrial and manufactured products. As Paul Gregory (1970, pp. 175, 180) has demonstrated, the speed with which they have oriented their economies toward industry and manufacturing is unprecedented. This foreign trade with each other also reflects the predominance in their economies of industry and manufacturing: In 1967, 70 percent of their trade with each other was in SITC categories 5 to 8, that is, in manufactured goods. This figure would undoubtedly have been even higher had intrabloc trade not included the large raw material shipments to the other nations from the U.S.S.R. The comparable figures for the percentage of manufactured goods in total exports of EEC and EFTA in 1967 were 80 and 79 percent, respectively—not too much higher in light of the aforementioned Soviet raw material exports. The problem of the CMEA nations in earning hard currency is reflected by the fact that the percentage of their exports of manufactured goods to EEC and EFTA were only 21 and 41 percent of totals to these nations (contrast with 70 percent intrabloc), whereas corresponding imports were 90 and 84 percent, respectively.[8]

Before leaving this section, it is important to square the above observations with received theory. At least two trade theories can be adapted to explain or throw light on the predicament of the Communist countries due to the factors elaborated above.

(1) Static comparative advantage theory, as noted above, is usually phrased in terms of relative production costs. The nations of Eastern Europe undoubtedly have the capability of producing and do produce many industrial and manufactured products "relatively" more cheaply than many Western nations. The several U.S.-U.S.S.R. purchasing power

parity studies which have appeared show a wide range of ruble-dollar ratios in manufactured goods and reveal that the U.S.S.R. produces many industrial products in which it appears to have a clear comparative cost advantage vis-a-vis the United States (Becker, 1959 and 1973; CIA, 1960). It is a long step, however, between producing cheaply and being able to compete successfully in world export markets. It is easy to ignore or assume away the "ability to sell" when this collection of traits (quality, service, advertising, packaging, et cetera) is relatively evenly distributed among nations. In the case of the centrally planned economies, this easy assumption is no longer possible. Comparative production costs no longer determine trade flows; salesmanship in all its many variants is also important. Problems in selling manufactured goods are compounded by relative inabilities to innovate and imitate. A static theory of comparative advantage modified to incorporate marketing and innovation activities would say that CPE's do have comparative advantages in production of many manufactured goods but lack the "factors" for comparative advantages in marketing and innovation. Such a theory would predict that in a properly functioning trading system, the CPE's would want to import from the West marketing and related services, high quality goods, and technology. Such import behavior is, in fact, observed and is steadily increasing. Unfortunately, the mechanism for importing marketing and other such skills are insufficiently developed to enable the CPE's to realize their potential comparative advantages in production of many manufactured products.[9]

(2) Linder's theory of trade and transformation on the face of it does not appear to fit the experience of the Communist nations in East-West trade. Linder argued that the Heckscher-Ohlin differential factor proportions theory of comparative advantage fails to explain the intensity of trade between developed industrial nations. Among such nations, trade is more intense in manufactured products, the more alike (rather than different) such nations are in factor proportions, per capita income,[10] and so forth. Similarity between two nations means that each has (1) the ability to produce the kinds of products demanded by the other as well as (2) a demand for the products produced by the other. Trade then takes place as a result of minor differences in tastes and of product differentiation—trading Chevrolets for Fiats. Intrabloc trade appears to have developed along these lines. For example, exports of manufactured goods increased from 53.5 to 70.4 percent of total intrabloc exports between 1957 and 1967. On the other hand, over the same period bloc exports to EEC changed from 26.7 to 26.6 percents, and to EFTA increased from 32.2 to only 40.6 percents.[11] How can East-West trade be squared with Linder's theory? To generalize this theory, one would have to account for the characteristics of nonmarket economies.

A broader formulation would have greater intensity of trade in manufactured products, a function not only of similarities of factor proportions
and per capita income, but of type of economic system as well.[12] Under
these circumstances, systemic differences would lead one to predict less
trade in manufactured goods as a percent of total trade in East-West
than in either West-West or East-East trade.

IV. The "Salability" Illusion

The main point of the preceding section is that the Socialist
nations have a comparative disadvantage in "selling" and in "developing
technology" and that this makes it difficult for them to compete in that
75 percent of world markets in which industrialized nations trade. It
is now necessary to show how this factor and other systemic problems
(below) have affected their balances of payments.

Historically, it is useful to distinguish between the period before,
say, 1955 and the years after 1965. Excess demand for Western goods
certainly existed in the early period but it was small compared with the
recent period. Several factors are responsible. First, Western controls on
exports of strategic materials to the Socialist nations were extremely
severe in the first decade after World War II and there was relatively
very little of interest available for import by the Eastern nations. Second,
there was considerable political pressure within the group of Socialist
nations to foster intrabloc trade (as opposed to East-West trade) to the
greatest extent possible. Therefore, even though the Eastern nations did
engage in some trade with the West, they undoubtedly repressed their
desires for Western goods far below the level which was possible even
with Western controls.

Developments in recent years have had, in Johnson's (1968)
terminology, a "pro-trade-bias" for Western products.[13] Several factors
were responsible. First, the decline of the cold war and development of
détente led to a substantial reduction in Western trade controls. As
more goods became available, Eastern interest in Western products
expanded. Second, the severity with which the Eastern nations repressed
demand for Western products was eased. This was due in part to the
developing détente with the West and in part to the fact that the U.S.S.R.
was simply neither willing nor able to exercise the same degree of political
control over the bloc after Stalin's death. Hence, demand for Western
products was no longer repressed to the same extent. Third, as the
Eastern nations developed, they became more interested in consuming
high-quality high-technology products than before. Fourth, this interest
which existed earlier, was intensified by the dramatic decline in growth
rates throughout Eastern Europe and the U.S.S.R. since about 1960.

This decline is quite generally attributed by both Eastern and Western economists to the fact that the major gains from extensive growth have been exhausted and that further rapid growth will have to be intensive. This will have to be achieved by raising productivity through the use of higher quality machinery and equipment and, in particular, products embodying advanced technology and generally available almost exclusively in the advanced Western industrial nations.

Now, in order to satisfy this both increased and less-repressed demand for Western imports, the Socialist nations have attempted to increase their exports to the West. They have succeeded in doing so but all indications are that the increase in exports has consistently lagged behind the increase in demand for imports. This in itself should not necessarily lead to deficits (although some deficits may be planned in advance to the extent that reserves or credit are available). For, to the extent that the CPE's are fully aware of their selling difficulties, they can tailor their planned imports to the amounts which can be financed through exports. "Salability" problems, in this case, would simply reduce the level of trade. To some extent, this has probably occurred.

Apparently, however, the planners also suffer from a "salability" illusion which leads them to overestimate the amount of exports they can sell each year in the West. When ex ante export plans are not fulfilled, the ex ante balanced trade plan becomes an ex post deficit (with unplanned drawing down of reserves or unplanned credits) and/ or import plans cannot be fulfilled. Support for the hypothesis that a "salability" illusion exists can be found in the Eastern literature. For example, the eminent Hungarian economist, the late Sandor Ausch (p. 109) has stated:

> In many cases . . . the extent of exports "planned" by individual CMEA countries exceeds what the capitalist market in question is able to absorb . . .

Speaking on the same issue, the U.N. Economic Commission for Europe (1970, p. 115) puts the problem as follows:

> . . . East-European planners and exporters experience considerable difficulties in assessing their possibilities for sales of manufactured goods to the industrialized countries of western Europe and also in selling their goods on the markets in question once decisions to export have been taken. These difficulties stem from uncertainty concerning terms of access to the markets, the small volume of present exports, the long-standing ties between west European enterprises, the keen competition in industrial goods in general and in technologically advanced products

in particular, and the lack of experience on the part of east European economic organizations in western forms of marketing.

One would think that the "salability" illusion would eventually disappear. At least four reasons can be given which may explain its persistence. First, and most important, Western markets account for no more than about 4 percent of Soviet-bloc sales (domestic and foreign), in the case of the U.S.S.R. less than 1 percent. The planners think that their products are salable in the West on the basis of the continuing experience that 96 percent of their products are salable either at home or in intrabloc trade. This experience is undoubtedly so overwhelming that it is difficult for the planners and especially plant managers to adapt in practice fully to the idiosyncrasies (to them) of Western markets. Second, some attempts are undoubtedly made by bloc producers and salesmen to improve the "quality" and "salability" of their products. But the quality, technology, et cetera "gaps" are probably perceived by bloc planners as stationary goals when in fact they are moving targets. When bloc products and techniques are improved, planners perceive equality but, in fact, a "gap" remains at a new and higher level. Third, many bloc foreign trade organization representatives undoubtedly do realize that the products they are trying to sell are deficient by Western standards. It is one thing to recognize the problem; it is another, however, to force producing enterprises, advertisers, packagers, servicers, et cetera to meet higher specifications when they have little or no motivation to do so. Finally, the foreign trade plans may be chronically too "taut" just as the national domestic economic plans are and for analogous reasons. Possessed of a great desire for imports from the West, the planners attempt to sell more to the West than is feasible; and the more they wish to buy from the West, the greater the temptation to try to export products which may be unsalable.

We have argued above that bloc exports to the West tend to fall short of plan because of their poor quality. No such market impediments exist on the import side. Imports are geared to the plan and transactions are consummated on the expectation that export earnings will be available. When it turns out that export earnings are falling behind, a deficit results and/or imports are repressed. It is, of course, hard to repress imports especially of intermediate products because negative repercussions on plan fulfillment can be very expensive possibly costing many times the market value of the import.

The problem generated by the "salability" illusion is presented diagrammatically in Chart 1. Let T be the CMEA transformation curve, with the X axis representing exportables, the Y axis representing importables. In order to simplify the presentation, we assume that the only

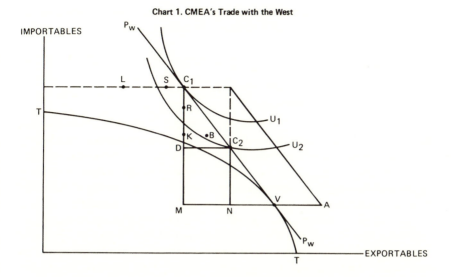

Chart 1. CMEA's Trade with the West

exportable is a low-quality low-technology manufactured product. Our importable can be any product that CMEA wishes to buy from the West. Clearly, we have in mind here primarily high-quality high-technology manufactured products. Let P_w represent the world price line, and V the production point. P_w is shown as tangent to T at V; it need not be, of course, and probably is not—but the argument is not affected by the assumption. Let the U's represent the set of CMEA community indifference curves in a choice between domestically-produced goods, including those traded within the bloc (called internal trade), and goods imported from the West.[14]

In effect, then, the CMEA nations establish plans which envisage exports totaling VM in exchange for imports totaling MC_1. They are frustrated in their attempt to carry out these plans because of the quality of their product and their inability to "sell." They find that at world price, P_w, they can only market VN of exports which brings in only enough foreign exchange to import MD $(=C_2)$ worth of goods. This leaves them with an excess demand for hard currency imports of DC_1. This excess demand may be satisfied through borrowing or drawing down reserves of hard currency or gold by an amount VA. Rapidly rising debt-service/hard currency export ratios (Farrell, 1973; Snell, 1974; Brainard, 1976; Zoeter, 1977) indicate that borrowing has been resorted to on a fairly large scale and much of this was "unplanned." The excess supply of exportables, MN, is not likely to be observable, however, since these are rapidly absorbed into the domestic economy when they prove unsalable at the going world price. The rationale for this statement is presented in section VI below.

V. Inability to Devalue and the "Terms of Trade Illusion": An Import-Export Asymmetry

In the previous section, we sidestepped the question as to whether or not bloc currencies were overvalued. As we shall demonstrate shortly, bloc currencies cannot be viewed as overvalued in the usual western sense. Nevertheless the foreign trade behavior as described in section IV which results in either unplanned deficits or the need to suppress planned imports does suggest the equivalent of overvaluation.

Another factor suggests the existence of (the equivalent of) overvaluation. We refer to the fact that the socialist nations can be viewed as a high-cost, low-variety, low-quality economic region relative to the rest of the world. In addition to factors cited in section III, this is due to their relatively small size (in world trade), to the fact that they concentrate their trade among themselves, and represent in effect the socialist version of a highly trade-diverting customs union.[15] As is well known, trade diversion implies higher costs; and a trade-diverting customs union is one in which members produce and sell to each other at higher than world prices. If one views the socialist nations as a high-cost enclave in the world economy, a situation perpetuated by implicit discriminatory quotas, then it follows that any relaxation of controls or mutual reduction of East-West barriers will lead to a tendency toward more imports by East than by West, a situation which will continue so long as East-West barriers exceed East-East and West-West barriers.

While under capitalist institutions, the above circumstances would spell currency overvaluation and would call for devaluation as a remedy, under present socialist institutions the same cannot be said. Bloc currencies are totally inconvertible and, in international trade, serve none of the usual functions of money (medium of exchange, store of value). By the same token, devaluation of these currencies (that is, changing official nominal values) has no impact whatsoever on bloc foreign trade. This peculiar state of affairs is a result of central planning with direct controls. One aspect of this problem has been dubbed "commodity inconvertibility." Commodity inconvertibility means that foreign buyers are not allowed to come into a centrally planned economy and shop around freely for goods as in capitalist countries. That is to say, foreign buyers are not allowed to compete with local enterprises for goods which have been allocated under the national plan since such competition would disrupt the carefully drawn fabric of the plan and lead to the undesirable repercussions noted earlier. Further, given irrational domestic prices, foreigners might purchase commodities at a price below the real cost of production—heavily subsidized commodities, for example. For these reasons, foreign importers are restricted largely to the commodities offered by the foreign trade associations as established in the State plan and usually under long-term agreement. Further, the Socialist nations don't allow foreigners to hold their currencies—in any case there wouldn't be any takers because of uncertainties as to what the money could buy, when, and at what price.

Inconvertibility is also a necessary consequence of the fact, described earlier (section II), that each Socialist nation has a set of irrational prices which differs unsystematically from that of other Socialist nations and from world prices. Obviously, an exchange rate which links a set of irrational prices to other sets of prices, rational or irrational, can have little meaning or function. The existence of commodity inconvertibility and irrational prices has forced these nations, as a last resort, to trade with each other (and with the West) at world prices or at some approximation thereto, and to settle their trade imbalances[16] either by deferred shipments of goods or by payments of convertible currency or gold.[17] That is to say, their currencies do not function as means of payment and their official exchange rates do not serve as real prices.[18] Now, while the use of world prices and convertible currencies effectively circumvents the need to use Socialist currencies and exchange rates, it does by the same token deprive these nations of an important instrument variable for improving their balances of payments, namely, devaluation.[19] Inability to devalue is a substantial handicap in the struggle to achieve payments balance.

Unable to devalue, Soviet bloc foreign trade planners largely trade with the West at a set of world prices which makes them deficit prone just as are Western nations with overvalued currencies. Under capitalism, maintenance of an overvalued exchange rate leads to deficits because the individual importers and exporters receive misleading signals and the capitalist nation, taken as a whole, operates under a "terms of trade" illusion. Importers are provided, in effect, with hidden subsidies which makes foreign goods look cheap and which leads them to import more than is consistent with payments balance; and exporters are saddled with the equivalent of a hidden tariff which makes foreign competing products look cheap and prevents them from selling as much as is consistent with trade balance. Western authorities become aware of overvaluation when deficits are incurred. Devaluation by the proper amount then eliminates implicit subsidies and tariffs and restores payments equilibrium.

Soviet bloc planners depend, like western authorities, on deficits to signal disequilibrium or the equivalent of overvaluation. Although they cannot devalue to eliminate a deficit, is it possible to simulate devaluation? The answer is yes particularly for exports but it is not clear that such a policy will be blessed with success.

Devaluation can be simulated on the export side by simply reducing below world prices the prices at which exports are offered.[20] There are several difficulties with such a policy. First, the question of "fairness." An Eastern ministry of foreign trade could hardly fail but be miffed at having to sell its exports at below world prices while having to pay world prices for its imports. World prices are looked upon, in the European socialist world, as representing an approximation to "fair" prices and it is these prices which are used, with some adjustments, in intrabloc trade. A bloc ministry of foreign trade would undoubtedly be reluctant to incur "discrimination" against its exports on such a wholesale basis.

Second, while pricing exports at below world prices is possible when the Eastern nation is exporting a product to a Western nation which does not produce that product domestically, it may not be possible where domestic competition exists because of antidumping rules. Given irrational prices and disequilibrium as well as nonfunctioning exchange rates, it is virtually impossible for a Socialist nation to refute a dumping charge even when the product in question is not being sold at a true loss. Because of the obvious difficulties in adjudicating such antidumping charges, the U.S.S.R. agreed, in its recent (now annulled) trade agreement with the United States, to withdraw any export which causes distress to a local U.S. producer. The United Kingdom and the original EEC nations also have agreements with the Eastern European nations which forbid the latter from exporting at below local domestic prices. These arrangements are much more restrictive than the antidumping laws themselves since the decision automatically favors the domestic producer against the exporter. In effect, some Socialist exporters are not allowed to compete effectively, if at all, in domestic markets in many Western nations and products.

So far, we have assumed that the Eastern nation or nations cannot eliminate excess demand for hard currency imports because they can't lower their terms of trade either by devaluation or by simply lowering the price of many of their exports because of Western market disruption laws. They can, however, lower the prices of some exports because some nations don't apply market disruption laws and others do not produce domestically some of the products imported from the East (and elsewhere). What sort of behavior and response might be expected?

Assume as before (chart 1) that a nation (or CMEA) plans to export VM with which to buy MC_1 of imports at world prices, P_w. At P_w, only VN can be exported and, therefore, only MD imported. Suppose that in order to increase exports, the nation lowers the price of unsold exportables. In the real world, some separation of markets might be possible and the prices of some of these goods might be lowered without affecting the prices of exportables in general. In terms of the assumptions of chart 1, however, the lowering of the price of our exportable product must be viewed as equivalent to a devaluation. In other words, from the standpoint of the nation lowering its prices, the slope of P_w shifts downward and to the left with its pivot remaining, in the short run, at V. The important question for the exporter is: How much of a reduction in prices is required in order to clear the market? If, for example, the market can be cleared by a shift in P_w to VR (not drawn), then it is very probable that prices would be reduced since the nation would end up on a U curve which is above U_2. If, on the other hand, market-clearing involves a $P_w=VK$ or any other price line below U_2, then the nation would clearly be worse off for lowering prices. In this case, prices might be lowered enough to sell part but not all of the unsold exports, if by this means additional exports can be sold and a position above U_2 achieved (say, B). If what we have said above (section III) is true, Western demand may be very inelastic with respect to price changes in CMEA exportables and it may be impossible to sell much more even at lower prices. We have already quoted Imre Vajda on this point—that lack of competitiveness of CMEA exports is due primarily to "factors other than price . . ." (Vajda, p. 53). If this is the case, then it may be impossible to export much more than VN at any acceptable price. Buyers in the advanced Western nations are either not interested at all or require an enormous price cut before they will buy automobiles which can't be easily serviced, machinery which breaks down frequently, equipment which is obsolete, and other relatively inferior manufactured products. The problem is exacerbated by Western antidumping laws and market disruption agreements. We pointed out that the short-run goal of lowering export prices is to clear the market of unsold exportables, MN. The achievement of this goal, it should be noted, would not enable the nation to fulfill its import plan because of poorer terms of trade. Thus, even if all exports are sold, imports will rise to MK or to MR but not to MC_1. If the planners are determined to achieve their import goal and to finance it by increased exports, then over the longer-run exports must be raised above VM. This assumes that the nation was able to profitably sell all of its exportables in the first instance by lowering prices—reaching a point like R. As with the short-run goal, success depends on whether the further lowering of export prices falls within the elastic range. If it does, then a point like S might be reached in which the import goal MG_1 is just reached by exporting more than VM. If on the other hand, achievement of the import goal requires the terms of trade to dip to, say, VL which is below U_2, the planners will not attempt it (if they are rational and have sufficient information). Finally, recall that the possibilities of lowering prices (rather than devaluing the currency) are severely limited by antidumping laws and market-disruption agreements.

The situation described above is akin to that of Western nations that have experienced so-called structural disequilibrium in their balances of payments (Kindleberger, 1968, pp. 487–488). This term has been used to describe nations whose exportables have been, among other things: First, products which have become obsolete, in some sense, and can no longer compete in world markets; or second, resources which have been exhausted; or third, temporarily reduced by wartime destruction and disruption (Europe after World War II). At the same time, nations in the first two categories have become accustomed to a certain level of imports either as crucial intermediate inputs into industry or as final products in the standard of living or, if in the third category, need imports for reconstruction, and find it difficult to cut back imports to the lower levels currently permitted by exports. Under these circumstances, devaluation is not likely to increase exports in the short- or medium-run—not until substitute exportables can be developed. Devaluation would, of course, reduce expenditures on imports if demand were sufficiently elastic—which may not always be the case. Hence strong balance of payments pressures may exist for some time.

We have discussed simulation of devaluation on the export side but not with regard to imports. Simulation on the import side is more difficult since if it is to be accomplished it must be done so in terms of shadow prices rather than real prices. Let me explain. Devaluation raises the actual prices of imports to buyers in the devaluing nation and this serves as a strong disincentive to importing as much as before. This cannot be simulated by a Socialist nation—that is to say, no nation would insist on paying more than the going price for imports. What the nation can do, however, is to raise the minimum level of profitability at which imports are allowed.[21] Such an effort is likely to be less than perfectly satisfactory. With prices as messed up as they are, profitability measures are unlikely to be taken very seriously.[22] It will be difficult, indeed, to reduce the level of desired imports when their ostensible hard currency cost has not changed. An overvaluation-type illusion that imports are cheaper than they really are undoubtedly remains under these circumstances. This illusion is fostered by the antimercantilistic approach to foreign trade taken by the CPE's. Central planners have been much more interested in importing than exporting, looking upon the latter activity as a necessary evil to acquire currency for imports.[23] This would give them a tendency to be overzealous importers and underzealous exporters particularly in the absence of clear terms of trade signals.

VI. The "Macro-Balance" Illusion

Overfull employment planning has already been mentioned as the cause of sellers' markets in the Socialist nations and indirectly, therefore, a cause of the reduced ability to export to the West. It also operates directly on the balance of payments. As noted, overfull employment planning means that planned demands exceed available supplies. Under these circumstances, as with inflationary pressures in Western nations, domestic producers and consumers compete for exportables and demand more imports and in the process create pressures which, if successful, cause deterioration in the balance of payments, including that with the West. These forces are most easily envisaged in terms of the "absorption" approach which, as is well known, tells us that even a devaluation is unlikely to improve a nation's payment balance under these conditions. The usual algebraic formulation of the absorption analysis is:

$$X - M = Y - A$$

where X and M denote exports and imports, respectively; Y denotes output and A is absorption or expenditures (for C + I + G). Clearly, if a nation spends more than it produces, that is $A > Y$, then it must run a deficit, $M > X$.

The situation can be demonstrated diagrammatically as follows (chart 2). Assume a nation on an actual transformation curve, T_a with domestic output at Y_a and an after-trade equivalent absorption, A_a. Assume that this nation planned to be on T_p with before-trade goal of Y_p and after-trade goal of A_p. If the nation actually ends up at A_a instead of planned A_p it will experience excess demand equal to BD of exportables + CE of importables[24] (or some equivalent combination at some other point such as the traditional A_pG of importables). Plans may be fulfilled by either dishoarding foreign exchange reserves or obtaining credits of an amount measured as either A_pG of importables or HA_p ($=FY_p$) of exportables.

In the discussion of overfull employment planning, we have abstracted from the balance-of-payments problems discussed earlier in connection with inability to sell and to innovate and with being in a high-cost customs union. In fact, these are different causes of excess demand even though, as indicated earlier, overfull employment planning

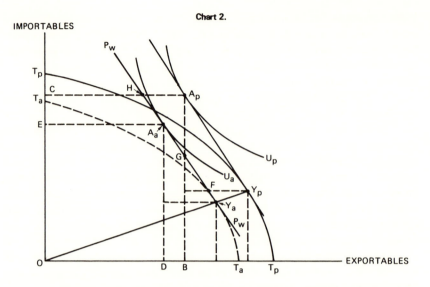

Chart 2.

is a contributing cause of the inability to sell. The balance-of-payments problem connected with inability to sell is a structural problem, one in which exportables cannot be converted into imports on the desired scale, leaving the nation with an excess demand for imports. Given favorable price elasticities, this problem, along with that connected with being a high-cost customs union, can be resolved in theory, though as we have seen not in practice, by devaluation. The excess demand generated by overfull employment planning cannot be resolved (without making special assumptions regarding real balance effects, et cetera) by devaluation.

VII. Rigidity in Face of the Western Business Cycle

It has long been a matter of faith that one great advantage of trade under central planning is that it tends to insulate the economy from the vagaries of Western markets, especially the Western business cycle. To some extent this is true. So, for example, with internal prices divorced from world prices, and with nonfunctioning exchange rates, clearly the CPE's are in little danger of importing Western inflation. But this may be as far as it goes. Soviet experience during the Great Depression provided ample evidence, ignored until recently, that: (1) A decline in economic activity in the West can cause an unplanned drop in CPE exports; and (2) changes in terms of trade can cause unexpected and unavoidable gains or losses from trade—in the 1930's, large losses. Soviet exports would have dropped by even more than they did in the

1930's had not Stalin determined to sell at all costs and at almost any price. Peasants starved so that grain would be available for export. Imports continued high for a few years to meet 5-year plan goals and then these also were abruptly cut back. Stalin had enormous power to generate exportables and control imports.

The Soviet experience of the early 1930's was repeated during the Western recession which began in 1974 and was shared by all of the CMEA nations. Each Eastern country experienced a sharp decline in its upward trend in exports; in fact, despite inflation, exports actually declined in 1975 in comparison with annual increases in the previous 2 years of approximately 40 percent. Moreover, CMEA raw material importers also experienced sharp deterioration in terms of trade. Since imports could not be reduced as rapidly as exports, very large hard currency deficits were incurred. These factors led to a doubling of hard currency debt over a few-year period.

In these respects, the CPE's proved themselves as vulnerable, if not more so, than capitalist nations. Vulnerability, as in the first 5-year plan, was partly due to inability mixed with unwillingness to cut back, on short notice, imports of intermediate products on which plans depended. To cut back such imports often involves very large losses— losses which can be many times larger than the cost of the imports. But vulnerability, this time, is also due to the fact that Eastern consumers are used to a rising standard of living and Eastern leaders are, unlike Stalin, unwilling or unable to disappoint them. Unplanned austerity is no longer in fashion in planned economies.

VIII. Export and Import Incentives at the Enterprise Level

A final factor, related to those mentioned in III above, is outlined briefly. Basically, there is a special asymmetry between exports and imports from the standpoint of equilibrium in the balance of payments. Producing enterprises whose products are exportable are usually paid in domestic currency and at the same price regardless of whether their products are sold in domestic, intrabloc, or Western markets. Therefore they are indifferent, on price grounds, as to which market their products are sold. However, they often prefer domestic or intrabloc markets as less demanding upon them and less risky.

Some enterprises which can use importables, on the other hand, have a strong preference for foreign goods, especially those from the West.[25] They are not concerned about the cost of the imports, especially the foreign exchange cost, since they are charged in local currency and often at the local price equivalent. The much higher quality of many imported inputs is a further inducement to managers to incur the higher costs of importing, if necessary.

The net result of the model just described is that there are stronger inducements to import than to export particularly to the West.[26]

IX. Concluding Remarks

How persistent is the socialist hard currency deficit likely to be? Is it a chimera like the permanent dollar shortage or will it continue into the foreseeable future?

With the political détente of the past 10 years, two classes of attempts have been made to grapple pragmatically with the problems. First, a considerable number of cooperation agreements have developed between Eastern European and Western enterprises in which the Western partner undertakes to assist in the production and marketing of products produced in the Eastern countries. Second, and related, there has been considerably more Western investment in Eastern Europe in recent years and, in fact, the proposed U.S. investments in Siberian energy resources are on an unprecedented scale anywhere. Further, these are to be repaid largely in kind, thereby presumably avoiding the convertible currency transfer problem.

It seems unlikely that the cooperative production and marketing agreements could ever develop on sufficient scale to overcome the socialist quality and inability to sell problems. Further, the technique is an inefficient way of earning hard currency since the Eastern European country loses a large share of the earnings to its Western partner—earnings which otherwise would accrue to it. Western investments in the socialist nations must also be viewed as suboptimal in terms of the problem at hand. The volume of investment which will flow under a repayment in kind constraint is bound to be much less than if repayment could be made in convertible currency. Further, repayment in kind has typically been most acceptable to Western enterprises in the case of products like oil and gas which could be expected to easily generate hard currency in the future. In this sense, repayment in kind provides no real relief from the convertible currency deficit, though the investment it induces may, if employed effectively.

Ultimately, it seems to me, hard currency balance of payments pressures of the socialist nations will not be eliminated until measures are taken to eliminate the root causes mentioned above. This would require a reform in which: The operation of the economy would be decentralized; prices would be freed; internal markets would be opened to foreign traders; exchange rates would become operational and internal and external prices would be organically connected; and overfull employment planning would be ended. The elimination of overfull employment by itself would reduce balance of payments pressures in the absence of other reforms but this appears a most unlikely possibility (Holzman, 1970; Grossman, 1971). A reform embodying the features noted above would increase ability to sell, to generate and adopt technology, and eliminate commodity inconvertibility thereby making it possible to effectively devalue a currency. It seems unlikely that such reforms are in the offing. In fact, current eastern interest in importing technology is widely viewed in the West as a substitute for full scale reform. A major reason why full scale reforms are unlikely to be undertaken is that they would lead fairly quickly to the near liquidation of the Soviet bloc preferential trading area. The reform would involve shifting the trading decisions of the nation from the central planning boards and foreign trade monopolies to thousands of enterprises. Faced with many more profitable opportunities to buy and sell in the West for reasons mentioned earlier, these enterprises would shift many of their transactions from East to West.

The big question is whether the U.S.S.R. would be willing to allow such a development. At this point in time it seems unlikely. For one thing, the Soviet internal reform has been extremely conservative and in fact, is presently backward-looking. Radical reforms, with the characteristics described above, would have a significant impact on the loci of power in government and society and is undoubtedly opposed by many of those currently in power (Burks, 1974). Further, the Soviet trade/GNP ratio is, like that of the United States, relatively small and the gains from a geographical restructuring of trade therefore of much less significance to them than to the smaller socialist nations. Their major concern, however, would be the possible weakening of political ties which might result from sharply lowered levels of intrabloc trade. However, the U.S.S.R. should be able to maintain political control over Eastern Europe without monopolizing the latter's foreign trade.

Notes

This paper benefited from the comments of Abram Bergson on two earlier drafts. Much of the material in Parts IV–VI appeared in Holzman, 1979.

1. Cf. Farrell (1973), Snell (1974), Brainard (1976), and Zoeter (1977).

2. Some LDC's have chronic balance of payments problems as do some advanced industrial nations. Many of the factors behind the socialist nations' problem presented below are unique to them, however. Other than systemic factors may also be responsible, of course. For example, the recent readier availability of western investments and credits on reasonable terms and the willingness of CPE's to entertain such relations with the West is one such factor.

3. While not precisely comparable, parallels with western experience may be drawn for illustrative purposes. A communist country with a "salability" illusion is one which faces balance of payments problems similar to those faced by a capitalist nation in "structural" disequilibrium. Nations which run deficits because their exportables have recently become obsolete or have been exhausted (raw materials) are cases in point. The "terms of trade" illusion is experienced by western nations with overvalued exchange rates. Western nations with full employment and inflation are apt to experience balance of payments problems related to those of communist nations with what we have called a "macro-balance" illusion.

4. The characteristics of central planning which are described directly below and foreign trade behavior described in later sections are a quite accurate description of present practice in all of the nations of the Soviet Bloc except Hungary which has undergone substantial economic reforms over the past five years. It is probably most descriptive of the situations in the U.S.S.R., Rumania and Bulgaria and somewhat less so of Czechoslovakia, Poland and East Germany. Nevertheless, it should be stressed that as a result of recent reforms, central planning in all of the Eastern nations is somewhat less rigid than described below.

5. Cited by Fallenbuchl, 1974, p. 104, from a 1971 Polish source. For a similar statement by two Soviet economists, see Alekseev and Borisenko, 1964, p. 47.

6. Inability to compete in Western markets is further aggravated by "commodity inconvertibility" to be discussed in section V. In effect, the Eastern nations find it difficult to make unplanned exports because of the disruptive effects on the central plan. This prevents them from taking advantage of many marketing opportunities and also often means that potential Western importers face longer than usual delivery times and may decide to buy elsewhere.

7. All figures estimated from United Nations, 1971, pp. 71–72. It is important to note that the rise in oil and other raw material prices over the past 5 years would reduce the percentage that manufactured goods are of total world trade.

8. All of the above figures are from the United Nations, 1979A, pp. 102–105. In 1968 the ratio of Western European imports from Eastern Europe relative to exports to Eastern Europe was .32 for all manufactures and .19 for engineering products. Corresponding ratios for the U.S.S.R. were .13 and .11. Cf. United Nations, 1970B, p. 75.

9. Prof. Edward Hewett who independently has developed similar views argues that "structure of organization" can be viewed as a "factor endowment" which differs among systems. CPE organization tends to be bureaucratic. Since production activity is more bureaucratically organized than marketing or R. & D., the CPE's will tend to have a comparative advantage in the former and disadvantage in the latter two. A brief summary of this view is contained in Hewett, 1974.

10. Closeness in per capita income will usually involve capital-labor ratios which are not too far apart, hence similar factor proportions.

11. On the import side, the increments were 11 and 16 percents, respectively, from EEC and EFTA, and were at the higher levels indicated above.

12. Following Hewett's formulation, one could argue simply that factor proportions are different—since he views "structure of organization" among the factors.

13. A "pro-trade-bias" on the import side means that the "income (output) elasticity of demand for imports" is greater than unity.

14. T and U are taken to represent CMEA rather than a representative CMEA nation in order to abstract from intrabloc trade. Alternatively, we might have either assumed a Communist nation which conducted all of its trade with the West; or added another dimension to the diagram to include intrabloc trade.

15. This is suggested by the following fact. Before World War II, they traded very little with each other—around 15 percent or less; the comparable percentages since about 1952 have been between 55 to 80 percent. Second, trade/GNP ratios have been much lower than they would have been had these nations not turned socialist and embraced each other as trading partners (Pryor, 1968). Trade creation implies rising trade/GNP ratios.

16. World prices provide the only consistent set of relative values upon which they can agree.

17. In intrabloc trade, an attempt is made to avoid imbalances and trade is usually within a few percent of perfect bilateral balance in world prices.

18. This is not strictly true for Hungary at present.

19. Evidence that past Soviet devaluations have not affected either the quantities or selling prices of exports or imports is presented in Holzman, 1973. The reasons for these devaluations are discussed in Holzman, 1968.

20. Other products might be offered for sale at world prices which previously would have been offered only if world prices had been higher.

21. Actually, many of the CPE's are reported to use foreign trade effectiveness indexes as a guide regarding what to import and export. In their simplest form, these are ratios of local currency prices of exports or import substitutes over foreign trade prices in foreign currencies. They tell the planners how much in domestic resources is required to earn a dollar of foreign exchange through exports of different products; and how much in domestic resources are saved by a dollar's worth of imports of different products. It should be profitable to export commodities with low ratios and to import commodities with high ratios. Simulation of devaluation means raising the maximum ratio at which exports are promoted and raising the minimum ratio at which imports are allowed.

22. Discussions with a number of Eastern and Soviet foreign trade specialists in June 1976 confirmed to me that in most of the CPE's, these indexes are either not used extensively or provide only one of many kinds of information upon which import and export decisions are based.

23. In contrast, Western capitalist nations are mercantilist or nonmercantilist largely because of their interest in freeing their domestic economic policies from balance of payments constraints.

24. This is illustrated by a Polish economist writing in 1968 regarding the situation in Poland in 1966–67. He states that industry, particularly the machine building industry ". . . did not have at its disposal the necessary production capacity and therefore was unable to meet its obligations for exports within the

group of commodities including machinery and equipment, and which also could not meet the demand of the domestic market. The result of the latter failure was that the plan of imports of machinery and equipment for the same period was exceeded . . ." (Gruzewski, 1968–69, p. 22).

25. Many managers, on the other hand, are not interested in imported equipment because of the weak ties between improving enterprise performance and management bonuses.

26. It has been argued that this model no longer applies at all to Hungary (Kover, 1971, pp. 174–75) and applies to a lesser extent than suggested above in some of the other smaller socialist nations. In particular, some exporting enterprises in some of the nations have been encouraged to export to the West by regulations which allow them to keep for their own (enterprise) use part of the foreign exchange earned.

References

Ausch, Sandor, *The Theory and Practice of CMEA Cooperation,* Budapest, 1972.

Alekseev, A. and Borisenko, A., "A Price Basis of Its Own," *Problems of Economics,* April 1964.

Becker, Abraham, *Prices of Producers' Durables in the United States and the USSR in 1955,* Rand Corporation (RM-2432), Santa Monica, Cal., August 1959.

————. *Ruble Price Levels and Dollar-Ruble Ratios of Soviet Machinery in the 1960's,* Rand Corporation (R-1063-DDRE), Santa Monica, Cal., January 1973.

Brainard, L., "CMEA: Rising Deficits," *East-West Markets,* January 12, 1976.

Burks, R. V., "The Political Hazards of Economic Reform," in Joint Economic Committee, U.S. Congress, *Reorientation and Commercial Relations of the Economies of Eastern Europe,* Washington, 1974, pp. 51-78.

Central Intelligence Agency, *1955 Ruble-Dollar Price Ratios for Intermediate Products and Services in the USSR and the US,* Washington, D.C., June 1960.

Fallenbuchl, Z., "East European Integration: Comecon," in Joint Economic Committee, U.S. Congress, *Reorientation and Commercial Relations of the Economies of Eastern Europe,* Washington, 1974, pp. 79–134.

Farrell, John, "Soviet Payments Problems in Trade with the West," in Joint Economic Committee, Congress of the United States, *Soviet Economic Prospects for the Seventies,* Washington, 1973, pp. 690–711.

Gregory, Paul, *Socialist and Nonsocialist Industrialization Patterns,* New York, 1970.

Grossman, Gregory, "From the Eighth to the Ninth Five Year Plan," in N. Dodge, ed., *Analysis of the USSR's 24th Party Congress and Ninth Five Year Plan,* Mechanicsville, Md.: Cremona Foundation, 1971, pp. 54–66.

Gruzewski, Stanislaw, "Direction of Export Specialization in the Machine-Building Industry," *Soviet and East European Foreign Trade,* Winter 1968/69. Transl. from *Handel Zagraniczny,* 1968, No. 9.

Hewett, Edward, "Economic Systems and East-West Economic Relations," in *East-West Trade and Technology Transfer,* ed. by Robert Campbell and Paul

Marer, Indiana University (International Dvelopment Research Center), May 1974, pp. 43, 55–57.

Holzman, Franklyn D., "Comecon: A Trade-Destroying Customs Union," 1975 (in progress).

———. "Some Systemic Factors Contributing to the Convertible Currency Shortages of Centrally Planned Economies," *Proceedings, American Economic Association,* May 1979.

———. "Foreign Trade in the Balance of Payments and GNP Accounts of Centrally Planned Economies," *Occasional Paper,* University Center for International Studies, Univ. of Pittsburgh, 1973, Part II.

———. "The Ruble Exchange Rate and Soviet Foreign Trade Pricing Policies, 1929–1961," *Amer. Econ. Rev.,* December 1968.

———. "Some Notes on Over-Full Employment Planning, Shortrun Balance, and the Soviet Economic Reforms," *Soviet Studies,* October 1970, pp. 255–266.

Johnson, Harry, "Economic Development and International Trade," in *Readings in International Economics* ed. by Richard Caves and Harry Johnson, Richard D. Irwin: Homewood, Ill., 1968, pp. 281–299.

Kindelberger, Chas. P., *International Economics,* (4th edition) Richard D. Irwin: Homewood, Ill., 1968.

Kover, Karoly, "Conceptual Changes in the Hungarian External Payment System Within the New Economic Mechanism," in I. Vajda and M. Simai (eds.) *Foreign Trade in a Planned Economy,* Cambridge, Eng. 1971, pp. 174–175.

Pryor, Frederic, "Discussion" in A. Brown and E. Neuberger (eds.) *International Trade and Central Planning,* Berkeley, Cal., 1968.

Snell, Edwin, "Eastern Europe's Trade and Payments With the Industrial West" in Joint Economic Committee, U.S. Congress, *Reorientation and Commercial Relations of the Economies of Eastern Europe,* Washington, 1974, pp. 682–724.

United Nations, Economic Commission for Europe, *Analytical Report on the State of Intra-European Trade,* New York, 1970 (1970A).

———. *Economic Bulletin for Europe,* 1970, Vol. 21, No. 1 (1970B).

Vajda, Imre, "External Equilibrium and Economic Reform" in Vajda, I and Simai, M., *Foreign Trade in a Planned Economy,* Cambridge University Press, 1971.

Vernon, Raymond, "International Investment and International Trade in the Product Cycle," *Quarterly Journal of Economics,* May 1966, pp. 190-207.

———. (ed.), *The Technology Factor in International Trade,* New York: NBER, 1970.

Wasowski, S. (ed.), *East-West Trade and the Technology Gap,* New York, 1970.

Wilcyznski, J., *The Economics and Politics of East-West Trade,* MacMillan and Co., London, 1969.

Zoeter, J., "Eastern Europe: Growing Hard Currency Debt," in Joint Economic Committee, U.S. Congress, *East European Economies Post-Helsinki,* Washington, 1977.

2
Creditworthiness and Balance-of-Payments Adjustment Mechanisms of Centrally Planned Economies

I. Introduction

The level of world external indebtedness is rising and presently exceeds all previous historical levels. The external public debt of 84 developing nations amounted to approximatley $174 billion in 1975 (IMF, 1977a, p. 177). As a result of the rise in raw materials prices, particularly of petroleum, many advanced Western industrial nations are rapidly liquidating external assets or are also going deeply into debt. At the end of 1975, Great Britain led the pack with a debt of about $45 billion, France was next with $20 billion[1]—an amount exceeded by Mexico and Brazil (*New York Times*, 1976). According to the same source, net foreign currency liabilities of Euromarket banks exceeded $275 billion. Finally, in tune for once with the capitalist world, the communist nations (referring here primarily to the USSR and the rest of Eastern Europe) have also been borrowing from abroad—and from the West at that—at unprecedented rates with debts, at the end of 1976, probably aggregating in excess of $40 billion[2]—and the end not in sight. This is surprising both because of the speed of the recent debt buildup and because until less than a decade ago, the Eastern nations followed policies largely designed to avoid any significant accumulation of external debt.

The issue with which we shall be concerned here is how to approach the question as to whether it is wise from an economic standpoint for the Western nations to continue to expand credits to the communist

Reprinted with permission from *Economic Welfare and the Economics of Soviet Socialism: Essays in Honor of Abram Bergson,* Steven Rosefielde, ed. (New York: Cambridge University Press, 1981), pp. 163–184. Copyright © 1981 by Cambridge University Press.

nations. Such an assessment requires us to examine the criteria by which loans are made and creditworthiness is judged in general and then to determine whether these criteria are equally applicable to all nations, planned and unplanned alike. Such a study necessarily involves examining balance-of-payments adjustment mechanisms, and this is done for the centrally planned economies in the latter part of the paper.

The basic aim of the paper is methodological-theoretical: to establish a more satisfactory approach, especially for centrally planned economies, to the question of international creditworthiness. However, particularly in the latter half of the discussion, which deals with adjustment mechanisms, I have gone beyond this limited purpose and made judgments regarding the empirical magnitudes of some of the more important parameters in order to draw tentative policy conclusions. These empirical judgments, although, hopefully, "informed," are nevertheless admittedly "casual," and I trust that the reader, forewarned, will keep the distinction between these two aspects of the analysis in mind.

II. The Debt Service/Export Ratio

It is typical in economic analysis to look for significant simple measures that provide criteria of performance. The criterion most widely used to measure creditworthiness of nations has been the debt service/export ratio (or, somewhat related to this, the total debt/export ratio). That is to say, a Western nation would be deemed creditworthy if current interest and amortization payments on its public and publicly guaranteed external debt[3] were less than a certain percentage (usually around 25 percent) of export earnings. This criterion is similar to the cash flow/liability ratio often applied to business enterprises.

How good a measure this is for enterprises will not concern us; as a measure of national creditworthiness, however, it is seriously deficient. This can be demonstrated empirically: Australia and Canada with ratios between 35 and 45 percent during the 1930s did not default, whereas various Latin American nations with ratios between 16 and 28 percent did default (Frank, cited in Portes, 1977). In recent years, Brazil with a ratio of 0.25 and Mexico with a ratio of 0.30 are still deemed creditworthy, Italy with only 0.10 is not, nor are Gambia and Mali with ratios below 0.10 because even so they are incapable of servicing their debts. There are several reasons why the debt service/export ratio (henceforth ds/x) is likely to be unreliable as a criterion of creditworthiness. First, it is a short-run cash flow concept. So a nation may have a 20 percent ds/x, which, depending on maturities and amortization rates, could represent a 5-year or alternatively a (say) 20-year annual burden. Obviously, the same ratio is less ominous in the former than in the latter case. In this sense, the ds/x is not unlike capital/output ratios, which abstract from the durability of the capital goods in question. Because the ds/x is a short-run concept, it abstracts from a second long-run feature of creditworthiness: namely, the prospective ability of a nation to transform its economy in such a way as to improve the balance-of-payments situation and/or repay its debts. Two nations may have identical ds/x's, but over a period of time one may go on to double it, the other to halve it, depending on policies, resources, potentialities for reducing imports and increasing exports (more on this below), and so forth. Third, the ds/x takes no account whatsoever of the relative profitability of the debt from the standpoint of either the lenders or the borrowers. Given high rates of interest relative to alternative investments either at home or in third nations, lenders may be perfectly content to see ds/x's rise still further. Similarly, given very high rates of return on investments financed by funds borrowed from abroad, a borrower may feel justified in further expansion, even with a high ds/x. Making this same point (with regard to the lenders) by analogy, Avramovic et al., 1964, p. 43, note that corporate investors do not look at cash flows but rather at potential growth, net earnings over time, diversification, and so forth.

Related to these points is another very important consideration: the question as to whether the excess of imports over exports results because a nation has to finance crucial consumption requirements and has large unexploited and profitable investment, *or* is simply overimporting because of an overvalued exchange rate.[4] This is not as serious an issue in the current era of greater exchange rate flexibility, but it has been in the past and still remains important. Although one can make a case for continuing to grant credit for urgent consumption and profitable investment needs, where the costs to lender and borrower are accurately reflected in relative prices under properly valued exchange rates, one cannot if exchange rates are out of equilibrium and deficits occur solely because buyers and sellers suffer from what amounts to a money illusion. Those who lend to nations with overvalued currencies in fact suffer a greater exchange rate risk.

Finally, even assuming that a borrowing nation's exchange rate is not overvalued and that debt-financed imports are invested profitably at home, it makes considerable difference whether the nation is investing adequately in exportables and import-competing products on the one hand, or in nontradeables on the other. The creditworthiness of the nation is greater in the former than in the latter case, of course.

III. The Transfer Problem:
An "Elasticity-Absorption" Approach

Basically, then, ds/x has to be rejected as an unambiguous indicator of creditworthiness of nations because it is exclusively a short-run measure and because it leaves out of account several important variables. This is not to deny that at times it may prove a useful warning signal. What alternative is there to the ds/x? In our opinion, there is no single measure that can be substituted. Creditworthiness must be judged with traditional balance-of-payments analysis tools, especially as these have been adapted to deal with problems relating to the transfer problem. For, essentially, what one wishes to know is whether the debtor nation can generate enough of a transferable surplus and earn enough foreign exchange to repay its debt within prescribed time limits. It is not proposed here to develop a quantifiable index but simply to try to spell out the differences between market and nonmarket economies in handling the transfer problem.

The international repayment of debt is then, like the transfer problem, a two-gap problem. The first gap is the savings-investment gap, or alternatively, the gap between income produced Y and income absorbed A ($A - Y$, where $A = C + I + G$ expenditures). That is, to repay a debt it is necessary, in the absence of past savings (reserves, stocks), for current savings to exceed current investment or for income produced to exceed income absorbed. If past savings do exist, they may be used to liquidate the debt even though current I exceeds current S. In fact, even though the macro conditions (just noted) for repayment exist, repayment also requires that individual private debtors in a capitalist nation be in a sufficiently viable financial position to make the necessary payments. There are, of course, no private debtors in socialist nations.

The second gap is that between international current account payments and receipts, $M - X$ for short. In the absence of foreign exchange reserves, debt repayment requires that $X > M$ by the appropriate amount.

In the absence of past savings of any sort (stocks, foreign exchange reserves, etc.) the two gaps are equated:

$$S - I = X - M \text{ or } Y - A = X - M$$

That is, at the macro level, foreign exchange can be earned to repay debts only by saving more than is invested or producing more than is absorbed.

The preceding analysis assumes that increasing Y and/or reducing A by the appropriate amount automatically results in an increase in $X - M$ which earns enough foreign exchange to service successfully the debt in question. This might be true for a small nation that faces perfectly elastic demands for its exports and can easily substitute domestically produced importables for its imports—but for many nations it is not. An improvement in the current balance may involve a loss in terms of trade either with or without a devaluation. In the case of a devaluation, of course, a given $X - M$ in domestic currency will exchange for less foreign currency than before and will be inadequate to service the debt denominated in foreign currency. This was termed, many decades ago, the secondary burden of a transfer and it is as relevant today as it was then. The common assumption is that a devaluation usually worsens the terms of trade because nations are usually more specialized as exporters than they are as importers; as a result, export prices are likely to fall (in foreign prices) to a greater extent than import prices are by efforts to improve the payments balance.

IV. The $A - \Upsilon$ Gap or Savings Gap

Before proceeding to discussions of the $A - \Upsilon$ and $M - X$ gaps, respectively, two additional preliminary comments are in order. First, in the discussion that follows we speak as though the current account consists exclusively of commodity trade and debt service. This is done primarily because there are so few data generally available on other invisibles; in fact, the debt service data presented below are all "estimated" by Western analysts. Second, the discussion proceeds on the assumption that the transfer problem facing a nation is the financing of the debt service. This ignores the fact that two nations with identical ds/x's may have different current account balances. For example, given a ds/x to begin with, three illustrative scenarios are:[5]

	(1)	(2)	(3)
X	$+50$	$+50$	$+50$
M	-40	-50	-60
ds	-10	-10	-10
K	0	$+10$	$+20$

Most centrally planned economies (CPEs) presently fall into classes (2) and (3), especially (3). The discussion that follows does not differentiate between these two classes. A major problem in including the deficit, over and above the debt service, is the fact that it can vary so much from year to year. In any event, because the primary purpose of this paper is methodological, this should not seriously limit the usefulness of the analysis.

The $A - Y$ gap of a nation is affected by at least two factors that are not totally systemic in nature: the intensity of its participation in trade or trade participation ratio (TPR $= X/\text{GNP}$ or M/GNP^6), and per capita income. As is well known, large and well-endowed nations such as the United States and the USSR trade a much smaller percentage of their GNPs than do smaller and less well-endowed nations. Ratios range from 6 percent for the USSR[7] and 7 to 8 for the United States to approximately 20 percent for the United Kingdom and West Germany and probably higher than 75 percent for many tiny nations and for nations such as Kuwait, whose production is confined almost exclusively to a single exportable. The debt service in any given ds/x ratio will amount to a smaller percentage of GNP for a nation with a small than one with a large TPR. Hence, all other things equal, the nation with the small TPR will find it easier to achieve the required $Y - A$ or $S - I$ gap. So, for example, if we take two nations, each with a ds/x ratio of 0.20, but with TPRs of 10 and 30 percent, respectively, the ds/Y will amount to 2 percent in the former case and 6 percent in the latter. This is a very significant difference; hence equivalent debt-service problems, measured in the usual ds/x fashion, can involve a much more serious internal strain to nations with large than with small trade participation ratios. Putting it another way, one could argue that this implies a serious shortcoming in the ds/x as a measure of creditworthiness.[8]

There are two systemic factors that, when taken account of, tend to reduce the $A - Y$ gap problem of CPEs relatively to market economies. First, there is a tendency for CPEs to have lower TPRs than comparable market economies. This tendency has been documented by many scholars and need not be elaborated here (see, e.g., Hewett, 1976). Second, and of much greater practical importance, our concern with CPE debt problems has reference exclusively to the hard currency deficits of these nations.[9] Since hard currency trade varies from around 20 to about 50 percent of the total trade of the Council for Mutual Economic Assistance (CMEA) nations, the hard currency TPRs are considerably smaller than the aggregate TPRs. Correspondingly, any given hard currency ds/x involves a much smaller $A - Y$ gap than in a comparable capitalist nation. These considerations suggest that the domestic financing of a given hard currency ds/x requires a savings effort in a CPE that is usually much less than that of a comparable Western nation.

Some crude indications of the magnitudes involved in the East are presented in Table 1 (but see the caveats to Table 1). In column 3, we present the X/GNP ratios for 1973, where X represents only Eastern *hard currency* exports. Compare the hard currency ratio for the USSR of 1.4 percent with that of the United States of 7 to 8 percent. Hungary has the highest ratio—11.2 percent. The ratio of a comparable small

Table 1. *Hard currency trade and debt service/export ratio relationships, mid-1970s*

	(1) $\frac{\text{Total } X}{\text{GNP}}$ 1973 (%)	(2) %X to developed West, 1973	(3) %X/GNP hard currency: (1) × (2)	(4) $\frac{\$ds}{X}$: 1975	(5) $\$\frac{ds}{\text{GNP}}$: (3) × (4)	(6) Average annual ΔGNP, 1971–5	(7) $\frac{\$ds/\text{GNP}}{\% \Delta\text{GNP}}$: (5) ÷ (6)
USSR	6.0	23	1.4	20	0.28	2.9	9.7
Bulgaria	26.4	12	3.2	66	2.09	6.7	31.2
Czechoslovakia	30.9	21	6.5	22	1.43	3.6	39.7
East Germany	20.5	24.7	5.1	27	2.97	5.0	59.4
Hungary	45.7	24.5	11.2	35	3.92	3.8	103.2
Poland	12.1	32	3.9	43	1.68	5.8	28.9
Romania	6.4	32	2.1	42	0.86	7.8	11.0

Caveat: The data used and methodologies employed in constructing this table leave much to be desired. The table is presented for illustrative purposes only, with the hope and conviction that the resulting errors are of lesser magnitude than the effects described in the text. Some of the problems are as follows. In column 1, the Soviet figure was constructed by converting Soviet exports to domestic prices and dividing by official Soviet figures of net material product (NMP), also in domestic prices. The IBRD figures for Eastern Europe, however, use NMP in domestic prices in the denominator but incorrectly (perhaps for lack of better alternative) use for numerators exports in Western prices converted to local currencies at official exchange rates. These exchange rates, in many instances, may be pretty far off correct purchasing power parities. This may account for the very low Romanian (and perhaps Polish) X/GNPs. Column 2 is calculated in dollars and is subject to the qualification noted above in the source but, additionally, should be calculated in domestic prices to be consistent with column 1. Column 3, then, as a product of columns 1 and 2, is also a hybrid of inconsistent units, even for the USSR with its consistent column 1 figure. Column 4 is calculated in dollars and, for what it signifies, is satisfactory. Column 5, however, as a product of columns 3 and 4, is also a hybrid of inconsistent units; similarly with column 7.

Sources: Column 1: USSR: Treml, 1980; Eastern Europe: IBRD, 1977, p. 415. Column 2: Calculated from CIA, 1975, p. 158. No allowance was made for the fact that the price level in intra-CMEA trade is higher than in East–West trade. Column 4: USSR: JEC, 1976, p. 738; Eastern Europe: Zoeter, 1977, p. 1367. Column 6: CIA, 1976.

Western nation would be upward of 25 percent. These small TPRs in hard currency translate into comparably small $ds/$GNP ratios, presented in column 5. These range from an insignificant 0.28 percent in the case of the USSR to, however, a moderately high 3.92 percent in the case of Hungary. The comparable figure for hypothetical small Western nations with TPRs of 0.25 to 0.50 and ds/x's of 0.20 to 0.30 would be 5 to 15 percent. More than 5 percent of GNP would be a substantial drain on current output;[10] 0.2 to 3.9 percent much less so.[11] Further, as Table 1 shows (column 5), these low $ds/$GNP ratios were generated by fairly large ds/x ratios, primarily much in excess of 0.20.

Another perspective on the primary burden of the $ds/$GNP is to compare it with the growth in GNP. In column 6 we present the average growth rates of GNP in the 1971–5 period, and in column 7, the ratio of $ds/$GNP to these growth rates. The percentage of an annual growth rate taken by the debt service ranges from 9.7 percent for the USSR to 103.2 percent for Hungary. Although the drains for nations such as Hungary and the GDR are large, it should be recognized that in terms of the growth of GNP, the resources devoted to a given amount of debt service take a once-and-for-all chunk. Assume a nation with a GNP of 100, annual growth of GNP of 6 percent, and annual debt service of 2. In the first year, although GNP would rise to 106, only 104 would be available domestically. In the subsequent year, domestically available GNP would rise by approximately 6 percent from 104 to 110.

In terms of GNP growth rates, $ds/$GNP ratios are perforce gradual and appear to be a small drain. Suppose, in the preceding example, that the debt service had risen from 2 to 2.5, an increase of 25 percent. Domestically available resources would rise from 104 to 109.5 instead of 110, an incremental loss of only 8⅓ percent of the increase in GNP.

The conclusion one reaches from these calculations is that the $A - Y$ gaps (uncomplicated by possible terms of trade losses) are not of large magnitudes, with the possible exceptions of Hungary and East Germany.

Given an $A - Y$ gap of specific magnitude, how difficult is it for a CPE to close (or reverse) the gap. If one examines the experiences of the USSR in the 1930s and some of the Eastern European nations during the 1950s, one might be inclined to argue that most gaps would be easily within the reach of CPE planners. On the one hand, Y was increasing rapidly in those periods, both through putting unemployed resources to work and getting closer to the production-possibilities frontiers; and through expanding the frontiers—the capacity to produce. On the other hand, the Eastern nations seemed to have had almost limitless power to reduce A, particularly by compressing standards of living. In the early 1930s, the USSR exported grain and other food products despite mass hunger. Under stress, in the early 1950s, some of the Eastern nations followed the Soviet example of the 1930s.

The possibilities of closing the gap appear to have lessened significantly in recent years. The goals of maximizing growth rates and achieving full employment (in practice over-full-employment planning) are pursued with such intensity under normal conditions that there is very little scope left for improvement either through growth or reducing unemployment. Further, the Soviet rate of growth has been in secular decline since the end of the 1950s. Eastern European rates of growth declined in the 1960s but have picked up again in the 1970s. However, no further increase appears probable in the near future.

The harsh measures once used to reduce A are probably no longer politically possible nor are most Eastern governments even interested in taking such extreme measures. Widespread expectation of improved living standards—the so-called consumerism movement—is evidence of loss of flexibility with regard to downward manipulations of A and C. Evidence: the USSR's huge grain imports since the early 1960s; inabililty of Poland to raise prices on foods and thereby eliminate enormous subsidies; the large food subsidies in most of the Eastern nations. The Soviet Union faces additional serious constraints on reducing A. Between the arms race with the United States and hostile relations with China, a reduction in military expenditures is unlikely. Further, the rate of investment appears to be creeping up slowly, probably in an attempt to offset the secular rise in the capital/output ratio and decline in rate of growth of GNP.

It need also be mentioned that reducing A in a manner that improves the balance of payments often involves diverting existing output from domestic use to export to the West and/or reducing imports from the West. Given taut planning, it is difficult to carry out such policies not only because of consumerism, already mentioned, but because in the short run at least, such policies could disrupt production. Actually, most products exported and imported are intermediate products, not final consumers' goods, and any reduction in availability of exportables or imports could have serious adverse effects on the plan and on GNP through the supply multiplier. In fact, a reduction in imports of intermediate products could even result in a reduction of exports to the extent that exports embody such imported goods.

Despite the loss in flexibility that the CPEs have experienced in the past decade or so in reducing absorption, it is worth noting that in 1975 and 1976, the growth in value of imports was substantially reduced in all of the Eastern nations, and in some cases absolutely reduced. It is also important to stress again the very small ds/GNP ratios vis-à-vis the West that these nations have.

V. The $M - X$ Gap: Overall View

We have just demonstrated that the $A - Y$ gap should not present serious problems to most Eastern nations, representing as it does a very small percentage of either current output or of the annual increment to output. The smallness of the $A - Y$ gap is in fairly sharp contrast with the hard currency $M - X$ gap plus the $X - M$ surplus required to finance the debt service. The latter is indicated in column 4 of Table 1. Ratios range in 1975 from 22 to 28 percent for Czechoslovakia and the USSR, respectively, to ratios in excess of 40 percent in the cases of Romania, Poland, and Bulgaria (which has a high of 66 percent). Still higher figures for all nations were recorded in 1976 (same source). By ordinary standards, the Romanian, Polish, and Bulgarian debt service problems would appear to be serious—but as we indicated earlier, the ds/x is not necessarily a good measure of debt service problems.

A major assumption of the discussion which follows is that the traditional CPE has to work through the market to increase its exports (i.e., by lowering prices) but can only adjust (reduce) imports by reducing import quotas. This is because, with the partial exception of Hungary, CPE exchange rates are not real prices, and devaluing the currency has no effect on exports or imports. Devaluation is, however, simulated on the export side by simply reducing prices. The analogous operation on the import side is obviously not a feasible policy. In the first part of this section we assume that reducing export prices is equivalent to a devaluation on the export side. In Section VII, we explore the special consequences of the fact that it is not.

The $M - X$ gap may be ameliorated even without changing the $A - Y$ gap by (1) diverting exports from Eastern to Western markets and imports from Western to Eastern markets. On the other hand, reversal of the $A - Y$ gap (ex ante), although necessary, may not be sufficient to reverse $M - X$ for two reasons: (2) the economy may have difficulty generating over the medium and long run more exportables and import-competing products; and (3) in the short run, the price elasticity of demand for exportables may be too low,[12] resulting in either no increase in foreign exchange or small increases because of the large adverse shift in terms of trade. (4) Finally, as a last resort, of course, the $M - X$ gap can be reduced by directly cutting back on M, as was done in 1975–6 in many CMEA nations. Let us discuss the first three of these issues in this order.

1. Diversion of exports from intrabloc to East-West trade faces the same obstacles as diverting output away from domestic markets. Taut planning and use of direct controls lead each CPE to be very dependent on planned imports of intermediate products from other CPEs. Consumerism also plays a constraining role here similar to that mentioned earlier. This is why the Russians import Western grain for domestic consumers *and* for *reexport* to Eastern Europe when their own crops fall short of commitments. It is worth noting, however, that the enormous increase in Western oil and gas prices after 1973 led the USSR to begin supplying a smaller percentage of Eastern Europe's needs of these products than had been the case!

The substitution of imports from the East or from other nondollar markets for imports from the West is also fraught with difficulty. Undoubtedly, attempts are made to implement such policies. Efforts along these lines would have the best chance of success in periods of Western recession during which Eastern hard currency balance-of-payments problems are widespread and are due to recession-induced declining exports to the West. Under these circumstances, both Eastern exporters and importers might be motivated to adopt the second best solution of trading with each other. There is undoubtedly a limit, however, to the substitutability of Eastern for desired Western imports, particularly of advanced machinery and equipment. It must be stressed that the shift of such imports from Western to Eastern sources undoubtedly involves a substantial reduction in gains from trade, a fact that creates resistance to change. It is, after all, the desire for Western products that creates the hard currency deficits in the first place. Data for 1976 show little or no shift in real terms to intra-CMEA trade, in aggregate, as a substitute for East-West trade.

2. The supply of exportables and import-competing products can be increased in the short-run by simply diverting output from the domestic market (as the USSR did with grain in the early 1930s) or, over the longer run, by transforming the structure of the economy (as the Polish government tried to do with its electrical golf carts). In the longer run, one might expect that part of Eastern imports from the West be allocated to try to improve the hard currency balance of payments.[13] We will not comment here on the short-run possibilities except to say that it seems highly probable—given the secular nature of Eastern deficits—that these possibilities have been by now largely exhausted.[14] Evidence regarding longer-run efforts is not plentiful, but what there is suggests that at least until 1975, new investment and imports were not concentrated as intensively as they might have been toward solving hard currency balance-of-payments problems. There is no question but that a substantial portion of CMEA imports are capital

goods and designed to increase productivity.[15] However, according to one authority, these imports are more often designed to increase productivity in industries that service domestic and intra-CMEA markets than hard currency markets (Snell, 1974, pp. 688–9). If this is generally true, the long-run creditworthiness of the Communist nations achieved by expansionary means is seriously compromised.

The longer-run picture with regard to hard currency imports must be qualified as was the case with exportables. To quote: "[CMEA] import of Western technology has not led to an effective program of import substitution" (Crawford and Haberstroh, 1974, p. 38). According to the same source, not only have imports not been used to develop import-competing industries, but in fact many of the industries established on the basis of Western machinery imports require continual additional hard currency imports of high-quality inputs for their operation. Further, it turns out that the faster-growing industries in Eastern Europe typically require a faster growth in supporting imports from the West—in effect, a high output elasticity of demand for hard currency imports.

Whether Eastern investment policies have recently changed to address more directly hard currency balance-of-payments problems has not been investigated. Some efforts along these lines certainly have been made in Eastern Europe via industrial cooperation agreements. But the Eastern nations may have found the recession plus rising Western protectionism very discouraging to the adoption of rational balance-of-payments investment policies.

3. It is one thing to increase the supply of products to be marketed for hard currencies, and another to actually sell them. There are several constraints.

First, although some exports can undoubtedly be expanded without lowering prices (e.g., oil, gas, and other raw materials), others cannot. Lowering prices in order to compete, if successful, may lead to Western antidumping or anti-market-disruption actions. Inability of the CPEs to prove that they are not selling below cost or below domestic market price (because of the irrationality of domestic prices) makes it difficult for them to refute antidumping charges successfully—even when they are not, in fact, dumping.

Second, the antidumping problem is exacerbated by the fact that CPE prices cannot be lowered on world markets by currency devaluation.[16] As noted above, CMEA exchange rates are not real prices (Hungary is a partial exception).

Third, a significant percentage of Eastern exportables are manufactured products. For reasons discussed elsewhere,[17] these products have not found easy markets in the West. It might therefore be difficult to expand sales at all or at prices that do not involve a prohibitive decline in terms of trade.

Fourth, as noted earlier, a major part of the responsibility for the recent rise in the ds/x has been the Western recession of the mid-1970s. Western imports fall below trend, partly because the rise in GNP is slowed or actually falls, and partly because under these conditions, nations have tended to increase protectionist curbs on imports (IMF, 1977b, p. 241). In periods like this, it becomes almost impossible to increase export earnings significantly. There is also some evidence that Western imports from the East decline more than Western imports from the West during recessions. That is to say, the East is viewed as the marginal supplier of imports.

VI. The $M - X$ Gap and Terms of Trade in Light of Static Price Elasticities

The first and third points just discussed can be illustrated using conventional analysis in terms of Figure 1. Let TT be the domestic transformation curve between importables M and exportables X for any Eastern nation. Let PP be the domestic rate of transformation and h the autarky production point. Abstract from the possibility of intrabloc trade—simplifying the analysis but not changing its essence. (If intrabloc trade were included, we could have assumed that PP was the intrabloc opportunity price.) Let $ae = mn$ represent the world price, P_w. The difference in slopes of PP and ae is large, reflecting the great profitability to the Eastern nation (E) of trade with the West. E would like to produce at a, export ac of X, and import ce of M. Such a policy would put it at welfare point e on I_3 as opposed to h on I_1. In fact, it can only export ab to finance bd of M. Borrowing is resorted to secure additional imports. If ce $(= bn)$ of imports is necessary to the plan (consumption and/or investment), then am $(= dn)$ is borrowed and E ends up at welfare level n on I_4. If, on the other hand, E just wishes to reach the equivalent of its original overall welfare target (but not its planned quantitative targets) of I_3, then ds is imported by borrowing av. Or if E does not wish to go further into debt, it will restrict imports to bd. In fact, E might well cut back M simultaneously with trying to increase X on the assumption, based on past experience, that ΔX will not bridge the gap. The trade data suggest that this happened in 1975–1976.

We have posited that E cannot export more than ab at going prices. More might be exported if E were willing to accept poorer terms of trade—in this case, by a uniform lowering of export prices equivalent to devaluation on the export side. The losses involved in accepting

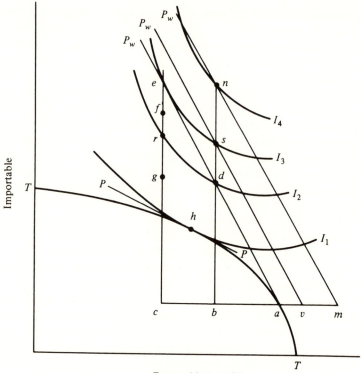

Figure 1. East–West trade of an Eastern nation (E).

poorer terms of trade would be, in effect, the secondary burden of the transfer problem mentioned earlier. If lowering export prices did not lead to antidumping action by the importing nations, then at least two sets of possibilities can be distinguished. First, if Western demand is sufficiently elastic, E could end up on a higher indifference curve (not shown)—passing through say point f. Because of the probable loss in terms of trade (from ae to af), that indifference curve (not shown) would be below I_3. Second, if demand is very inelastic, the terms of trade would drop to, say, ag, at which point E would be at a welfare level below I_2—and the additional trade would not be worthwhile.[18] In my opinion, it is entirely conceivable that the Eastern nations face such a situation for a large number of manufactured products which they have attempted to market in the West. This is one reason why an expansionary solution to the deficit problem may not be promising (but see below).

It is illuminating to look at these issues using the conventional static price elasticity approach (see Kreinen and Heller, 1974). The elasticity of balance-of-payments formula is

$$b = k \frac{s_x(d_x - 1)}{s_x + d_x} + \frac{d_m(s_m + 1)}{s_m + d_m}$$

where given balanced trade to begin with, b is the percentage improvement in the balance of payments from a k percent devaluation, d_m and d_x are the price elasticities of demand for imports and for a nation's exports, and s_m and s_x are the corresponding supply elasticities.

An expansionary solution in this formulation requires that the price elasticity of foreign demand for a nation's exports, d_x, be greater than 1. This is because if $d_x < 1$, then the first (or export) term on the right side of the equality is 0 or negative. The preceding discussion, centered on Figure 1, argues that for many products which the CPEs are trying to sell to the West, d_x may indeed be less than 1 and certainly less that for a comparable market economy. As noted earlier, devaluation cannot be simulated on the import side (i.e., the CPEs have no mechanism or motivation for paying higher prices for imports). Import quotas are simply reduced, so the second term on the right is inoperative as a measure of market response. However, the magnitude of d_m suggests whether it is easy (large d_m) or hard (small d_m) for the CPE to reduce imports, and this suggests the extent to which M is cut back as a substitute for ΔX. The magnitude of s_m suggests whether the price of imports is likely to be much affected by the reduction in imports. Generally speaking, the likelihood is that d_m (price elasticity of CPE demand for Western products) is low for several reasons: prevalence of taut planning, excess demand for Western products, consumerism, and the need to avoid (or remedy) bottlenecks (the so-called supply multiplier). On the other hand, s_m—the price elasticity of supply of imports from the West—is undoubtedly very high simply because the CPEs are, for most imported products, a very small part of the market. So reducing imports probably has little or no effect on world prices (i.e., prices are not reduced by the loss of part of the CPE market).

These same elasticities can be used to gauge the change in terms of trade which probably would be experienced by a CPE *if* it could devalue. The terms of trade, t, improve after a devaluation if

$$d_m d_x > s_m s_x$$

There seems to be little doubt that t would deteriorate if there could be a devaluation because both d_m and d_x are likely to be relatively very small, whereas, as we have seen, s_m is probably very large. On a priori grounds it is difficult to assign a value to s_x. Tautness plus lack of responsiveness to market conditions suggests a smaller s_x for some CPEs than for market economies. On the other hand, to the extent that the planners earmark existing output to foreign trade organizations (fto's) for additional exports or new investment to increase the supply of exportables, s_x might be interpreted to be either elastic or inelastic: elastic if the products are offered at a given price with the quantity to be determined by demand; inelastic if the amount offered is fixed and price depends on what buyers are willing to pay. The latter case seems more realistic. But whatever the value of s_x, the large size of s_m and the relatively small values attached to d_x and d_m would suggest a probable large drop in terms of trade if devaluation were possible, larger than that which would be experienced by a comparable market economy.

VII. The CPE as Price Discriminator

In the real world, as we have noted, a CPE does not devalue to increase export earnings but simply reduces prices. What this means, in effect, is that the CPE is automatically put into the position of a price discriminator to the extent that it is dealing in markets in which the products are not homogeneous and/or markets can be effectively separated. As we are primarily discussing exports of manufactured products, the nonhomogeneity condition holds and some separation of markets can be assumed possible. As a price discriminator, the CPE can drive a much better bargain for itself than the market economy devaluer.[19] This can be illustrated in terms of Figure 1.

Suppose that P_w is not very elastic and at going terms of trade, E can only sell ab for bd and is left with bc of unsold exportables. If E devalues from ae to ar, it will be no better off than before because gains from the increased quantity of exports sold are just offset by the reduction in price of all goods due to devaluation. If, on the other hand, E is able to continue to sell ab at ad prices, and then sell bc additional exportables at a lower price, such as, say, df, which is parallel to ar, then the same drop in the prices of bc exportables enables E to come much closer to its target.

The point can also be made on a partial equilibrium diagram (Figure 2). Assume that E is faced with a $d_x = 1$. If it devalues from OA to OA', it earns no additional foreign exchange because $CDEF$, the gain on additional exports, is just offset by the lower earnings $ABCA'$ on existing exports. If it successfully price discriminates, however, $CDFE + GHTF + $ etc. foreign exchange is earned without losses on previous markets. In fact, if discrimination were continuous rather than discrete, the supply curve would be continuous and negatively sloped (i.e., $ABDH$),

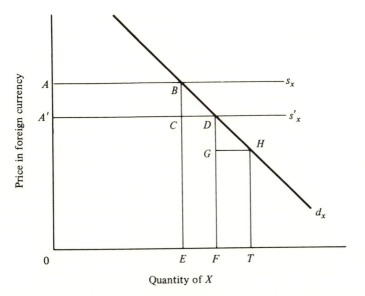

Figure 2. CPE as price discriminator in X market.

thereby increasing foreign exchange earnings by $EBHT$. This process would stop when the real cost of foreign exchange, hence of imports, in terms of resources embodied in exports, becomes too high. (As noted earlier, the value of d_m suggests when it may make sense to cut back imports rather than try to expand exports.) In effect, at some point along $ABDHD_x$, the supply curve turns positive. The s_x might also turn positive if the foreign exchange target were exhausted. A negatively sloped s_x must have characterized the USSR in the early 1930s when exports were increased sharply in the face of rapidly falling prices and terms of trade.

Whether a nation devalues or price discriminates makes a dramatic difference in the cost of earning additional foreign exchange through losses in terms of trade. Suppose that E is a devaluer and desires to increase exports by 20 percent. If it faces a $d_x = \infty$ and has an $s_x = \infty$, it can do so without devaluing—just selling 20 percent more exportables. The burden of the transfer is just the 20 percent increase in exports. Suppose that it faces a $d_x = 2$. In this case, to increase the quantity of exports sold by 20 percent would require a 10 percent devaluation. Increasing the quantity of exports by 20 percent, would however, only increase the value of foreign exchange earned by approximately 10 percent because of the lower price now received on the previous volume of exports. In effect, E has to export twice as many goods to earn the same amount of foreign exchange as before—the terms of trade cost of a 10 percent devaluation is 50 percent. The secondary burden of the transfer in this case is as large as the primary burden. If $d_x = 3$, a 6⅔ percent devaluation is required to increase exports by 20 percent. In this case the terms of trade cost amounts to about 35 percent.

The price discriminating CPE fares much better. The cost of additional foreign exchange earnings through one-time price reductions in the preceding two cases are 10 and 6⅔ percent, respectively. For the perfect discriminators, the losses would be one-half of these amounts, 5 and 3⅓ percent. The secondary burden of transfer in these instances is obviously quite small.

The advantages accruing to the CPE price discriminators may be reduced by their relatively (to a comparable market economy) inelastic d_m. This could throw a larger burden of the balance-of-payments adjustment on increasing exports, where, as we have seen, the d_x is also relatively inelastic. With so much of the adjustment required on the export side, prices are more likely to be pushed down to the very inelastic segments of d_x, even in the case of those products in which it was elastic to begin with.

The extent of CPE terms of trade losses and secondary transfer burdens depends very heavily on the extent to which the CPE is able to play the roles of devaluer and price discriminator, respectively, in East-West trade. The burden of achieving balanced payments for a CPE price discriminator may well be much less than that of a comparable market economy, despite the fact that it faces less favorable elasticities.

It might appear, at first glance, that the CPEs are in a superior economic position by virtue of not having real exchange rates that can function to equilibrate trade and thereby being put into the position of price discriminators. This is not necessarily true. In a well-functioning market system, a devaluation of the exchange rate efficiently eliminates marginal importers and induces entry of marginal exporters over the whole range of potential traders as well as serving to reduce purchases and increase sales in the cases of existing imports and exports. In the case of imports, the interests of individual enterprises and of the nation coincide. That is, the devalued exchange rate makes it unprofitable for some importers to continue buying from abroad. By maximizing profits under these conditions, they save the nation foreign exchange. In the case of exports, this coincidence of interests also exists when the price elasticity of demand is greater than unity: higher profits and increased foreign exchange earnings both result. National interests diverge from those of enterprises, however, when $d_x < 1$. Expansion of exports always leads to higher enterprise profits in local currency; on the other hand, these translate into smaller foreign exchange earnings at the new exchange rate when d_x is inelastic. This is another aspect of the rationale for price discrimination, particularly in cases of low aggregate d_x.

The CPEs have no choice: they cannot obtain the benefits of a market exchange rate. The irrationality of domestic CPE prices and exchange rates plus the fact that convertible currencies are undervalued to them at world prices[20] (or why such convertible currency deficits?) makes it rational for them, as a second best strategy, to sell at varying amounts below world prices where necessary. This is particularly advisable in light of the low d_x's they appear to face on many products. By price discriminating, they can make the best of a nonoptimal situation, but not achieve an optimal solution.

VIII. The Special Case of Hungary

The People's Republic of Hungary is something of an exception to the foregoing generalizations. The basic difference is that Hungary has more market and less planning by direct controls than other CMEA nations. In terms of data presented in Table 1, Hungary's hard currency debt service appears to represent a substantially larger savings problem than those of the other CMEA nations. This is partly attributable to the fact that Hungary has the most "open" economy of the group— with a TPR of approximatley 0.45. The openness is partly due, of course, to Hungary's small size and lack of diversified resources, but it may also be due to greater reliance on market mechanisms. Evidence suggests that the use of planning and direct controls reduces foreign trade below what it would be under market mechanisms (Hewett, 1976). If this is the case, then perhaps Hungary's gains from greater trade provide some compensation for its more severe balance-of-payments problem.

With regard to price and exchange rate adjustments, it is not obvious to what extent internal Hungarian prices are rational market prices; nor is it obvious just what role the dollar and ruble exchange rates of the forint play in restoring balance-of-payments equilibrium (I suspect not very much). The question is: What is the optimum policy for a halfway house? In light of the preceding discussion, it seems reasonable to argue that if internal prices are rational, it would pay to take advantage of this fact by using market exchange rates and decentralizing foreign (as well as internal) trade. If, on the other hand, internal prices are not rational market prices, it would be second best to control trade centrally in order (1) to avoid purchases and sales based on improper price information as well as to encourage purchases and sales that are discouraged by improper price information and (2) to reap the benefits of price discrimination on exports.

IX. Concluding Remarks

The Eastern nations have large ds/x ratios and, by traditional standards, some of them might be considered serious credit risks. The ds/x is, however, a very poor measure of creditworthiness. Viewing creditworthiness as a transfer problem, it was concluded that, unlike the LDCs, the primary internal "savings" burden of the CPEs is not large relative to the size and growth of GNP. Converting these saved resources, particularly into exports but also into import replacements, thereby rectifying hard currency balances of payments and financing debt services, was deduced to be a much more difficult problem because of the assumption of relatively low values of the demand elasticities. By free-market standards, the CMEA nations might (1) find it extremely difficult to rectify their hard currency deficits and especially without (2) very large adverse shifts in terms of trade and resulting large secondary burdens of transfer. Sufficiently large secondary burdens of transfer could actually raise the savings burden ($ds/$GNP) for some of the CPEs (e.g., Hungary, East Germany) to levels more like those of the LDCs. It may not be appropriate to use free-market standards in judging the CPEs, however, because they are not devaluers but, in part, price discriminators. To the extent that they are price discriminators, they are in a position to reduce, substantially, their terms of trade losses.

Notes

An early version of this paper was sponsored by the Bureau of East-West Trade, U.S. Department of Commerce. A later version was presented to the Fourth US-Hungarian Conference in Economics in Budapest in November 1978. I am indebted to members of that conference and to Rachel McCulloch, Steven Rosefielde, and Gordon Weil for helpful comments.

1. The debts of some other advanced industrial nations must be viewed with less concern than those of LDCs because the former are lenders as well as borrowers and own large external assets.

2. Forty billion dollars in external debt amounts to 4 to 5 percent of GNP, whereas the corresponding figure for the developing nations exceeds 15 percent.

3. All CPE debt is publicly guaranteed, so ratios in the West are usually relatively understated in comparison with CPEs as measures of total debt service, public plus private.

4. This point has been made by Brainard (1975).

5. K stands for capital flows.

6. Although in theory X and M include goods and services, in this chapter we deal only with commodity trade because of the absence of reliable data on invisibles for the Eastern nations.

7. The 6 percent refers to $X/$GNP. The $M/$GNP ratio for the USSR is about twice as high (see Treml, 1980).

8. As noted above, the ds/x ratio fails to indicate the magnitude of the $A - \Upsilon$ problem for still another nonsystemic reason, one that does not concern us here. Two nations with identical or similar ratios might have quite different per capita incomes. Consider the relative problems faced by two nations with vastly different per capita incomes, each of which has to reduce the level of absorption relative to income produced by the same percentage. Certainly, the problem would be simpler *ceteris paribus*, for a nation with a per capita income of $4,000 than one with a per capita income of $500. Eliminating the *ceteris paribus*, of course, might create a new ballgame. The ability of nations to collect taxes, reinvest profits, and so on, varies for many different reasons, political and social, as well as economic.

9. Since the 1973–4 price increases, many of the CMEA nations have developed deficits and debts with the USSR. Although these are not unimportant, we ignore them here.

10. This is not meant to imply necessarily that the gains from the imports financed by borrowing are not large enough to carry the debt service.

11. In a recent paper on LDC debt problems, Robert Solomon (1977) concerns himself almost exclusively with $A - \Upsilon$ problems to the neglect of the $M - X$ gap. This is probably largely because for the poor LDCs, the relatively large ds/Υ ratios represent serious resource drains.

12. Obviously, when demand curves are shifting to the left because of recessions—as in the West during 1974–5—the relevance of price elasticities is sharply reduced.

13. To make an obvious point, it is not necessary for imports from the West to be directly usable in investments designed to improve the hard currency balance of payments; they can serve this function just as well by efficiently satisfying domestic requirements and thereby freeing up additional domestic resources for developing foreign trade industries. This qualification should be kept in mind in the discussion that follows.

14. Admittedly, the incentive to make short-run adjustments may have been blunted by the ready availability of relatively cheap hard currency credit.

15. However, on balance the percentage does not appear greater for the CMEA nations than it is for many Latin American and Asian middle-level developing nations (see Brainard, 1978).

16. On the other hand, since internal price inflation is not a serious problem— nor would it affect foreign trade if it was—the need for devaluation is much less acute in the CPEs.

17. See Holzman (1979a,b). Basically, the argument is that CMEA exports are hard to sell for nonprice reasons (quality, marketing, servicing, packaging, etc.), implying a low price elasticity of demand.

18. If the imports that would have to be foregone were intermediate products essential to domestic production, this conclusion might not follow so easily. The losses to the economy from a reduction in imports, in this case, could be much greater than the value of the foregone imports themselves. This effect could, of course, be included implicitly in the indifference curves.

19. By concentrating exports in products with a high d_x, in products not previously sold, in markets in which a product has not been previously offered, and in markets in which the d_x is relatively higher. As a serious caveat to the argument of this section, one must question whether the foreign trade planners have sufficient flexibility in the market to successfully price-discriminate on a large scale.

20. One meaning of this statement is that CPEs are willing to export at very low prices if they estimate that the gains to them from imports, which otherwise could not be imported, are very high.

References

Alton, T. 1974. "Economic Growth and Resource Allocation in Eastern Europe." In Joint Economic Committee, U.S. Congress, *Reorientation and Commercial Relations of the Economies of Eastern Europe.* Washington, D.C.

Avramovic, D., et al. 1964. *Economic Growth and External Debt.* John Hopkins Press, Baltimore, Md.

Brainard, L. 1975. "Criteria for Financing East-West Trade." In John Hardt (ed.), *Tariff, Legal and Credit Constraints on East-West Commercial Relations.* Carleton University, Ottawa.

Brainard, L. 1978. "Eastern Europe's Indebtedness Policy Choices for East and West." In C. T. Saunders (ed.), *Money and Finance in East and West.* Springer-Verlag, New York, pp. 79–98.

CIA. *Handbook of Economic Statistics, 1975.* Washington, D.C.

CIA. *Handbook of Economic Statistics, 1976.* Washington, D.C.

Crawford, J. and Haberstroh, J. 1974. "Survey of Economic Policy Issues in Eastern Europe: Technology, Trade and the Consumer." In Joint Economic Committee, U.S. Congress, *Reorientation and Commercial Relations of the Economies of Eastern Europe.* Washington, D.C.

Hewett, Edward. "A Gravity Model of CMEA Trade." In Josef Brada (ed.), *Quantitative and Analytical Studies on East-West Economic Relations.* 1976. Indiana University Press, Bloomington, Ind.

Holzman, Franklyn D. 1979a. "Some Theories of the Hard Currency Shortages of Centrally Planned Economies." In Joint Econ. Committee, U.S. Congress, *Soviet Economy in a Time of Change.* Washington, D.C.

Holzman, Franklyn D. 1979b. "Some Systemic Factors Contributing to the Convertible Currency Shortages of Centrally Planned Economies." *Proceedings of American Economic Association,* May.

International Bank for Reconstruction and Development. 1977. *World Tables,* Washington, D.C.

International Monetary Fund. 1977a. *Survey,* June 6.

International Monetary Fund. 1977b. *Survey,* August 1.

Joint Economic Committee, U.S. Congress, 1974. *Reorientation and Commercial Relations of the Economies of Eastern Europe.* Washington, D.C.

Joint Economic Committee, U.S. Congress. 1976. *The Soviet Economy in a New Perspective.* Washington, D.C.

Joint Economic Committee, U.S. Congress. 1977. *East European Economies Post-Helsinki.* Washington, D.C.

Kreinin, M. and Heller, H. R. 1974. "Adjustment Costs, Optimal Currency Areas, and International Reserve." In Willy Sellssekaerts (ed.), *International Trade and Finance (Essays in Honour of Jan Tinbergen).* International Arts and Sciences Press, White Plains, N.Y., pp. 127–40.

New York Times. 1976. November 11, p. 60.

Portes, Richard. 1977. "East Europe's Debt to the West: Interdependence Is a Two-Way Street." *Foreign Affairs,* July.

Snell, E. 1974. "Eastern Europe's Trade and Payments with the Industrial West." In Joint Economic Committee, U.S. Congress, *Reorientation and Commercial Relations of the Economies of Eastern Europe.* Washington, D.C.

Solomon, R. 1977. "A Perspective on the Debt of Developing Countries." *Brookings Papers on Economic Activity 2.*

Treml, Vladimir. 1980. "Foreign Trade and the Soviet Economy: Changing Parameters and Interrelations." In E. Neuberger and L. Tyson (eds.), *The Impact of International Economic Disturbances on the Soviet Union and Eastern Europe: Transmission and Response.* Pergamon Press, New York, pp. 184–207.

Zoeter, J. 1977. "Eastern Europe: The Growing Hard Currency Debt." In Joint Economic Committee, U.S. Congress, *East European Economies Post-Helsinki.* Washington, D.C.

3

Commentary on Richard Portes' "Internal and External Balance in a Centrally Planned Economy"

Richard Portes has produced a paper which does for CPEs what Mundell, Swan, and others have done for market economies—he has shown the interrelationships between internal and external balance. He has had to provide much more complete specifications of these relationships than individual Western economists have because of the very little previous theoretical work on these matters; and he has succeeded. His paper represents, in my opinion, a considerable achievement.

Portes does not compare his model with similar market economy models. I found such a comparison useful for understanding what his model accomplishes and particularly "how." In figures 1 and 2, graphic representation of Swan- and Mundell-like models,[1] respectively, are presented; figure 3 reproduces Portes' figure 5.7.

Figures 1 and 2 have the same goals—balance in payments (BB) and stable-priced full employment (YY). The latter, presented as a single goal, is, of course, a prestagflation objective. Figure 1's policy variables are the exchange rate (r) and government expenditures (g); r is used to steer the economy on to BB and g to steer it on to YY though each policy variable affects both targets. Both goals are achieved simultaneously at E.

Figure 2 assumes fixed exchange rates and the interest rate, i, substitutes for r as one of the two policy variables. i affects YY by its effect on investment. Through the same channel it affects BB since ΔI

Reprinted with permission from *The Impact of International Economic Disturbance on the Soviet Union and Eastern Europe: Transmission and Response,* Egon Neuberger and Laura D'Andrea Tyson, eds. (Elmsford, N.Y.: Pergamon Press, 1980), pp. 113–118. Richard Portes' article "Internal and External Balance in a Centrally Planned Economy" is Chapter 5, pp. 93–113, in the same book.

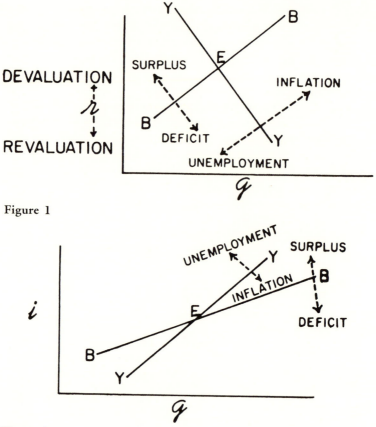

Figure 1

Figure 2

$\longrightarrow$ ΔY $\longrightarrow$ ΔM (imports). It also affects BB more directly by encouraging or discouraging capital flows. Since it is assumed that i has a greater impact on BB than g does, and g has a greater impact on YY than i, the assignment of policy variables to goals is obvious. Both goals are achieved simultaneously at E. If the proper policies are assigned to the various goals, E can be achieved under the assumptions of the models, and even sometimes when policies are not assigned efficiently.

Portes' model, as represented in figure 3, does not use r or i, and properly so. As Portes notes, the CPEs do not have functioning exchange rates so r is out as a policy variable. In recent years, i has been used in the limited sense that the CPEs have been willing to borrow in Western financial markets at market rates of interest. However, the lack of internal financial markets and the fact that i has virtually no

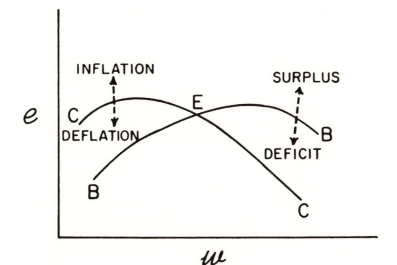

Figure 3

impact on the domestic CPE economies makes it an unlikely policy variable for a CPE seeking simultaneous internal and external balance.

Figure 3 nevertheless bears a strong superficial resemblance to figures 1 and 2. It has a BB goal (which need not express balance but could reflect planned imbalance). It also has a CC goal which represents equilibrium in the consumer goods market. This is, of course, different from figures 1 and 2 in which YY represents aggregate macroequilibrium; Portes ignores the problem of achieving equilibrium in the nonconsumer goods market in his figures. Since he is not concerned with equilibrium in the nonconsumer goods market, that market can be manipulated to achieve his specified YY and CC goals—hence g is one of his policy variables. Dealing in the two-dimensional space of figure 3, g is held constant and changes in g may be represented by shifts in the CC curve. For example, a reduction in g would be shown as an upward shift in CC. In effect, if some g is shifted to c, equilibrium in the consumer goods market becomes consistent with a higher level of exports (e). Assuming that g is constant, internal and external equilibrium is achieved by manipulating e and w (real wages), and that is the situation shown in figure 3.

At first glance, the task of achieving E in figure 3 would appear to be much simpler than the same task in figures 1 and 2. The decentralized planners have two goals and two policy variables; the central planners, two goals and three policy variables.[2] However, it is not quite proper simply to add policy variables because of the systemic differences in their nature. In figures 1 and 2, r, i, and g are parameters which, when altered by government action, set off a chain of reactions in the economy which presumably lead to a real market equilibrium. In figure 3, w is such a parameter and, in fact, it works a little like g does in figures 1 and 2. An increase in w, the real wage, affects the labor supply and increases the output of the economy (as well as the demand for consumer goods). Eventually, as Portes notes, if w is pushed high enough, output no longer increases because of diminishing returns to labor and backward-sloping supply curve effects. Much of the shapes of BB and CC seem to be determined largely by changes in w.

What about g and e in figure 3? In fact, g and e are not parameters which, when changed by the planners, set into motion equilibrating behavioral market forces; they are direct controls like price controls. In fact, e is one side of BB. I hesitate to make these statements categorically because when one opens the black box—the first four sections of Portes' essay—and looks at the network of equations and interrelationships which Portes has laid out, changes in e or g are going to have impacts on the economy, and therefore on trade, which, however, are not immediately obvious.[3] Of course, some of these may be technical, not behavioral. Nevertheless, changes in e and g do not appear to affect the slopes of BB and CC as drawn in figure 3 (as w does and as r, i, and g do in 1 and 2) except insofar as they affect w—and this is evidence of their primary character as direct controls which do not set into motion equilibrating market mechanisms.[4] I think Portes would agree with me.

What I believe has emerged is the rather obvious point that under central planning with direct controls, the planners naturally try to reconcile conflicts among goals in part by nonmarket means. A realistic CPE model, then, could be expected to include among its major policy variables direct controls which are not designed to affect market behavior. Along the same line of reasoning, it is worth noting that Portes' CC goal is of a piece with the BB and YY goals in figures 1 and 2 in that they all envisage equilibria based on market forces. On the other hand, I do not believe that the same can be said for Portes' BB goal, whether that goal represents balanced or unbalanced trade. The absence of organic ties between domestic and world prices, the lack of real exchange rates, the irrationality of domestic prices, the artificial separation of intra-bloc and East-West trade, and the rigid bilateralism within CMEA all lead one to believe that market forces are not fully expressed in exports, imports, and in BB. In effect, BB is a target which, while set in cognizance of market constraints, does not represent the outcome of market forces but is largely implemented by direct controls which do not set in motion equilibrating market mechanisms.

I would like to make a final point on these matters. Portes relies heavily on changes in w and resulting changes in labor supply (output) and consumer-demand as his major market mechanisms for reconciling conflicting objectives. This gives his BB and CC much of their shape. It would be my judgment that the planners would get very little leverage from the labor supply equation, much less than Western policy-makers would get from r, i, or g.[5]

Portes' model is very complicated and, in order to present it within reasonable space bounds, he has chosen to emphasize some aspects of it at the expense of others, although for the most part he has been careful to indicate other possibilities. For the sake of realism, as I view it, I would have preferred it if some of the following approaches had been tried.

In the model, imports are a linear function of income, exports a function of the balance-of-trade target and of the terms of trade. Portes has chosen exports as one of his three major policy variables. For the sake of argument, why not imports? I think it is the case that at present, every CPE would prefer to increase exports over reducing imports, especially over the long run. Portes' model, however, is a short- to medium-run model. It is hard to say which variable is more important over the short and medium run in intra-bloc trade, since intra-bloc trade is always in balance due to inconvertibility. But certainly in East-West trade, and especially during the recession-generated crises of the past few years, imports (and debt) have had to bear most of the burden of adjustment. In many respects, imports (of intermediate products) are more interesting than exports because of their impact on output, as in equation 8 which embodies the supply or bottleneck multiplier.

Secondly, Portes' model is, like Western models, a macro model which concentrates almost exclusively on final products. This fact, plus the fact that balance in the g sector is not explicitly considered, leads Portes to (knowingly) ignore one of the central features of a CPE, namely supply planning; and certainly foreign trade plays an important role in supply planning, especially among the smaller CPEs. Unlike Western policy-makers who can concentrate on the macro variables and let markets and prices take care of shortages of intermediate products, central planners are daily and intimately concerned with preventing bottlenecks, including those generated by a shortage of imports as well as those which are relieved by an increase in imports. It is not clear to me that it would be possible to take this problem into account in a Portes-type model, but if it is, it would add substantially to its realism.

Thirdly, I am not happy with Portes' decision to concentrate on equilibrium in the consumer goods market and to largely ignore equilibrium in the nonconsumer markets, particularly after admitting (pp. 102–103) that the former is probably adjusted to the requirements of the latter. Having always believed that most of the CPEs have tended to be "taut" most of the time in both sectors, I think it would have been more interesting to have had, like Swan and Mundell, a YY curve rather than a CC curve. Admittedly, the exposition might have been less interesting since it would be impossible, with overall tautness, to achieve internal and external equilibrium simultaneously (as in Portes' figures 5.3 and 5.4 where BB and CC do not cross). However, one could still demonstrate how w and e might be manipulated to minimize, though not eliminate, the contradictions among objectives.

Notes

1. Figures 1 and 2 are adaptations of the Swan and Mundell models taken from Caves and Jones (chapter 18). These versions were used because they were more comparable to Portes' model than the originals. So, for example, Portes uses government expenditures (g) as a major instrument variable. Swan in his original article used real expenditures and Mundell used the budget surplus or deficit. The Caves-Jones versions use government expenditures in both cases.

2. In fact, given stagflation, the decentralized planners' YY goal becomes two separate goals. The central planners, on the other hand, avoid this problem by using wage and price controls, in effect a fourth CPE policy variable and one not acceptable in the market economies.

3. In fact, a difficulty with Portes' graphic representations is that they simply cannot do justice to the underlying complexity of his model. For example, in his graphs, changes in w have their effect by changing output and consumer demand. Output is also affected by whether there is repressed inflation or not—whether the economy is above CC or not. This is taken into account in equation 11—the supply of labor equation—but not in the diagram. Of course, Portes is only using the diagrams for illustrative purposes and cannot be faulted for the two-dimensional character of plane geometry.

4. g probably has an impact on YY and CC through equations 15 and 16 and Portes' figure 5.1 which gives the trade-off between g and c.

5. In my opinion, changes in real wages would not be used as a short-run policy variable as in this model but mostly for achieving longer-run goals. In those instances in which real wages have been changed in the short run, it has been primarily as a defensive move, as, for example, when real wages were cut back in the USSR in 1930–33 in order to finance grain exports; or as in Poland in 1976, when prices of food were not raised for political reasons. The tenor of Portes' remarks suggests that he had in mind primarily a positive use of changes in real wages.

References

Caves, Richard, and Jones, Ronald. *World Trade and Payments*. Boston: Little, Brown, 1973.

Part Two
FOREIGN TRADE BEHAVIOR
AND COMMERCIAL POLICY

4

A Comparative View
of Foreign Trade Behavior:
Market Versus
Centrally Planned Economies

Capitalist Market Economy

In the basic model of free market capitalism, enterprises are privately owned and independently determine what and how much to produce in response to the market demands of other enterprises, households, and the government. Changes in demand are reflected not only in changes in quantities produced and purchased, but in changes in prices and, therefore, in profits. These changes in turn lead to further changes in quantities. Within limitations imposed by costs, availability of communications (information), and transportation, each nation tends to have a unified market with similar prices for similar goods, and to engage in specialization and division of labor. As part of this process, capital flows freely between regions within a nation in response to investment opportunities and also because some regions may buy more from other regions than they sell to them.

Introduce a second market economy. In many fundamental respects international commodity and capital transactions are motivated and take place on the same bases as inter-regional trade: prices and profits, specialization, and division of labor. A major difference results from the fact that, for reasons of sovereignty, each nation has its own currency. This requires the introduction of exchange rates for translating the prices of one country into those of another and for setting the terms of currency exchanges. As with inter-regional trade, changes in exports and imports follow from changes in demands, prices, and profits, and— here there is a difference—from changes in exchange rates. And changes

Reprinted with permission from *Comparative Economic Systems: Models and Cases,* Morris Bornstein, ed. (Homewood, Ill.: Richard D. Irwin, Inc., 1985), pp. 367–386.

in exchange rates often follow from changes in the other variables just mentioned. This is especially the case under floating exchange rates. Under pegged rates, the central bank or treasury buys or sells foreign exchange to prevent the exchange rate from fluctuating outside specified narrow limits. Should a nation with a pegged exchange rate experience deficits that eventually exceed available stocks of foreign exchange plus credits from other nations, then the exchange rate must be devalued or exchange controls be imposed. The imposition of exchange controls on imports amounts to import rationing or so-called resident inconvertibility of the currency.

Sovereignty is responsible not only for the existence of separate national currencies but also for protectionism. The result is that regulated market economies impede imports by the use of tariffs, import quotas, and other such devices. Exporters are also assisted in foreign competition, most prominently by credit subsidies.

Because of the distorting effects of governmental interferences in currency and commodity markets and the need to harmonize the conflicting interests of different nations, two major international economic organizations were created: the International Monetary Fund (IMF) and the General Agreement on Tariffs and Trade (GATT). The IMF was designed to keep order in world currency markets and to assist nations with balance-of-payments problems. GATT's primary role is to reduce impediments to free multilateral trade by negotiating reductions in tariffs and quotas, curbing export subsidies, and so forth. Impediments to trade have also been reduced by the formation of customs unions in which a number of nations cut and eventually eliminate barriers among themselves while maintaining common barriers, at GATT levels, to the rest of the world. To the extent that lowering of barriers increases trade among customs union members through reducing protection of domestic economic activity, the results are salutary. However, trade between members may also be increased at the expense of more efficient non-members—so-called trade diversion—an action which reduces welfare.

Domestic Features of Centrally Planned Economies

Certain domestic characteristics of the CPEs affect their foreign trade behavior. Some of these characteristics should not be viewed as absolutely necessary to central planning, nor are they present to the same degree in each of the CPEs. They are included because they have been relevant in most East European nations and the U.S.S.R. until the present. The major exception is Hungary since 1968.

Material Balance Planning

There is virtually no private ownership of means of production in a CPE. Non-agricultural enterprises are the property of the state and are run by state-appointed managers. State managers do not determine independently, on the basis of market conditions, what and how much to produce, to whom to sell, from whom to buy (inputs) and at what prices. Rather, they take orders on these matters from the central planners, particularly on transactions with other enterprises. Since there are no real markets between enterprises, the planners have the enormous task of balancing supplies and demands for thousands of commodities—so-called material balance planning.

They also have the task of supply-planning—telling each enterprise where and when to ship its output and from which enterprise to obtain its inputs. Should supplies and demands for individual commodities fail to balance—and this seems to be the rule rather than the exception—the planners have to try to make adjustments. Such adjustments are often difficult because, for example, to increase the output of a deficit input requires increases in the outputs of many other inputs, and in a process of many stages. Problems like these, solved quietly and anonymously by the invisible hand in market economies, are a major headache of central planners.

Overfull Employment Planning

The problems of material-balance planning are made all the more difficult by another feature of central planning—the tendency to over-commit resources. In this respect, CPEs resemble market economies during wartime. The resulting excess demand by consumers for final products and by enterprises for factors and intermediate products expresses itself, given rigid price control, as repressed inflation. Moreover, the "taut" plans lead to sellers' markets and to a resulting relative lack of concern for the quality of output, including exportables.

Quantity Targeting

The major goal of enterprises is their output or sales targets. In the scarcity context of "taut" plans, of course, usually everything that is produced can be sold, so that output and sales usually amount to the same thing. The emphasis on output and sales, rather than on profits, cost reduction, and numerous other "success indicators," is due to the need of the planners themselves to equate supply and demand through material balances. The use of quantity targeting, however, reinforces the tendency, noted above, for management to be less concerned with quality than it otherwise might.

Irrational Pricing

The prevalence of "irrational" costs and prices in CPEs is almost universally acknowledged. Basically, it is due to (a) extensive use of differential excise taxes and subsidies; (b) failure, because of the influence of Marxian ideology, to account properly and fully in the price structure for rent, interest, and profits; and (c) insensitivity to the changing influences of supply and demand forces. With regard to (c) one need only note that since 1950, the Soviets have had only three major industrial producer price reforms: in 1955, 1967, and 1982. In between reforms, the prices of 95 (or more) percent of commodities remained unchanged.

Foreign Trade Behavior of Centrally Planned Economies

With these characteristics of central planning by direct controls in mind, we now turn to the resulting foreign trade behavior of CPEs.[1]

State Trading

It has been said that ". . . economic planning of the type practiced in Russia is not feasible without the use of a foreign trade monopoly. . . ."[2] Like all other major economic activities, foreign trade is nationalized in the centrally planned economies and is usually conducted by combines which function as agents of the state. This has at least three major consequences for foreign trade behavior.

First, among the Eastern nations, foreign trade is conducted primarily to obtain essential imports. Exports are considered not as an end in themselves but as a means to finance the necessary imports.[3] This view of the foreign trade process seems natural enough since the CPE nations, typically pursuing overfull employment policies, can hardly be interested in mere employment effects of exports. If, notwithstanding this, some of the CPE nations have led intensive export-promotion campaigns, it was because of balance-of-payments pressures—that is, to pay for rising imports. In the West, the level of exports is just as (if not more) important a goal as the level of imports. Some individual traders export, others import, with gains to the economy, presumably reflected in private profits, in either case. Western policymakers are motivated to encourage exports for both their employment effects and their balance-of-payments effects.

Second, the CPEs often take a barter-type approach to foreign trade and view exports and imports as interdependent. Profitability is assessed primarily with respect to overall "terms of trade" rather than on the basis of profit on each individual transaction. This is a consequence of the import orientation of trade (above) as well as of "irrational" internal prices, and of the predisposition, inherited from internal planning, to operate in categories of physical allocations.

Third, because foreign trade is run by a state monopoly, tariffs are basically redundant; trade is controlled by implicit import and export quotas. The decisions to trade are made directly by the government, often without the mediation of price comparisons. In the absence of such explicit decisions, trade will not take place—a reaction equivalent to that achieved by employing prohibitive quotas. By comparison, in market economies profitable opportunities for trade may be pursued unless the government makes an explicit decision to the contrary. Such decisions may be implemented by tariffs, quotas, or exchange controls.

Level of Trade

The desire for self-sufficiency in some commodities produced at a comparative disadvantage motivates all nations to some extent, thereby reducing the possible volume of world trade. The nations with centrally planned economies appear to be more strongly motivated in this direction than market economies, for the following well-known reasons.

First, because of the complicated input-output interrelationships among intermediate products, most of which are directly allocated, central planners try to avoid heavy dependence of the domestic economy on foreign supplies and, thus, to insulate it from the vagaries, both imaginary and real, of the world market.

Second, all nations endeavor to achieve a certain degree of self-sufficiency for reasons of military security—to diminish the risks of economic warfare. Owing to this universal desire, countries where all industry is nationalized are likely to reduce trade to a greater extent than those in which a large part of economic activity is in private hands.[4]

Third, in a market economy competition exists naturally and protection requires an explicit act by the government. Under central planning as it is presently practiced, protection is the rule unless the government makes an explicit decision to allow imports to replace domestic production.

Fourth, the anti-trade bias of CPEs may possibly be enhanced by their irrational price systems; in fact, it is often very difficult for the planners to decide what they should trade. These are significant impediments to trade.

Inconvertibility

Currency convertibility in its commonly used meaning refers to the right or possibility of the holder of a currency to exchange it for gold or for "hard" currencies. Limitations are placed on convertibility when a currency is in excess supply on foreign exchange markets or, what amounts to the same, when other currencies or gold are in excess demand by the holders of the currency in question. Among market economies such limitations on convertibility are likely to be put in force if a currency is overvalued, owing to inflation or to more fundamental structural factors. With overvaluation, there is a tendency for imports to exceed exports. Usually, nonresidents are allowed to convert current earnings of the currency in question into their own currencies. Balance is maintained by restricting imports, that is, by placing limits on convertibility for residents.[5]

Why are the currencies of the CPEs, say, the ruble, inconvertible? Overvaluation, although a sufficient condition for inconvertibility in a market economy, is neither necessary nor relevant, given the foreign trade institutions and practices of the CPEs. So long as internal prices are disorderly and world prices are used as the basis for trade, and the composition and volume of trade are determined by direct controls and administered by a foreign trade monopoly, the exchange rate remains merely an accounting device. Its changes have no effect on trade. Thus, for instance, the substantial devaluations of April 1936 and January 1961, both of which brought the ruble into rough equilibrium in a purchasing-power-parity sense,[6] had no discernible impact on the volume or composition of Soviet foreign trade, or how it is conducted.

Currency inconvertibility in CPEs is in part a reaction to balance-of-payment pressures and the lack of sufficient foreign exchange reserves. Yet, although these factors (related to rapid growth, overfull employment planning, inadaptability of exports, and repressed inflation) might partly justify the prohibition against converting domestic currency into foreign exchange by residents, they can hardly be adduced to explain the existing convertibility restrictions on nonresidents. Typically, the Soviet Bloc laws do not permit nonresidents to convert domestic currencies into foreign exchange or gold, nor do they even allow them to accumulate such currencies.[7] These extreme legal restrictions on convertibility (to be explained below) obviously reduce the demand for bloc currencies. Their effect, additionally weakening the international financial standing of the bloc nations, has been superimposed on other factors discouraging the potential nonresident demand for bloc currencies. Clearly, even if foreigners were allowed to accumulate rubles, for example, their demand for Soviet currency would be blunted by circumstances always present under central planning.

First, there would be the considerable uncertainty on the part of nonresidents regarding the possibility of purchasing goods with bloc currencies. Nonresidents are quite limited in the scope of possible purchases from the East European nations, not because the latter do not have large amounts of potential exportables, but because most commodity flows are directly planned and it is difficult to buy items not earmarked for export (implicit trade controls). That is to say, within the existing system of allocation, foreign holders of, say, rubles (or, for that matter, of hard currencies), are not allowed much, if any, opportunity to compete for goods with Soviet enterprises and domestic consumers. Their difficulties are compounded by shortages resulting from "tautness" and might be additionally increased by the fact that trade negotiations are usually conducted with special foreign trade organizations subordinate to the foreign trade monopoly rather than directly with producing or distributing enterprises. This substantial limitation on purchases by nonresidents was aptly called by Oscar Altman "commodity inconvertibility," in contrast with "currency inconvertibility."[8]

Second, uncertainty generated by inaccessibility of bloc exportables is compounded by the irrationality of internal pricing and absence of functional exchange rates which make it difficult to determine in advance of negotiations the prices at which goods may be bought or sold. The foreign trade prices, therefore, usually deviate considerably from domestic prices and are, as a "first approximation," based on "world prices." Although this practice largely eliminates the overvaluation problem and may, additionally, reduce somewhat the uncertainty (due to irrational internal prices) in the case of simple standardized commodities, the prices of complex products remain quite conjectural. Finally, uncertainty as to the "value" of a ruble, for instance, is still further increased by factors mentioned above concerning the quality, delivery, and general unadaptability of exports to foreign markets. To sum up, from the point of view of nonresidents, bloc currencies are not only inconvertible in the usual sense, but also undesirable because of the substantial uncertainties regarding their exchangeability for goods.

Owing to the significance and uniqueness of "commodity inconvertibility" of bloc currencies, it is impossible to explain its existence and implementation without discussing the foreign trade monopolies of CPEs.

First, and most important, since central planning is implemented primarily by direct allocation of resources, the planners deem it necessary to insulate the flows of products from external disruption. This is accomplished by the Soviet foreign trade monopoly by prohibition of foreign-held ruble balances and by inconvertibility of rubles into other currencies as well as commodities.

Second, when internal prices are not "rational" as indicators of the relative values of goods to the planners or in terms of some measure of "real costs" (for reasons discussed earlier), free trade (commodity convertibility) cannot be allowed (nor can the foreign trade monopoly be dispensed with) because it would lead to a pattern of trade disadvantageous to the CPE and productive of large gains for the Western trading partners.

Let us sum up these conclusions in another way. Given the irrationality of internal prices, resident convertibility (free imports) cannot be allowed because it will lead to large-scale importation of commodities which have relatively high prices but which, in fact, may be more cheaply produced at home (for example, many consumers' goods). On the other hand, strict controls over Soviet exports, discouraging potential ruble holdings by foreigners, must be maintained lest nonresidents compete in domestic markets for goods which, owing to subsidies or some other costing quirk, have a low price but, in fact, are expensive to produce.[9] Nonresident "free" expenditure within the bloc countries cannot be allowed, because it may involve losses to their domestic economies. As noted earlier, the bloc nations do not grant convertibility rights to nonresidents except in the special instance when the swing credit limits of a bilateral agreement are exceeded. Moreover, foreigners are usually prohibited from accumulating bloc currencies, whether within or outside the centrally planned economies. The only exception to this prohibition is that made for temporary imbalances within the rigid framework of bilateral trade agreements. Presumably, this is because the availability of bloc currencies to outsiders might lead to discounts in world currency markets, something the East European planners undoubtedly wish to avoid.

In the case of Western nations with inconvertible currencies, nonresidents are encouraged to hold, or spend, the "inconvertible" currency—the problem is that they don't want to. The CPEs are in the peculiar position of being unable to try to boost their exports—thereby improving the position of their currency—by allowing nonresidents freely to import from them.

Bilateralism

The percentage of bilaterally conducted trade is much higher among the CPEs than among either the Western industrial or the developing nations. Intrabloc trade is more bilateral than East-West trade. Institutionally, the high degree of bilateralism is implemented by means of annual and long-term trade and payment agreements which attempt, within limits and after taking account of credits, to keep trade between the two participating countries in balance over the period in question. These agreements are implemented, of course, by direct governmental controls over the level and composition of imports and exports.

The CPEs recognize the advantages of multilateralism and have taken steps toward increasing its scope in intrabloc transactions. Why, despite those steps, bilateralism is still so strongly adhered to can be attributed primarily to currency inconvertibility and the factors behind it discussed above. Since no nation is willing to hold balances in rubles, zlotys, and so forth, payments of the CPEs must be balanced insofar as they are unable to produce gold or develop export surpluses with convertible currency nations.

A second factor leading to bilateralism in intrabloc trade is the tendency among bloc countries to strive for overall payments balance among themselves. Now, the necessity or desire to achieve overall balance does not logically require bilateral balancing by nation. Among market economies, however, it has been observed that nations with export marketing problems sometimes resort to bilateral balancing by individual trading partner. The propensity to do so is much stronger among the planned economies. In fact, it is difficult to see how a substantial degree of multilateralism could be achieved by CPEs simultaneously with the desired overall balance. The twin objectives are accomplished imperfectly in a market economy via the automatic operation of price, income, and capital flow adjustment mechanisms that do not function under central planning. The easiest way to achieve overall balance in the latter case is undoubtedly by planning for a high degree of bilateral balance.

Envision the difficulty of planned multilateralism with overall balance. Suppose country A trades with B, C, and D. Overall balance can be achieved by relatively simple balancing with each nation. This is not to say that bilateral balancing is easy, for it undoubtedly requires considerable negotiation and, on the part of one or both partners, either some uneconomic trading or the foregoing of some profitable trading. On the other hand, suppose A runs a surplus with B. This means that A (B) goes into negotiations with C and D requiring a net deficit (surplus) equal to the surplus (deficit) with B (A). But there may be no particular reason why C and D should want to run surpluses with A exactly to offset deficits with B.

Under central planning, where domestic prices are misleading and only the relatively few goods specifically earmarked for export or import can be traded, nations may be loathe to accept a surplus (deficit) with another nation because of the subsequent difficulty of buying (selling) more than can be sold to (bought from) third countries. This, in effect, is equivalent to a situation in which the various inconvertible currencies have different expected values to different holders. If interest conflicts occur along these lines, there is no economic adjustment mechanism to resolve them. An administrative reconciliation, if any, would undoubtedly involve a substantial reduction of profitable trade and/or addition of unprofitable trade. The problems are likely multiplied as the number of nations in the system increases. (In a system with economic adjustment mechanisms, the problems would probably be lessened as the number of nations increased.)

Inconvertibility and bilateralism are among the major international economic problems facing the Soviet Bloc nations. They have been actively concerned for many years over the disadvantages of their rigidly bilateral trading system. Early evidence of this concern was the establishment in 1963 of an International Bank for Economic Cooperation (IBEC) the major purpose of which was to overcome rigid bilateralism in trade among the member countries of the Council for Mutual Economic Assistance (CMEA). The members of CMEA provided the Bank with capital consisting of their domestic currencies and gold. With these as backing, the Bank created an all-CMEA currency unit called the transferable ruble or TR. Intra-CMEA trade was to be transacted in TRs, and members were encouraged to trade bilaterally with each other but without attempting to balance exports and imports. These original annual bilateral negotiations were to be followed by an all-CMEA session in which the resulting surpluses and deficits in TRs would be canceled out multilaterally. Imbalances which still remained were to be eliminated by additional exports by the overall deficit nations to be paid for with the TRs accumulated by those nations with overall surpluses.

This attempt failed and trade remained as rigidly balanced as before. The TR, operating within a context of national irrational prices and commodity inconvertibility, proved to be as inconvertible as CMEA internal currencies and, therefore, could not facilitate multilateralism. Those nations which would have had overall surpluses under the above plan would have been faced with the same problems that had to be faced by nations holding inconvertible national bloc currencies before 1963. Each nation had an incentive to run a deficit, but not a surplus. There was no mechanism under the new scheme to insure that deficits and surpluses would, in the aggregate, balance out. And so, to avoid an aggregate surplus, each nation strove for bilateral balance whenever it was in danger of running a surplus.

In fact, over the past 20 years, the rigidity of bilateral balancing has been increased in the following respect: Not only must exports and imports with each trading partner balance but, additionally, it has been the practice to have at least two sub-balances—one for so-called hard goods (goods that can be sold in the West for hard currencies) and one for soft goods (that cannot be sold for hard currencies). Where a commodity balance in hard goods cannot be struck, the deficit nation must either pay in hard currency or forgo the purchase. This practice is carried to an extreme in which, if one nation sells another a product which includes inputs that have been imported from the West and paid for in hard currency, the cost of those inputs has to be reimbursed in hard currency even though the product as a whole is viewed as "soft."

Attempts to reduce bilateralism have continued. The CMEA "Complex Program" adopted in 1971 specified a gradual shift to multilateralism by requiring that 10 percent of bilateral trade imbalances be paid for in hard currencies, and that this percentage be gradually increased. But, since nations refuse to run surpluses and deficits in the first place, such an administrative solution was bound to fail, and it did. CMEA economists also talk about planning in real terms for multilateralism. This is equivalent to planning for a tradeoff in which the hatmaker buys a pair of shoes from the shoemaker, the shoemaker buys 2 shirts from the shirtmaker, and the shirtmaker buys 1½ hats from the hatmaker! And these same economists speak as though such planning would make the TR more transferable. But surely, this is putting the cart before the horse—if the TR were convertible, trade would be more multilateral.

In 1976, an attempt was made to get Western enterprises to accept TRs in partial or full payment for their exports. Foreign holdings of TRs in IBEC would earn one percent per annum in interest. The purpose of this new regulation appears to have been to secure cheap credit, as the United States has because so many foreigners are willing to hold dollars. Needless to say it failed. The one percent rate of interest was much too low. In addition, foreign holders of TRs could not convert them into hard currencies, but could only use them to import goods from the one CMEA nation from which they had received the TRs.

Clearly, central planning by direct controls is incompatible with currency convertibility. Unless the CMEA nations abandon central planning in favor of decentralized markets, free prices, and exchange rates which function to relate, organically, internal and external prices, the twin goals of convertibility and multilateralism will remain a chimera. This is in striking contrast to the situation in a market economy. In the latter, inconvertibility (and resulting bilateralism) owing primarily to overvaluation can be eliminated by devaluation. And deeper-seated disequilibria (owing to shifts in international supply and demand) can usually be worked off or adapted to over time, given the application of a proper assortment of policies including devaluation.

Exchange Rates

The CPEs all publish exchange rates and, in fact, often make changes in these rates as a nominal adjustment to changes in world prices. What meaning can such exchange rates have if the prices of the nations in question are irrational? The answer is: very little. There is no point in comparing prices which are irrational and which are largely irrelevant to foreign trade. This is the reason why CPE exchange rates serve almost no function.

It is worth mentioning, however, that the official exchange rates are used (a) for such "invisible" transactions as purchases of the CPE currency by visitors to (and business and diplomatic residents in) the country; and (b) for translation of foreign trade figures in foreign currencies into figures in the national CPE currency.

The absence of a functional exchange rate is finessed in different ways in intrabloc and in East-West trade. The annual trade between CPEs ordinarily is balanced (in world prices) for the very purpose of avoiding the necessity to hold another nation's currency. Were it not for commodity inconvertibility, CPEs might accept each other's currencies or TRs and store them for later use. But, as noted earlier, this is not the case. Normally, each CPE carefully avoids running a surplus with every other CPE—a state of rigid bilateralism. In contrast, East-West trade is also conducted at world prices *but* in world currencies. Trade is not balanced bilaterally. Rather, each CPE is free to spend its earnings of convertible currencies in any other country—that is, trade is conducted multilaterally. Since a CPE's trade with the West is entirely in Western currencies, there is still never any question of having to use its official exchange rate for converting domestic (CPE) currency into a Western currency.

Further, because CPE exchange rates serve no real economic function, a CPE which experiences persistent current account deficits, cannot improve its balance of payments by devaluing its currency. In fact, it is possible that absence of realistic functioning exchange rates has contributed to the Eastern balance-of-payments problems with the West. A rational exchange rate along with rational internal prices enables one to estimate what might be profitably exported and imported. Absence of such exchange rates and prices makes it very difficult to come to rational judgments on these matters.

If a market economy with a deficit devalues, its exports become cheaper to foreigners and imports become more expensive. In the case of CPEs, no guidance is provided by exchange rates. Because a CPE's trade is conducted in foreign currencies, a change in the CPE's exchange rate does not alter the price in foreign currency of an export or import and thereby lead to changes in the quantity of goods traded. In turn, because a CPE's domestic prices of exports and imports in domestic currency are set independently of the foreign-trade prices in foreign currency, changes in the foreign-trade prices do not automatically affect the domestic prices of the same goods. Therefore, a devaluation of a

CPE's exchange rate will not reduce a trade deficit by increasing exports and decreasing imports.[10]

MFN Clause Tariff Problems

The nations of Eastern Europe customarily request most-favored-nation (MFN) treatment on tariffs in their exports to the West.[11] In return, they purport to reciprocate in ways described below. The question is of importance today because so much of the increase in world trade and reduction in trade discrimination has come about through the mutual lowering of tariff barriers in which the MFN clause plays an obvious role.

The basic difficulty faced by the CPE nations in adapting to the MFN clause on tariffs is quite obvious. Whereas in the West the mutual cutting of tariffs provides a free-market price criterion of the appropriate change in volume and distribution of trade, in the CPEs the decisions (a) to import or not to import and (b) from whom to import[12] are made quantitatively by quotas that are implicit in the planning process. It is well known that sensitivity to price is in this case much lower than in market economy countries.

It is also worth noting that, regardless of the level of tariff, in a CPE[13] imported commodities are ordinarily sold at the same price as comparable domestically-produced goods. Differences between the "import price plus cost of distribution plus tariff" and the price of the comparable domestically produced goods are "equalized" by offsetting taxes or subsidies. When the planners finally decide to import a commodity, tariffs have no impact on final domestic price—nor is the domestic price necessarily affected (in the short run, at least) by the decision to increase through imports the availability of a commodity. Last, but not least, import decisions continue to be largely "quantitative." Tariffs cannot be allowed to assume their usual market functions so long as exchange rates are in disequilibrium and the relationship between internal prices and costs of production is distorted.

In the 1960s, several CPEs, including the Soviet Union and Hungary, introduced double-column tariffs with the clear purpose of providing bargaining weapons against discriminatory treatment by the European Economic Community (EEC) and the European Free Trade area (EFTA). Goods of those nations which did not grant the Soviet Union and Hungary MFN treatment were subject to duties according to the higher of the two tariff schedules, all others according to the lower. The foreign trade combines presumably have an incentive to shift their purchases to countries whose goods receive the lower schedule of duties, because both their profits and the managerial bonuses based on these profits are greater on the same goods imported from lower-tariff instead of higher-tariff countries.

It may appear that granting MFN status under these double-column tariffs is equivalent to granting MFN status under free market conditions, but in fact it is not. First, it is unlikely that the extensive planned bilateral intrabloc trade would be disrupted or altered for small price differentials, which may develop in favor of Western nations as a result of granting the latter MFN status. Second, for reasons already mentioned, the lowering of a tariff would have no effect on the decisions "how much" and "what" to import—that is, competition with domestic suppliers would not be allowed. The only possible effect of the system, then, would be to redistribute trade among a nation's Western trading partners—but not to increase it.

To get around this problem, the Soviet Union attempted to reciprocate MFN status with some nations by agreeing to increase the value of its imports from them. In effect, the increase in imports is designed to simulate the trade-creating effects of lowering tariffs. This technique has been adopted by GATT and is the basis upon which Poland, Romania, and Hungary have been allowed to join. Although this method satisfies some nations and does appear to bridge the systemic gap, it deviates from the ideal in at least two respects in the case of bilaterally-negotiated MFN treatment.

First, in theory a mutual bilateral lowering of tariffs should increase trade between the participants as a result of both trade creation (competition with domestic suppliers) and trade diversion (at the expense of other nations). In fact, there is nothing in these agreements to ensure such results, and it may be that a preponderance of the bilateral increase of trade is at the expense of other nations. This would foster bilateralism and would be contrary to the "equal treatment" and antidiscriminatory spirit of MFN clauses.[14]

Second, once MFN is in effect, the Western partner has no way of knowing whether the Eastern partner has actually increased access to its markets by third nations, an access which should be extended equally to the Western nation in question, as a privilege of MFN status.

Under GATT, the CPEs pledge to increase imports from GATT members as fast as their overall trade increases or at some specified rate of increase. If one can assume that they trade primarily for commercial considerations, then the increase in imports should be non-discriminatory and multilateral, although perhaps not at the volume which would result if real tariffs were being lowered. Since the early 1970s, however, balance-of-payments stresses have undoubtedly caused the expansion of trade of Eastern GATT members to deviate sharply from the GATT ideal. Undoubtedly, much trade has flowed not toward the cheapest markets but in the direction of credits and counter-trade agreements. In this respect, however, the CPEs are not much different from market economies with balance of payments problems.

Dumping

Dumping is usually defined as selling abroad at a lower price than at home. When the commodity is not sold domestically and therefore has no home price, "domestic cost of production" or "export price in third markets" is sometimes substituted. The Soviet Union has been accused of dumping in Western markets a number of times, for example, in regard to aluminum, tin, glass, and so forth.[15] That the Soviet Union and other state traders have the power to dump[16] is unquestioned. Whether the above criteria of dumping are proper for a centrally planned economy is a more difficult question.

First, to the extent that the currencies of the CPEs have often been or are substantially overvalued by official exchange rates, comparison of domestic and export prices is a misleading criterion of dumping. Under these circumstances, exports must be nominally subsidized. The nominal losses on exports are matched, of course, by large nominal profits on imports.

Second, as noted above, relative domestic prices in the CPEs reflect subsidies and excise taxes introduced to satisfy domestic fiscal and other requirements. Here again, comparison of domestic and export prices is a misleading criterion of dumping even when exchange rates are not overvalued.

Third, the CPEs, following the labor theory of value, have a different concept of "cost of production" from that of the West. This makes the use of "cost" an imperfect substitute for "price" in assessing dumping. The problem can be exemplified by commodities like petroleum whose "cost" does not adequately include the quantitatively important categories of rent and interest.

Fourth, and in many ways most difficult to deal with, is the fact that export and import decisions are not always independent of each other as in capitalist market economies; instead, state monopolies view exports as payment for imports. The connection is especially close in bilateral agreements. Thus, for example, a state trader who sold a commodity at one half of domestic cost could hardly be accused of "true" dumping, if the foreign exchange earned were used to import goods purchased at one third of domestic cost. A nominal financial loss on exports would be, in this case, more than offset by the financial gain on imports.[17]

Although this approach may seem fair from the point of view of the CPEs, it fails to take account of the rationale behind antidumping legislation in market economies.[18] A major purpose of antidumping legislation is to prevent the disruption of domestic markets and loss of domestic production facilities as a result of what might be termed unfair competition. If one's markets and production facilities are lost in (fair) competition with a truly lower-cost producer, one can expect, in return, assured imports at lower prices. If, however, a foreign supplier sells below domestic price because of a temporary surplus or in an attempt to break into a market, the low price is not likely to be maintained and the disruptive effect is without compensating benefits. CPE exports offered at a loss in order to reap a large profit on imports would seem to fall into the second category. They would not necessarily reflect a stable comparative advantage position. They are, therefore, potentially "disruptive" and should not be allowed. Finally, data on the domestic prices, taxes, and subsidies for commodities exported by CPEs are not easily available. Consequently, an evaluation of dumping charges is difficult, if not impossible, using traditional criteria.

Because of the difficulties in assessing dumping charges by CPEs, the U.S. Government has developed some alternative methods of evaluation. Find a country at a comparable level of development as the CPE charged with dumping. For example, Spain has been used as Poland's proxy nation.

If the proxy nation produces the allegedly dumped product, take its domestic price of the product in question and translate it through its (proxy nation's) exchange rate into the currency of the nation into which the product allegedly has been dumped—in order to get a "test" price for comparison with the actual export price. If the proxy nation "test" price is equal to or below the actual export price, the verdict is "not guilty" of dumping; if above—"guilty." For example, suppose Poland was attempting to sell electrical golf carts in the United States for $1,000. Suppose further that these carts were produced in Spain for 200,000 pesetas. If the peseta exchange rate were 150 p = $1, the test price would be $1,333 and the Polish enterprise would be considered to be dumping. If the carts were produced in Spain for 100,000 pesetas, the test price would be $667 or below the Polish price. Verdict: not dumping!

A problem arises if the proxy nation does not produce the allegedly dumped product. In this event, a 1979 U.S. regulation stipulates that the actual physical inputs required by the CPE to make the product be measured and then be costed at prices of the proxy nation. To the cost so determined, add estimates of a fair profit, selling costs, packaging, and the like. The resulting price is then converted through the proxy nation exchange rate to provide the test for dumping, as above.

While in theory the two variants of this method do bridge the systemic gap, it is a far from satisfactory solution. There is no reason to believe that just because two nations are at approximately the same level of development, their costs of production of any particular product would be comparable. This is particularly true, given the significant differences between market and non-market economies in the organization and management of production. Perhaps even more important, one must question the assumption that the exchange rate of any particular market economy is relevant for a non-market economy. This is especially the case when one considers the different degrees of disequilibrium in the exchange rates of various nations.[19]

Competitiveness in World Markets

Given their levels of development and especially their emphasis on rapid industrialization, the CPEs export relatively few industrial and manufactured products to the West and import a relatively large amount. Lack of success in these markets is due partly to central planning with direct controls. Basically, CPE enterprises do not have to compete in domestic markets because (1) purchases and sales are guaranteed by the central plan and (2) "taut" planning implies sellers' markets—demand usually exceeding supply. Moreover, enterprise targets, upon which bonuses are based, are primarily quantitative—a natural consequence of central planning implemented by material balances. This contributes to a focus on quantity rather than quality, and to a lack of interest on the part of management in improving technology. Since most CPE enterprises, especially Soviet enterprises, operate primarily in the non-competitive environment just described, they find it difficult to compete in Western markets for manufactured markets. This helps explain their hard-currency balance-of-payments problems, and the development in the 1970s of various kinds of industrial cooperation agreements designed to overcome the East-West gaps in salesmanship, quality, technology, packaging, and the like.

CMEA, the Communist Customs Union

The Soviet Bloc CPEs comprise a kind of customs union called the Council for Mutual Economic Assistance (CMEA). Among market economies, customs unions are defined as a group of nations that reduce or eliminate tariffs (and other trade barriers) among themselves and maintain a common tariff barrier to the rest of the world. CMEA cannot, of course, be considered a customs union so defined in market categories.

However, the members of CMEA have always traded more with each other and less with the rest of the world than could be explained in economic terms (see below), and in this sense constitute a preferential trading area like a Western customs union. The CMEA countries' preferences are not expressed in heights of tariffs but in the implicit discriminatory quotas that result from the decisions of foreign-trade planners.

While both political and economic factors motivate the formation of Western customs unions, the political factors played a much more dominant role than the economic in the formation of CMEA. On the one hand, for military and political reasons, the Soviet Union forced the other CMEA nations into high levels of intrabloc trade; on the other, Eastern Europe was pushed into Soviet arms by Cold War ostracism. From an economic standpoint, the Eastern nations had little interest in trading with each other—and hardly did so before World War II (with the exception of a modest German trade with Bulgaria, Hungary, and Romania). The large increase in intrabloc trade which did take place after World War II was primarily at the expense of (a replacement for) former trade with Western nations. This so-called trade diversion, while perhaps better than no trade at all, represents a substantial reduction in gains from trade relative to the much more advantageous East-West trade it replaces.

While the basis for this intra-CMEA trade is largely political, one institutional factor strongly encourages intrabloc economic relations. Central planners find it very convenient, when drawing up their annual material balances, to be able to trade with other central planners. Further, as noted above, trading with other CPEs in large bilateral bargaining sessions results in large economies of scale in negotiating and much reduction in effort.

Regardless, the data suggest that, from an economic standpoint, intra-CMEA trade has been excessive. Hewett[20] has shown that as of 1970, whereas the EEC and EFTA almost doubled the trade among their respective members, CMEA increased trade among members by almost 16 times. While this emphasis on intrabloc trade was certainly substantially reduced during the détente period as East-West trade expanded, it still must be excessive by several orders of magnitude—implying very large trade diversion, less than optimal geographic trade structures, and hence reduced gains from trade. The above statements should not be taken to mean that the CMEA nations engage in too much foreign trade in the aggregate, for they do not, but simply that their trade patterns are very distorted.

Attempts have been made, especially since 1970, to integrate some economic activities within CMEA. But aside from some showcase examples like the intra-CMEA oil and gas pipelines and electricity grid which have been "naturals" for integration, little has been accomplished. Irrational prices, absence of functional exchange rates and interest rates, and the various rigidities of national central planning have posed obstacles to long-run cooperative ventures which have proved very difficult to overcome.

In market economies, members of customs unions achieve integration primarily by reducing barriers to trade and to flows of factors (labor and capital). Where barriers to factor flows are removed as well as tariffs and quotas on imports, the customs union becomes known as a "common market." Nations which agree to being part of a customs union or common market give up, in effect, some sovereignty to impersonal market forces. So, for example, a nation which wants to have a steel industry and has been protecting an inefficient steel industry knows that when it enters a customs union it will probably lose at least part of that industry.

Subjecting private industry to such market risks is difficult for the government of a capitalist regulated market economy, but not as difficult as agreeing to give up a nationalized enterprise or industry is for a CPE. CPEs have shown themselves willing to agree to some intraindustry specialization (A produces 2½-ton trucks; B, 5-ton trucks; and C, 10-ton trucks), but not to give up large enterprises or industries.

Since the CPEs don't have "impersonal" market forces to guide and implement integration, the only feasible alternatives would seem to be to set up a supranational authority with the power to make such decisions. Or, more modestly, in the case of joint ventures, to force all member nations to go along with majority rule. Supranationality was rejected early on by the smaller nations in CMEA which feared that their interests would be subordinated to those of the larger nations, especially the U.S.S.R. The CMEA Charter, finally completed in 1960, reaffirmed national sovereignty. A bitter three-year fight then ensued over majority rule. This fight, primarily between the U.S.S.R. and Romania, was won by the latter nation, and "unanimity" has since been required for all joint projects undertaken officially under CMEA's banner. As a result, only a few percent of all investments undertaken by the CMEA nations have been on a cooperative basis.

Finally, factor flows among the CMEA nations have been minimal. In addition to all of the other inhibiting factors mentioned above, the extremely low rate of interest prevalent in CMEA is not conducive to medium- and long-term loans for foreign investment. And, given the attitude in the Soviet Bloc toward emigration, it is no surprise to find few CMEA workers gainfully occupied anywhere but in their home countries.

Notes

This essay includes material reprinted by permission from the writer's "Foreign Trade Behavior of Centrally Planned Economies," in *Industrialization in Two Systems: Essays in Honor of Alexander Gerschenkron,* ed. Henry Rosovksy (New York: John Wiley and Sons, Inc., 1966; copyright by the President and Fellows of Harvard College), pp. 237–65, and "Systemic Bases of the Unconventional Trade Practices of Centrally Planned Economies," *Columbia Journal of World Business,* vol. 18, no. 4 (Spring 1984), pp. 4–9.

1. For a somewhat different approach to some of the issues in this paper, see Edward A. Hewett, "Foreign Trade Outcomes in Eastern and Western Economies," in *East European Integration and East-West Trade,* ed. Paul Marer and John Michael Montias (Bloomington, Ind.: Indiana University Press, 1980), pp. 41–69.

2. Alexander Gerschenkron, *Economic Relations with the U.S.S.R.* (New York: Committee on International Economic Policy, 1945), p. 18.

3. "Russia exports solely in order to obtain the wherewithal for payments for imports. In this sense, she is likely to live up to the classical doctrine of foreign trade and to reject the tenets of mercantilism. This, no doubt, sounds paradoxical, but is undeniable. From the Russian point of view exports are a loss and not a gain." (Ibid., p. 47.)

4. This factor operates to curtail Eastern trade with the West much more than intrabloc trade. Along these same lines might be mentioned the desire of many nations to industrialize at any cost rather than submit to comparative advantage, even when long-run comparative advantage suggests less industrialization. Romania was a case in point. The strategic controls imposed by Western nations on trade with the East also contribute somewhat to the low level of East-West trade, although much less so now than in the past.

5. Under extreme circumstances, nonresidents may be denied convertibility into their own currencies, particularly on capital account. Whether nonresidents are allowed to transfer the currency in question to residents of third countries depends on the degree of overvaluation with respect to all other currencies. Usually, conversion is allowed into "softer" but not into "harder" currencies, or into gold. At present, any bloc currency is probably equally "soft," relative to the major Western currencies, since general convertibility prevails in the West. On the other hand, my guess is that some bloc currencies are less desirable than others in intrabloc trade.

6. By this we mean that the foreign trade prices (that is, world prices) of goods exported and imported are, on the average, approximately equal to the domestic prices of the same goods at the given exchange rate. Given the controls which exist over Soviet trade, this appears to be the only operational definition of exchange rate equilibrium which is possible. Equilibrium, under this definition, may deviate substantially from "true" equilibrium, of course.

7. Exceptions to this rule occur in the use of temporary imbalances in bilaterally-balanced trade relationships as well as according to provisions in some bilateral agreements for payment in gold or convertible currency if imbalances exceed prescribed limits for a period of time.

8. Oscar Altman, "Russian Gold and The Ruble," *International Monetary Staff Papers*, vol. 7, no. 3 (April 1960), pp. 430–31. Note that "commodity convertibility" essentially means absence of restrictions on exports. The term "free trade" on the other hand is typically used to denote absence of restrictions on imports, though in theory it encompasses exports as well.

9. Exports also have to be controlled, as noted above, because of the factors associated with "commodity inconvertibility."

10. The problem facing the foreign trade planners regarding what is profitable to import is analogous to that which faced Soviet industrial ministries attempting to choose among investment projects in the 1930s without an interest rate. Each ministry had thousands of projects, but no way of scaling them according to profitability. Similarly, the foreign-trade planners are faced with many more potentially profitable imports than they can finance. In the case of investments, the ministries developed a "coefficient of relative effectiveness" which enabled them to rank projects. Foreign-trade coefficients for ranking exports and imports have also been developed but, according to my information (personal interviews), they are little used.

11. The effect of the most-favored-nation clause is to place on the conceding state the obligation to grant to the nationals and goods of the beneficiary state, either in general or in certain specified respects, the treatment accorded or in future to be accorded to the nationals and goods of the state receiving most favorable treatment in the territory of the conceding state.

12. The decision "from whom to import" is probably less centralized than the one dealing with "what and how much to import" in CPE trade with the West. The foreign trade combines are often told to buy or sell such and such commodities but are left to themselves to seek the best market.

13. Not all of the centrally planned economies have, or have had, tariffs. Note also that since the introduction of economic reforms in Hungary in 1968 much of this section no longer is strictly applicable to that nation.

14. "When we recognize that the most-favored-nation clause does not serve its purpose in trade relations with a foreign trade monopoly, and have introduced quantitative stipulations into trade agreements, we have still not established equality of trading opportunity. We have merely provided for a certain volume of trade . . . there is no reason to assume that quantitative regulations embodied in agreements concluded between pairs of countries would provide for equality of trading opportunity." Gerschenkron, *Economic Relations*, p. 29.

15. The East European nations have sometimes been forced to sell below world prices in Western markets because of real or imagined inferiority of Eastern goods, for political reasons, and so forth.

16. That is to say, they have sufficient monopoly power to separate the various markets in which they sell, as well as to prevent the reimport of goods. They also can easily subsidize losses on dumping out of the general treasury.

17. It is this view of the trade process which has enabled the centrally planned economies to maintain overvalued exchange rates and still engage in a reasonable volume of trade.

18. The centrally planned economies would, of course, welcome Western dumping. Their major foreign trade objective is to get as good terms of trade as possible, and they have no fear of market disruption.

19. For a more extended discussion of these issues, see Chapter 6, "Dumping by Centrally Planned Economies: The Polish Golf Cart Case."

20. Edward A. Hewett, "A Gravity Model of CMEA Trade" in *Quantitative and Analytical Studies in East-West Economic Relations,* ed. Josef C. Brada (Bloomington, Ind.: International Development Research Center, Indiana University, 1976), pp. 1–16.

5

Trade, Technology, and Leverage: The Limits of Pressure

Any particularly horrible crime gives ammunition to proponents of the death penalty. Any particularly egregious Soviet violation of the so-called "spirit of détente" provokes Western analysts to seek a suitable punishment, or at least a threat short of military force, that would induce the Russians to be less beastly and more cooperative. The simple and understandable desire to do something is usually accompanied by an implicit theory of deterrence and, less often, by evidence that the proposed deterrent will be effective.

There is little economic reason to believe that any threat of restricting technology transfer to the USSR and Eastern Europe could extract significant noneconomic concessions from the East. Nor are there any great benefits for the West in such technology transfer beyond the normal economic gains from foreign trade. But the benefits to the East of technology imports from the West are similarly limited, so that Western restrictions on technology exports cannot be a serious deterrent or bargaining counter.

Technology is the knowledge and the techniques with which inputs into the production process are transformed into output. Technology can be transferred from one country to another: the supply of information and knowledge (publications, personnel, technical assistance, and so forth); the licensing for a fee of production processes or advanced techniques; the sale of machinery and equipment embodying sophisticated technology; the sale of advanced production processes, as in the construction of turnkey plants (factories that are bought and sold as complete units, ready to operate as soon as they are completed); and the transfer

Written by Franklyn D. Holzman and Richard Portes. Reprinted with permission from *Foreign Policy* 32 (Fall 1978): 80–90. Copyright © 1978 by the Carnegie Endowment for International Peace.

of related management and marketing systems, as well as technical personnel. Such large-scale transfers often take the form of joint ventures.

It is often argued that exporting technology is different from exporting other commodities. A machine (or its blueprints) embodying advanced technical development may give a buyer greater potential returns than can be had from importing other goods. Having already realized on their investment in research and development, companies may be ready to sell or license their technology for fees that are much less than the productivity gains to a buyer in a technologically less advanced economy. If the imported technology can be copied and spread widely through the economy, the gains to the importing country may be multiplied many fold. This can be especially important if the initial holder of the technology is unable to establish his own production facilities in the buyer's market, as is largely true in the case of Eastern countries.

The flow of technology runs primarily from West to East. The West has an advantage in technology, partly because it represents a larger pool of industrially more advanced nations. But the underlying reason for the West's advantage is that the organization and systems of incentives in the centrally planned Eastern economies are less suited to invention, innovation, and the diffusion of technology than their private enterprise counterparts. Typically, central planning is preoccupied with quantity rather than quality or cost targets; enterprise managers tend to avoid the disruptions and risks associated with introducing new production methods; lack of competitive pressure and poor communication and cooperation between research and development organizations and the users of technology also hinder change. The result is a lag in both the development and the spread of technology. Without belittling the often impressive achievements of central planning, it can be said that this lag is perhaps its weakest feature.

Although the USSR's achievements in the military and aerospace industries provide evidence of a capability for better performance, elsewhere in Soviet industry there has been no narrowing of the West's technological lead over the past two decades, either at the prototype level or in the diffusion of advanced technology.[1] Good performance in highest priority areas is clearly due to the mission-oriented organizational and incentive structures used there, which could not be extended throughout an entire centrally planned economy.

Small Impact

East European interest in importing technology has undoubtedly been enhanced by the desire to modernize more quickly, thereby raising economic growth rates. The slowdown[2] of the late 1960s probably made imports of Western technology more attractive, especially to the USSR, which, unlike its neighbors, has experienced a continuing decline in its growth rate since the early 1950s.

Concerns about economic growth led to attempts at economic reform by all of the Eastern nations in the 1960s. In most instances the aim of reform was merely to make central planning less cumbersome. The more fundamental changes that were being introduced in Czechoslovakia were cut short by the 1968 Warsaw Pact invasion. Hungarian reform measures constitute something of an uneasy, though fairly successful, middle way between centralized and decentralized planning.

Many Western observers believe the present Eastern, especially Soviet, interest in importing technology reflects the failure of economic reforms as well as the need to compensate for the slowdown in the growth of the labor force. This may be true, although the Soviets would be importing technology even if their system had been effectively reformed. Trade in technology is worldwide. Even the United States imports many kinds of technology, some from the USSR.

In any case, the import of technology has not succeeded in reversing a downward trend in the Soviet growth rate. To what extent are technology imports likely to affect the future rates of growth of the Eastern economies? For the USSR, the answer is probably very little, though perhaps the effect will be somewhat greater in the smaller countries of the Council for Mutual Economic Assistance (COMECON)—even Poland.

In most Eastern countries, imported technology makes up a very small fraction of total annual investment outlays. Soviet imports of machines from the West have amounted to about 2 percent of their total machinery investment. Even if the productivity of these imported machines were two or three times as great as that of new domestic production equipment, the impact on the rate of growth could only be marginal. Recent calculations suggest that variations in Soviet machinery imports from the West within any plausible range in the foreseeable future would affect the annual 5 percent growth rate of Soviet industry by only .1 or .2 percent. The effect on the overall growth rate of the gross national product would be about half as great.[3]

In the case of Poland, where Western machine imports rose to almost 30 percent of total machinery investment in 1972–1976 (more than double the 1961–1971 average), the impact was materially greater. This new policy appears to have raised the annual growth rate of industrial labor productivity by an additional 1 percent, the previous trend rate having been slightly under 6 percent per annum.[4] To maintain permanently the increased level of machinery imports from the West, the Eastern countries will have to export more manufactured goods. Poland could not do this and has had to cut back such imports. The hard currency debt it incurred in the meantime is onerous (estimated at $12.6 billion net by the end of 1977, roughly two-and-a-half times the annual value of hard currency exports).

Other East European countries, also with already large hard currency debts, could not possibly import Western machinery on the scale of the Polish experiment. Thus the hard currency constraint alone will severely limit the macroeconomic effects of Western machinery imports on the East, whatever Western policies on such exports may be.

Even when the volume of imports is relatively large, the potential impact of imported technology on the rate of growth tends to be grossly overstated. Even if the imports are obtained at favorable prices, the resources used to pay for them must be offset against the gains they supposedly produce. Imported mchinery or techniques must be combined with domestic factors—labor, materials, management skills—to be useful. Thus it is inappropriate to attribute the full gain in productivity only to imported technology. The same factors that tend to hamper domestic innovation and technical advancement also reduce returns from imported technology. Finally, technology imported from abroad usually will have been designed for use in the West and not for the quite different environment of the nonmarket economies. One study of Soviet manpower problems done for the Joint Economic Committee of Congress in 1973 cites the example of five imported chemical plants originally designed to require 91 auxiliary workers for maintenance and repair work. This requirement was revised upward in the USSR, first to 430 auxiliaries and again, after the equipment was put into operation, to 732.

Societies that rely on central planning tend to be unable to spread technology very effectively through their economies. Their rigidities have also limited the updating and improvement of imported technology. The developers of a new technique or item of equipment will commonly seek to reap the benefits for themselves until a further technical advance has taken place. An importing nation will thus be getting products or processes that are already outdated in the originating country.

In itself, this built-in lag may be of smaller consequence, but this has not been the case in Eastern countries. Their organizational and incentive systems are powerful inhibitions to the diffusion of new techniques. Travel restrictions limit an important source of technology transfer and diffusion—the exposure of trained domestic personnel to their foreign counterparts. Imported technology is used mainly to produce output for the domestic economy rather than for export. As a result, the products usually do not face foreign competition and the consequent need to keep up with the continually advancing level of foreign technology. Whatever technology they import from the West, the Eastern countries will therefore probably be unable to diffuse and improve upon it as, for example, Japan has done so successfully. The major exception is again in the military field, in which the East faces direct foreign competition. Thus a major study recently concluded that "other than the gains from trade, the net benefits from the foreign technology that succeeds in penetrating the economic structure will be very modest. Borrowed technology is no substitute for structural change."[5] Exporting technology to the East is likely to make it more dependent on the West in the long run.

There is very little reason to believe that imported technology will affect the internal organization of the Eastern economies. In fact, a primary reason for importing technology may have been to avoid making more fundamental changes in the organization of the economy. Any substantial organizational alteration would involve profound changes in the political power structure, as was evidenced by the abortive 1968 Czech reforms. Nor is there much reason to expect that marginal improvements in economic growth and income levels that technology imports might assist would make the USSR and its allies softer or more cooperative with the West. These are not serious arguments for a liberal export policy.

Ineffective Monopoly

Technology transfers affect exporters as well as importers. It is often argued that by exporting technology to the Communist world, the West not only reduces its product markets in the East but also creates competition for itself in third markets as well as in its domestic markets. Such concerns seem to be largely unwarranted. In a dynamic trillion dollar trading world, disturbances from the East can only be minor in the foreseeable future. This is all the more likely because of the difficulties that the nonmarket countries have in exporting to market economies. In any case, to the extent that imported technology does increase exports of goods and services from these countries, the East will be able to pay for additional imports. The effect will be to increase trade in both directions, and any loss of markets through Eastern competition is likely to be offset by the expenditure of increased export earnings in the West.

So far the effects of Western exports of technology to the East have been considered in aggregate, at a macroeconomic level. Clearly, the overall impact of these exports on the Eastern economies is very marginal indeed. There is little basis for special concern about the export to the East of technology, as contrasted with the general range of goods and services. But at the individual, microeconomic level, might not a particular product or process be of critical importance to the USSR or its allies? Items with more or less direct military applications, data processing and computing equipment, and oil production equipment require special attention.

Weapons and equipment suitable only for the production or operation of weapons are usually not exported to the East. But virtually every good has some impact on the ability of a nation to build up its military strength. To single out those exports that have a direct and substantial relationship to Western security interests calls for highly sophisticated assessments, with emphasis on both economic and technical considerations. Conspicuously nonmilitary products like feed grains may be among the imports most essential to the East.

So far as the Soviets are concerned, military research, development, and production have the highest priority for scientific workers, skilled manpower, materials, and equipment, and must meet the highest quality standards—all in contrast to the civilian economy. With a far less developed economy than those of the advanced industrialized states, the USSR has shown that it can equal and even surpass the West in some of the critical dimensions of military and aerospace performance. There is not much in these areas that the USSR does not have, or could not produce, if that were considered necessary. The West can delay the acquisition or increase the cost to the USSR of some items by prohibiting exports; but to deny anything of high and direct military importance is not likely to be feasible for very long.

Data processing is a military-related field that has attracted much attention. Restrictions on the export of computing equipment might appear to have considerable justification on strictly defense or security grounds. But when a group of experts in computer and military technology considered this issue, they were unanimous in their judgment that, except for data processing networks for anti-ballistic missile (ABM) systems on which opinions differed, the USSR's domestic computer capability was adequate to its tasks. To the extent that the best Soviet computer fell short of meeting needs, greater inputs of time, labor, and other resources enable the Russians to produce "achievements comparable to those of the West's more computer-intensive defense policy."[6] A sufficiently strict export control system might deny the Soviets least-cost solutions to their military data processing problems, but it probably could not prevent the Soviet military from achieving satisfactory solutions. If this is so in the case of advanced computer technology, it seems likely that the same judgment applies in other fields.

A similar argument may be made for other supposedly essential items, such as oil production equipment. How long it would take the Soviets to produce a substitute for a given item and what it would cost them are questions less for economists than for technological specialists. Economists can, however, warn against ceteris paribus arguments of the form, "If we do not send them a particular type of drilling equipment, pump, etc., their oil output will be x million tons lower or their production plan will be delayed n years." In many cases, the centrally planned economies have demonstrated their capacity for quick, massive redirection of resources to deal with specific bottlenecks. To be sure, this may be costly, but the burden imposed by such limited export restrictions cannot be very large overall, and it is more likely to fall on consumers than on the military.

Might the possibility of withholding technology exports nevertheless increase the bargaining power of the West on noneconomic issues? This seems doubtful for several reasons. First the technology in demand in the East is usually available from many nations and through a variety of channels, varying from technical publications to turnkey plants. It is likely to be difficult to gain the cooperation of competing technology suppliers (either countries or firms) to organize an effective monopoly. At best such an attempt would only delay, rather than deny, access. Further, such arrangements would encounter difficulties with antitrust laws in many Western countries. They might also lead to an unhealthy growth in monopoly power in the West. Most important, given the relatively modest gains likely to accrue to the East, and particularly to the Soviets, from imported technology, and given the strong commitment of the Eastern bloc to political objectives, it seems unlikely that real concessions on noneconomic issues could be gained by using technology as a bargaining chip.

For such bargaining, the West has potentially more powerful economic instruments at hand. Placing controls on the export of grain or the provision of hard currency credits would probably be more effective than denying export licenses for oil drilling equipment or a computer—how much more effective, however, is difficult to say. But there are evidently strong domestic and international political pressures against the use of such policies in the United States and among other Western countries.

Notes

Richard Portes is professor of economics at Birkbeck College, University of London. This article is adapted from a report on "Economic Relations Between East and West: Prospects and Problems," drawn up at a conference in Kiel,

West Germany, last June, sponsored by the Kiel Institute of World Economics, the Japan Economic Research Center, and the Brookings Institution, which has published the report in English. The authors, who participated in the conference, take full responsibility for the views expressed here. The first draft of the report, which provided the basis of discussion for the conference, was written by Franklyn D. Holzman.

1. R. Amman, et al., *Technological Level of Soviet Industry* (New Haven: Yale University Press, 1977).

2. Abram Bergson, "The Soviet Economic Slowdown," *Challenge,* Vol. 20, No. 6, Jan.-Feb. 1978.

3. See Donald W. Green and Herbert S. Levine, "Macroeconomic Evidence of the Value of Machinery Imports to the Soviet Union," in John R. Thomas and Ursula M. Kruse-Vaucienne, eds., *Soviet Science and Technology: Domestic and Foreign Perspectives* (Washington, D.C.: George Washington University, 1977). The methodology of their model may be questioned, but it is generally believed that their estimates are if anything on the high side.

4. Stanislaw Gomulka, "The Growth and the Import of Technology; Poland 1971–1980," *Cambridge Journal of Economics,* Vol. 2, No. 1, March 1978, p. 2.

5. Joseph Berliner, *The Innovation Decision in Soviet Industry* (Cambridge, Mass.: MIT Press, 1976), p. 518.

6. R. E. Klitgaard, *National Security and Export Controls,* RAND Corporation, Report #R-1432-1-ARPA/CIEP, April 1974, p. 46.

6
Dumping by
Centrally Planned Economies:
The Polish Golf Cart Case

Alex Erlich did not learn to play golf when he was growing up in Poland before World War II. This was not necessarily due to lack of aptitude. In fact until this day no Polish youngster, nor adult for that matter, has had the opportunity to learn golf because in Poland there are no golf courses—none with the exception of a two-hole course in Warsaw set up within the past few years to demonstrate to potential foreign buyers the electrical golf cart that the Poles have been producing and exporting to the United States since 1971.[1] Had the Polish golf cart not been of such superior quality and exported at a relatively low price, this story would be over. With both of these conditions present, however, U.S. producers were moved to resist the Polish competition by invoking various categories of foreign trade and antitrust legislation, particularly the antidumping laws. The Poles have fought back, and the case has become something of a cause célèbre, the notoriety of which has been limited only by the fact that the market for golf carts is so modest. The importance of the case goes far beyond golf carts, however. First, a new method was devised to assess dumping charges against centrally planned economies (CPEs). Second, the CPEs have serious balance-of-payments problems with the West. They need hard currency badly. The success with which Poland resists dumping (and other) charges has significance for the future of eastern attempts to compete in U.S. markets for manufactured products.

Reprinted with permission from *Marxism, Central Planning and the Soviet Economy: Economic Essays in Honor of Alexander Erlich,* Padma Desai, ed. (Cambridge, Mass.: MIT Press, 1983), pp. 133–148. Copyright © 1983 by The Massachusetts Institute of Technology.

1. Dumping Defined

Dumping is usually defined as exporting in a foreign market at below the exporter's domestic price for the same product. This is the most common basis of complaint under the U.S. Antidumping Act of 1921 and under GATT's Article VI. In cases where the exporter has no domestic sales, Article VI further defines dumping as the export price that is either less than cost of production (plus selling costs and profits) in the country of origin or less than the export price to a third country. The cost of production test was introduced into U.S. law in 1974. Exporting at discriminatorily low prices or at below cost of production is viewed as selling at "less than fair value" and therefore as unfair competition. If import-competing enterprises are distressed by the dumping and can prove "material damage," the government is obliged to levy antidumping duties which bring the prices of the imports in question up to "fair value."

Dumping is generally viewed as an exercise in price discrimination by private enterprises. Related to this, most nations, including the United States, and the GATT prohibit government subsidies by other nations designed to promote exports and provide for countervailing duties to remove the advantages of the subsidies when such subsidies cause material injury to importing nations' industries.[2] One would have expected that legislation relating to government subsidies and countervailing duties rather than to dumping would have been applied to presumed "less than fair value" sales in the United States by communist foreign trade organizations since these are nationalized enterprises, but this has not been the case. Several possible explanations come to mind. First, it is difficult to verify dumping by centrally planned economies and even more difficult to establish the existence of subsidies since data of this sort have been unavailable. Second, since the U.S. countervailing duty code did not require injury until the Tokyo Round a few years ago, it might have been viewed by the administration as opening the way to a more restrictive import policy than even the most hidebound protectionists would desire. Third, for reasons which are not at all clear, low-priced Soviet sales in the West, especially in the United States, during the 1930s and 1950s, were always discussed primarily as possible cases of dumping even though it was often recognized that, if dumping was being practiced, it might well have been due to government subsidies (Feller 1967, p. 134). This tradition may well be the major reason for the use in recent years of dumping rather than countervailing duty statutes against low-priced CPE exports.

2. The Systemic Gap

Products entering the country from CPEs at below the market price are viewed with more than the usual amount of suspicion by import-competing enterprises for nontrivial reasons. CPE-exporting enterprises are virtually all state enterprises with potentially the full power of the state purse behind them. Further it is well known that very commonly in the CPE world enterprises operate for long periods of time at losses covered by state subsidies. Hence it would not be at all surprising to find that enterprises having difficulty selling in western markets are being subsidized to facilitate price competition.

Further suspicion is aroused by the fact that CPE domestic markets are largely insulated from world markets, and domestic prices are not organically related to world prices. In the words of three Polish economists (speaking of price and cost comparisons between the CPE nations): ". . . because of the autonomous system of domestic prices in each country and the automatic and purely internal character of the monetary system and arbitrary official rates of exchange which do not reflect relative values of currencies, it is impossible to compare prices and costs of particular commodities in different countries."[3] Domestic prices in the CPEs do not reflect market forces, either supply or demand, to any great extent. Prices in the U.S.S.R., for example, have been largely frozen since 1967 despite the enormous changes in basic economic conditions since that time. Relative prices cannot help but be irrational. Obviously, under such conditions, an exchange rate has little meaning as a monetary price through which actual internal commodity prices may be compared with external commodity prices. In fact Soviet foreign trade planners have used some 250 commodity group price adjustment coefficients to compare internal and external prices.

The exchange rate also fails to serve any role in the balance of payments. Changes in the exchange rate do not affect the supply of exports or demand for imports through market forces.[4] The exchange rate is only a unit of account and not a very accurate one at that.[5] If the exchange rates of the CPEs were real prices, they would of course be significantly overvalued vis-à-vis western currencies as indicated by the serious hard currency deficits and large external debts of each CPE nation.

While western business men typically are not aware of the full complexity of these differences, they know that internal CPE prices (or costs) are not relevant to trade, that they are generally unavailable, and that converting them into western currencies via official exchange rates is, in any event, not a meaningful procedure. A western enterprise, when threatened by imports from CPEs (or from other western enterprises), does not need a valid excuse to call for antidumping relief. The U.S. Treasury, which must determine whether the alleged dumping has taken place, is faced, however, with the fact that the usual methods of evaluating dumping charges do not work with nations that have nonmarket costs and prices, nonfunctioning exchange rates, and, in any case, have usually not been willing to disclose industrial accounting information to outsiders.

Evaluation of dumping charges is not the only issue raised by systemic differences. Motives behind dumping may also be different. A western enterprise may dump for several reasons: to eliminate competition, to get rid of a temporary oversupply, or to use price discrimination as a way of increasing one's market in order to achieve economies of scale. The U.S.S.R. was first accused of dumping raw materials and grain on world markets during the Great Depression. Its purpose was to earn hard currency to buy the machinery and equipment required to achieve the industrialization targets of the First five-year plan. While it might appear to others that they were exporting at a loss, from the standpoint of the planners, the gains from the imported machinery paid for by their exports were adequate compensation. That is to say, in the final analysis the planners viewed the exchange of grain and raw materials for machinery and equipment in barter terms rather than as independent transactions.[6] Their motive was not that of a classic dumper even though their impact on the markets where they dumped was no different from that of a classic dumper—and should therefore have been subject to the antidumping laws. This was the period of beggar-thy-neighbor policies, but even in normal times many transactions are undoubtedly rationalized in barter terms.

Dumping charges were levied against the U.S.S.R. again in the 1950s particularly in connection with sales of petroleum. Again the motivation was not that of a classical dumper. Before World War II (and also before World War I) the Russians had a substantial share of the world petroleum market. They simply wanted that share back again. They had no interest in selling at below the market price, but they had no other way of gaining entry. It is significant that just a few years later, a huge field of industrial diamonds was discovered in Siberia. Shortly thereafter it was announced that Soviet diamonds would be marketed by De Beers. Clearly, the capitalists and communists had both learned a lesson and were benefiting from it.[7]

3. Exchange Rate Overvaluation and the Inability to Devalue

In theory a proper evaluation of dumping charges should—but never does—take account of over- or undervaluation of exchange rates.

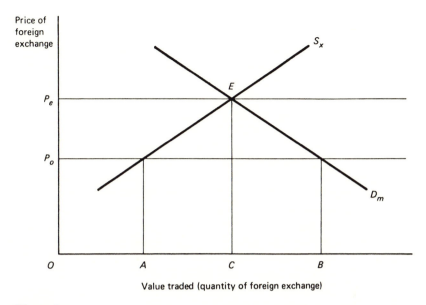

Figure 1

An undervalued exchange rate implicitly subsidizes all exports and levies a sales tax on all imports, while an overvalued exchange rate subsidizes imports and levies a sales tax on exports. Such implicit sales taxes and subsidies lead the market to distort true comparative advantage and thus to surpluses in the case of undervaluation and deficits in the case of overvaluation. In figure 1, at an overvalued exchange rate, P_o, the nation would export OA and import OB for a deficit of AB. Devaluation to an equilibrium exchange rate, P_e, would decrease imports and increase exports both to OC, thereby balancing trade. True comparative advantage is revealed at P_e. At P_o, AC of exports are priced out of the market by the hidden sales tax of a macrodisequilibrium. In fact at P_e all of AC but the marginal sale could be made at below the world price without a loss.

Most market economies do not boast of exchange rates that are in equilibrium. Nevertheless, most have the option of changing their exchange rates to approach equilibrium. The CPEs have no such option. As noted earlier, their official exchange rates are not real prices and have little or no effect on foreign trade decision making (Hungary excepted). They simply trade in world currencies at world prices. At world prices they have been experiencing large trade deficits with the West for about a decade.[8] Now a market economy experiencing such deficits would have an overvalued exchange rate and would be suffering from a terms-of-trade illusion due to the implicit subsidies to imports and implicit sales taxes on exports. Devaluation eliminates this illusion. The large trade deficits persistently experienced by the CPEs suggest that they experience something of a terms-of-trade illusion in trading without a real exchange rate at world prices (Holzman 1979, pp. 307–311).[9] In any event, faced with a desire to import more than can be financed by exports or by prudent borrowing, it would not be surprising if they showed an inclination to sell at below world prices to expand exports. They know that, since the value of additional imports (beyond *OA*) is sufficiently great, it would be worth lowering the price of, say, *AC* of exports, to finance them. This would not be true dumping although it might appear to be so.[10]

4. Polish Golf Carts and the Antidumping Statutes

Approximately a dozen companies in the United States produce some 40 to 50 thousand golf carts annually. Most of these are electrically powered like those imported from Poland. The possibility of producing and exporting golf carts to the United States was suggested to the Poles around 1970 by an American distributor who was dissatisfied with the domestically produced versions he was handling in the United States. A Polish light aircraft enterprise, which exports crop dusters to the United States and other western nations on a fairly large scale felt, after some investigation, that it could compete successfully in the U.S. golf cart market. Exports to the United States were begun in 1971 and since 1972 have amounted to 5 to 10 thousand units annually.

The first of several dumping charges were brought against Pezetel, the Polish foreign trade organization, by Outboard Marine Corporation, a company that went out of the golf cart business because, they claimed, Pezetel was selling its carts at less than fair value. This led to several attempts to find a satisfactory way of determining whether or not Pezetel was dumping to get around the price-cost exchange rate problems:

1. The statutes on dumping provide that, if an exporting nation does not sell its product in its home market, then the price of its export in third nations can be used to assess dumping charges. This alternative could not be used in the present case because all of Polish exports were directed at the U.S. market. In any case this approach has been rejected for CPEs because of the judgment that costs of production in the usual sense are not a controlling factor in the prices charged in third nations, and those prices are therefore not reliable for the purpose at hand.

2. The Antidumping Act of 1921 was amended in 1974 so that the fair value of CPE export prices could be determined from the prices charged by non-CPE producers in other countries, including the United States. At this time the main non-CPE producers were Marathon in Canada and some small companies in Brazil, Mexico, and Japan. The companies in the latter three countries sold their carts at very high

prices in protected domestic markets and were not competitive in foreign markets. Marathon's carts sold in both Canada and the United States, and its price was used as a basis for determining the fair value of Polish carts. Adjustments were made for differences between the Polish and Canadian carts as well as for the fact that the relatively much larger number of carts annually produced by the former (10,000 versus 250) entitled them to economies of scale. Marathon went out of business shortly thereafter forcing all parties to seek a new measure of fair value.

3. An attempt was made at this point to use the prices charged by U.S. golf cart producers as a basis for determining the fair value of Polish carts. It was argued that U.S. producers were, after all, non-CPE producers and their prices were relevant. Under this interpretation Polish carts would have been priced out of the U.S. market because fair value, as determined by this method, was based on full costs of production by U.S. producers not including transport costs to the market. Since Polish transport costs to the U.S. market are so much higher than those of U.S. producers, their selling prices in the United States would necessarily be correspondingly higher. The Polish representatives raised this objection. This method was withdrawn in treasury regulations dated September 8, 1978 (Soltysinski 1980, p. 3).

Objections were raised to attempts 2 and 3 on the grounds that it was unfair to use the costs of production of advanced capitalist countries (Canada, United States) to determine the fair value of a similar product produced by a less-developed nation. Because of differences in factor proportions and factor prices, one could not assess Poland's comparative advantage—in this case fair price—by looking at prices in advanced capitalist nations. In the golf cart case, unfortunately, no nation at a comparable level of development produced a competitive product. In 1979 Poland was accused also of dumping carbon steel plate. Spain was taken as a nation at approximately the same level of development and the price of carbon steel plate at the one Spanish plant that produced it was taken as a measure of fair value.[11] This price was converted from pesetas to dollars at the going Spanish exchange rate, and by this measure it appeared that the Poles were dumping. However, the International Trade Commission determined that the domestic U.S. industry did not suffer material injury, and the case was dropped.

4. As a last resort, if a product is not made or sold in other countries, the law provides for an estimate of the cost of production in a comparable (level of development) third country to be determined. This is the so-called "constructed value" approach. The Polish golf cart case was the first in which this approach was used for a CPE. Implementation involved the following steps. The specific physical components required to produce the golf cart were estimated. These included hours

of labor, quantities of raw materials, amounts of energy, among other factors. These were then valued in prices of a "comparable" market economy, in this case Spain. To the total direct value so obtained were added markups for general expenses (notably, overhead, profits, packaging). The overall total was then converted into dollars through the surrogate nation's exchange rate.[12] The dollar price thus obtained was not above the price at which the golf carts were being sold in the United States; hence by this measure a charge of dumping could not be sustained.[13]

5. Evaluation of Comparable Nation and Constructed Value Approaches

The U.S. Treasury and the Polish Government both appear to be satisfied with the methods used in both the carbon steel plate and golf cart cases. Here are methods which appear to have bridged the systemic gap, providing proxy costs (prices) and proxy exchange rates by which dumping charges can be assessed. The question is, How good are these proxies?

Use of proxy costs from nations of comparable levels of development are based implicitly on a simple Heckscher-Ohlin static comparative advantage model (H-O) with the dynamic properties of Ray Vernon's product cycle model (Vernon 1966). That is to say, nations at different levels of development are likely to have different factor proportions (capital and labor) and different factor prices; at similar levels of development, similar factor proportions and factor prices. Therefore an accurate representation of CPEs product price is more likely, but not necessarily, to be obtained by using either the constructed value (in golf cart case) or actual price of the same product produced in a third nation of similar level of development (in the carbon steel plate case) than in third nations at different levels of development. Nevertheless, there is no special reason to believe that such an H-O approach will always lead to a favorable result (low price) since, with different factor proportions and factor prices, different methods of production may be used which may or may not be more efficient in some comparative advantage sense. The likelihood of a more favorable result is no doubt based intuitively on the Vernon conception that, after new manufactured products have been around a while, less-developed nations with their lower-wage costs gradually begin to outcompete the higher-wage cost advanced nation innovators. This theory assumes that wages are the major cost of production—for most not-too-advanced products, a good assumption.

Using a proxy nation like Spain which is at a similar level of development probably makes more sense than judging Polish costs or prices by data obtained from more (or less) advanced nations. Nevertheless, this approach has serious limitations. In the first place it is subject to all of the well-known criticisms of the oversimple H-O factor proportions theory. Literally hundreds of articles have been written since Leontief's classic study to demonstrate that other considerations than pure factor proportions and prices play a role in determining which nations and enterprises have a comparative advantage. Two nations could be identical by these and other macroindicators and still produce the same product at widely different costs and by different methods. Even within a nation many industries are characterized by large differences in costs between the more and less efficient producers of the same product. How often are firms outcompeted (pricewise) and either bought out or forced into bankruptcy? How often does one hear references to high- as opposed to low-cost producers? Such differences exist for many reasons including those relating to differences of scale, technology, management efficiency, position on the learning curve. Further, between nations with widely different factor proportions and factor prices the most unpredictable product price relationships are found to exist. For example, Abram Becker of Rand Corporation compared ruble/dollar ratios of prices of some 500 producer durables produced in both the U.S.S.R. and United States in 1955. The variations were striking. The overall weighted average ruble/dollar ratio was 0.69 with a low of 0.15 for steam engines and turbines to a high of 1.81 in communication and X-ray equipment. The differences within categories were even more striking: motor vehicles, 0.34 to 2.28; internal combustion engines, 0.42 to 2.09; metal working machinery, 0.42 to 2.09; and so forth.[14]

A final bit of evidence against putting too much faith in the comparable level of development approach is contained in table 1, where sixteen nations are ranked by level of per capita GDP and then their prices compared for two products that might be viewed as industrially comparable to golf carts, tractors and metal-working machinery. The prices are selling prices and may not always reflect domestic production costs—but probably in most cases, they do. The striking fact revealed by the estimates in table 1 is that there appear to be virtually no linear relationships between relative price and level of development. Regressing price on per capita GDP resulted in r^2 coefficients of 0 and 0.0168 for tractors and machinery, respectively. Eliminating the seven poorest nations from the regressions raised r^2 insignificantly to 0.0394 and 0.0172, respectively. One might argue that these figures are distorted by the fact that different nations support different degrees of disequilibrium in their exchange rates, thereby distorting relative prices. The reply to this argument is that in practice the dumping laws do not distinguish between equilibrium and disequilibrium in exchange rates.

Table 1

Purchasing-power parity comparisons for tractors and metal work machinery, 1970 (U.S. prices = 1.00)

	Per capita GDP (U.S. = 100)	Tractors	Metal work machinery
Kenya	6.33	0.96	0.63
India	6.92	0.70	0.67
Philippines	12.0	1.30	0.77
Republic of Korea	12.1	1.10	0.35
Colombia	18.1	1.06	0.75
Malaysia	19.1	0.85	1.70
Iran	20.3	0.58	0.58
Hungary	42.7	1.02	0.97
Italy	49.2	0.89	0.48
Japan	59.2	0.87	1.14
United Kingdom	63.5	0.77	0.71
Netherlands	68.7	1.01	0.94
Belgium	72.0	1.01	0.89
France	73.2	0.88	0.51
West Germany	78.2	0.95	0.74
United States	100.0	1.00	1.00

Source: Irving Kravis, Alan Heston, and Robert Summers, *International Comparisons of Real Product and Purchasing Power* (Baltimore, Md.: Johns Hopkins University Press, 1978). Prices in local currencies were taken from appendix table 4.3. These were converted into dollar relatives by dividing by dollar exchange rates from table 1.1. Per capita GDP figures taken from table 1.2. It should be noted that the price relatives listed here represent domestic selling prices and some nations may not produce either or both products.

Clearly, there is a lack of what might be called uniform cost hierarchies within and among products between different nations, whether these nations are at the same or different levels of development. Poland relied on the price of carbon steel place produced by a Spanish company and on the constructed value of a golf cart estimated from Polish factor proportions and priced by Spanish engineers. Had there been several Spanish companies producing carbon steel plate, there might have been as many estimates as companies, and estimates might have varied significantly. Had France or India been chosen as surrogates instead of Spain, the results might have been even more or less favorable to Poland. It would be difficult to guess which nation's costs would be lower or higher than Poland's. Different factor proportions are likely to be offset in unpredictable ways by different relative factor prices. So, for example, higher wage costs in France may be more than offset by labor-saving production techniques.

Had there been more than one set of Spanish engineers estimating the cost of producing Polish golf carts, there might also have been several widely differing proxy prices, for most of the same reasons mentioned in the case of carbon steel plate. In the golf cart case, however, it is methodologically relevant to use a nation that is at a comparable level of development, certainly not one at a higher level of development. This is because the lower-income CPE is likely to use more labor and less capital than an advanced proxy nation. Valuing the CPEs physical mix of labor and capital at the higher-wage levels and lower-capital costs of the more advanced nation would result in an inappropriately higher-cost estimate.

We have argued that the connection between levels of development and costs of production or prices of specific products is very weak. There would also appear to be no necessary relationship between levels of development and exchange rates of any two nations. This could be either because (1) the equilibrium exchange rates differ or (2) because the two nations maintain exchange rates with different degrees of disequilibrium.

Suppose a CPE (Y) and a capitalist nation (Z) have identical monetary units, factors of production, structures of demand, and so forth. Then, if the two nations had similar organizations of production, the equilibrium exchange rates (notional rate in the case of the CPE) of the two nations should be unit equivalents and should bear identical relationships to other currencies. Suppose now that, with all other things still equal, there is a large autonomous capital inflow into Z.[15] The currency of Z would immediately appreciate relative to that of Y and other western currencies as well. Under these circumstances, Z's exchange rate would not serve as an accurate surrogate for Y's but would be overvalued. Because two nations are never identical in the ways assumed, and in addition differ with regard to goals, management, distribution of income, and so forth, there are many potential differences, given identical levels of development, that could affect their relative equilibrium exchange rates.

Suppose now that Y and Z have unit equivalent exchange rates (notional in the case of Y) in balance-of-payments equilibrium, but macro policies (or lack of same) dictate that one or both are in disequilibrium. In fact it would be an improbable coincidence for two countries to have the same degree of balance-of-payments disequilibrium at the same time, and therefore it is unlikely that the exchange rate of Z would ever precisely represent that of Y. It would also probably be impossible to say when the degrees of disequilibrium in the two nations are approximately the same for many reasons, including the fact that the CPEs repress balance-of-payments disequilibriums by methods invisible to the outside world. A CPE, seeking a surrogate exchange rate, should try to select a nation that is in approximate balance-of-payments equilibrium. Such an exchange rate would in theory provide it with (1) a lens through which it could view its trade without the terms of trade illusion discussed earlier and (2) a relatively low export price. From this standpoint the selection of any surrogate nation with less overvaluation than the CPE exporter would improve its chances of avoiding a determination of dumping. Should the surrogate nation have a more overvalued exchange rate than the CPE (an unlikely possibility), then the latter would find itself handicapped in exporting and forced to charge higher prices than are warranted to avoid a dumping determination. However, regardless of whether the surrogate nation's currency is more or less overvalued than the CPEs, its state of disequilibrium would undoubtedly be totally unrelated to its level of development.

Before leaving this discussion, it is important to mention an important empirical barrier in the identification of dumping, namely, that manufactured products are not usually homogeneous and prices therefore cannot be expected for this reason alone to be identical. Under ordinary circumstances, one might expect in two market economies a reasonably even distribution of high- and low-"quality" products.[16] As is well-known, however, manufactured products sold by the socialist countries tend to be of lower quality and must be sold in the West at lower prices than comparable western products. Examples of Soviet discount pricing in 1974 to 1975 are transformers, 30 percent; resistors, 30 percent; tractors, 20 to 40 percent; machine tools, 40 to 50 percent; turbines and compressors, 40 to 50 percent; and so forth (Ericson 1976, p. 723). How can one tell whether these lower prices reflect quality or are evidence of dumping? It is almost impossible to make such a judgment from the cost side (How to price such things as servicing convenience and frequency of breakdown). If the value of quality differentials can only be determined by the market, then in these cases differential prices cannot be taken as evidence of dumping (within reasonable limits of course).

6. Concluding Remarks

The third-country and constructed-value approaches are clever attempts to bridge the systemic gaps that impede the application of antidumping laws to CPEs. They are based implicitly on H-O model mechanisms, and this leads to the selection of nations at comparable levels of development to provide proxy costs or prices and proxy exchange rates. The H-O model is too weak to do a reliable job on costs and prices and has no mechanisms through which an appropriate surrogate exchange rate might be generated. So far the results from these approaches have been mixed: the third-country approach provided evidence that Poland was dumping carbon steel plate; the constructed value approach, on the other hand, exonerated Poland from the dumping charge. Polish representatives appear satisfied with these approaches, particularly the constructed value approach. That the third country approach sustained a dumping charge indicates, in my opinion, the weakness of the general framework, for it seems highly unlikely that Poland or other CPEs are engaged in dumping. Apparent dumping by CPEs is unlikely to be true dumping because (1) CPE foreign trade behavior typically reflects notional exchange rate overvaluation, (2) most CPE manufactured products are of lower quality than similar western products, and (3) because of overfull employment planning CPEs tend to generate shortages rather than surpluses of goods, so they are unlikely to be seeking temporary external markets. If third-country and constructed-value approaches continue to result in "satisfactory" dumping decisions, then it might be worth staying with them since in a technical sense they bridge the systemic gap. I would be surprised, however, if other future applications of these techniques didn't indicate dumping whether or not true dumping was taking place.

Two possible substitutes to these procedures come to mind. First, there is Richard Cunningham's proposal that imports from CPEs be exempted from dumping charges so long as they are not priced below all other imports.[17] This would take care of most imports from CPEs, and would probably be more than fair to U.S. producers because of the CPE bias against dumping. It would not take care of those instances, like the Polish golf carts where for several years there were no imports from other nations. The third country and constructed value approaches could as a last resort be reserved for such special circumstances. A second possible approach is to discontinue using the antidumping (or countervailing duty) statutes against CPEs and handle all cases of injury to domestic producers under the antimarket disruption clause, Article 406, of the Trade Act of 1974. This has the disadvantage to the CPEs that, if injury is determined, they cannot clear themselves by proving that they are not dumping. On the other hand, (1) domestic industries have access to Article 406 and (2) the techniques developed to determine whether a CPE is dumping, while ingenious, must be recognized as relatively inadequate expedients.

Addenda

1. In May 1980 the U.S. International Trade Commission determined that Polish golf carts were not causing distress to the U.S. industry, thereby removing another basis for the dumping charges.

2. Polish golf cart competition in the United States is still clouded by antitrust action which has been taken against the Poles by the American producers under both the Clayton Act and the almost forgotten Antidumping Act of 1916 which allows treble damages if dumping can be shown to have been motivated by an attempt to destroy competition. Most of the charges by the American companies have been, at present writing (June 1980) refuted, and Pezetel has instituted a countersuit against these companies. Since the purpose of our antitrust laws is to foster domestic competition, it is a little paradoxical to find them being used to prevent foreign competition. Apparently, this is the first time they have been so applied (Schwartz 1980).

3. It is unfortunate that, just as Poland seems to be winning its long fight against its U.S. competitors, it must now face new competition from the Japanese firm, Yamaha.

Notes

1. As my good friend, Dr. James Finkelstein, has noted, "This may be putting the cart before the course!"

2. GATT's Article VI requires material injury for the levy of a countervailing duty. The basic U.S. legislation the Tariff Act of 1930, does not require material injury. However, at the Tokyo Round the United States agreed to require injury also.

3. Cited by Fallenbuchl (1974, p. 104) from a 1971 Polish source. Polish prices have been moving toward greater rationality but, in my opinion, still have considerable way to go.

4. This statement, and other such statements in this paragraph, are less true of Hungary than of the other CPE nations. Also in the few years before August 1980, it was claimed that Polish planners had largely relied on a single notional exchange rate and actual industrial prices to make many of their foreign trade decisions. This notional rate was not published and was unknown to foreigners. It is also not clear how many exceptions to this procedure there were and how reliable the procedure was. Further the rate used must be suspect in light of the large Polish hard currency deficits.

5. The exchange rate in used to convert trade in world prices (dollars, pounds, etc.) into so-called foreign trade valuta (rubles, zlotys, etc.). For integrating the trade accounts with the GNP accounts in internal prices, further conversion coefficients are required.

6. This can be rationalized as a case of exchange rate overvaluation, as discussed in the following section.

7. In the late fifties the U.S.S.R. allegedly dumped aluminum and tin on the world markets. In both of these cases they were getting rid of temporary surpluses and, according to the philosophy behind the antidumping laws, should have been subjected to sanctions.

8. Actually, the basic disequilibriums of the CPEs are probably sharply understated by the sizes of their external debts and hard currency deficits. It is my opinion that imports are repressed and, if the desire to import were given free rein, would be much larger than has been the case.

9. The evidence is also consistent, for some CPEs, with a decision to borrow to expand imports.

10. To some extent the CPEs use foreign trade efficiency indexes to guide their external trade decisions. In their simplest form these consist of a fraction, in which the numerator is the cost of producing an export or import substitute in domestic currency (adjusted for estimated price irrationalities) and the denominator is the hard-currency price at which the export is sold or import purchased. High-ratio products should be imported; low-rate products exported. Such indexes would suggest how much world prices might be undercut, if necessary, to finance desired imports.

11. This approach was initiated by the U.S. Treasury in 1960.

12. This approach was devised and accepted by the U.S. Treasury in fall 1978. The constructed value approach has been used for some time for capitalist countries where neither exporter's domestic nor export to third country prices were available. In these cases, however, the values are constructed directly from the domestic costs of the local producer-exporter.

13. Implementation of this method of evaluating dumping charges requires that the exporting country be willing to allow U.S. customs officials on site access to its factories to determine the physical quantities of inputs. The Polish government granted permission in this case. There is some question as to whether all other CPEs would grant such permission.

14. Although these ruble/dollar ratios are based on Soviet 1955 reform prices, the irrationality of Soviet prices certainly contributes to the scatter of ratios.

15. Alternatively, we could have supposed that like Great Britain Z suddenly discovered and exploited North Sea petroleum reserves.

16. We use the term here to include many dimensions such as durability, servicing, and packaging.

17. A bill (S. 958) introduced in February 1981 by Senator Heinz would accomplish this by levying a countervailing tariff on CPE products priced below all other imports. This bill unfortunately does not provide for an injury test. It also abolishes the market disruption clause (Article 406) of the Trade Act of 1974.

References

Abram Becker, 1959. *Prices of Producers' Durables in the United States and the USSR in 1955.* RM-2432, Rand Corporation, August.

Richard Cunningham, 1980. The need for "rules of conduct" approach to the regulation of U.S. trade with non-market economies—orderly expansion versus unpredictable shifts in policy. Paper presented to *Interface Two* Conference in Poznan, Poland, June.

Paul Ericson, 1976. Soviet efforts to increase exports of manufactured products to the West. In JEC, U.S. Congress, *Soviet Economy in a New Perspective*, Washington, D.C.

Z. Fallenbuchl, 1974. East European integration: Comecon. In JEC, U.S. Congress, *Reorientation and Commercial Relations of the Economics of Eastern Europe*, Washington, D.C.

Feller, Peter, 1967. The antidumping act and the future of East-West trade. *Michigan Law Review* (November), 115–133.

Franklyn D. Holzman, 1979. Some theories of the hard-currency shortages of centrally planned economies. In JEC, U.S. Congress, *Soviet Economy in Time of Change, II*, Washington, D.C.

Louis B. Schwartz, 1980. American antitrust and trading with State-Controlled economies. Paper presented to *Interface Two* Conference in Poznan, Poland, June.

Stanislaw Soltysinski, 1980. The Application of U.S. antidumping and other foreign trade competition laws to the so-called state-controlled economy enterprises. Paper presented to *Interface Two* Conference in Poznan, Poland, June.

Raymond Vernon, 1966. International investment and international trade in the product cycle. *Quar. Jl. of Econ.* (May), 190–207.

U.S. International Trade Commission, 1980. *Electric Golf Cars from Poland.* Publication 1089, June.

Background References
on Polish Golf Cart Case

Robert Hudec, 1980. Interface revisited: "unfair trade" policy after the Tokyo Round. Paper presented to *Interface Two* Conference in Poznan, Poland, June.

Subcommittee on Trade, House Committee on Ways and Means, 1977. *Hearings: Oversight of the Antidumping Act of 1921*, November 8, pp. 106–123.

Donald Wallace, George Spina, et al. (eds.), 1979. *Interface One*. Georgetown Institute for International and Foreign Trade Law, Washington, D.C.

7
Commentary on Jacob Dreyer's "Countervailing Foreign Use of Monopoly Power"

I shall restrict my comments on Jacob Dreyer's paper to the part on state trading. I shall first consider the exercise by the Soviet bloc foreign trade organizations (FTOs) of monopsony power—the issue considered by Dreyer—and then broaden my remarks to consider briefly some of the other challenges to the liberal order posed by these nations.

The belief that Eastern FTOs exert monopsonistic power in East-West trade is fairly common among Western economists and has several sources. First, because the FTOs all have monopolies in their own countries of trade in particular products, it is assumed that they therefore have monopsonistic power in dealing with the West. Obviously, there is no basis in either economics or logic to support this reasoning. Second, at the time of the so-called great grain robbery of the early 1970s, the Russians bought an enormous amount of grain from the United States and other nations to supplement the very poor harvest of 1972. By very cleverly making simultaneous secret purchases from many different American grain exporters, they were able to hide the size of their total purchase and thereby avoid driving up the price. This was a clever end run around the price system that was possible only because one giant buyer could coordinate the operation. It was, however, an exceptional case, and the U.S. government has taken steps that should prevent the recurrence of such an event in the grain market. Third, fuel was added to the belief that Eastern FTOs exercise monopsonistic power when the U.S. government's General Accounting Office (GAO) asserted that this is indeed true.[1] In no uncertain terms, the GAO attributes monopsonistic powers

Reprinted with permission from *Challenges to a Liberal Economic Order*, Ryan C. Amacher, Gottfried Haberler, and Thomas D. Willet, eds. (Washington, D.C.: American Enterprise Institute for Public Policy Research, 1979), pp. 348–353. Jacob Dreyer's article "Countervailing Foreign Use of Monopoly Power" is found in the same book, pp. 317–347.

to the FTOs and contends that U.S. commercial and banking interests are manipulated, with the result that profits are lower than they should be and both products and technology are transferred at much too low a price. So serious does the GAO consider the problem that it proposed that:

> The Secretary of the Treasury, in his capacity as Chairman of the East-West Foreign Trade Board should . . . review all transactions involving . . . national interests, such as commodity price stability and supply, technology seepage and security of investments, as well as transactions requiring credit or export licenses. Criteria for involvement could include size of transaction and credit, nature of product or technology, number of firms competing, and structure of transaction (product payback, for example). *The intensity of involvement could vary from indirect guidelines for the firms, to observer status at commercial negotiations, to direct negotiations with Soviet officials, to disapproval of the transaction.*[2]

Dreyer attempts an empirical assessment of Soviet FTO buying power by comparing the prices at which the USSR imports a wide range of products from the United States with the prices Western European importers paid us in 1975–1976. He finds very little difference, but where differences exist the Soviets appear to pay less. He correctly notes, however, that these lower prices might well reflect quantity discounts, lower quality of imported products, and substitution of domestic for American storage facilities. He concludes, in direct contrast with the GAO (whose report he does not mention), that intervention by the U.S. government is not called for.

The Department of Commerce Advisory Committee on East-West Trade came to similar conclusions. In the publication mentioned in note 2, above, hearings on the so-called whipsaw controversy are reported.[3] These hearings consider the returns on a questionnaire sent out to some 500 American enterprises exporting to the USSR. The majority of the respondents reported generally profitable trade with the USSR and either no whipsawing or no more whipsawing than experienced in other markets. Bankers on the advisory committee further reported that they did not experience any significant amount of whipsawing. In conclusion, most members of the committee took the same position Dreyer takes—that U.S. government interference with U.S. sales to the Eastern bloc is not generally warranted since the evidence of exercise of monopsonistic buying power is not very strong.

Dreyer does not consider the possibility that American importers may be hurt in dealing with Soviet exporter FTOs. This omission may be for the very good reason that Eastern exporter FTOs appear to possess much less monopolistic power than the importer FTOs possess monopsonistic power. In a pair of studies by this writer cited by Dreyer, it was shown that Soviet and other Eastern European exports usually had to be sold at below world prices in order to break into Western markets in the 1950s and early 1960s. While the situation may have improved in recent years, no one to my knowledge has ever claimed that Eastern FTOs were extracting monopoly profits. To the contrary, any complaints have been directed at alleged Soviet dumping. The potential for dumping by a state-owned exporting agency is much greater than for a private exporter, of course. The obstacles to adjudicating a dumping charge against an Eastern FTO are substantial because of the unavailability of cost and price information. Even if such information were available, the fact that internal costs and prices are not rational or market clearing and that exchange rates are not real prices but simply units of account would make it almost impossible to interpret the information. Under the U.S.-USSR Commercial Agreement of 1972, the USSR simply agreed to withdraw exports that cause distress to domestic American producers. While this arrangement sidesteps the problems mentioned above, it is important to realize that any solution which in effect automatically rules out the import of goods that compete with domestic products is protectionist to the extreme.

I should like to consider briefly a number of potential challenges to a liberal economic order posed by the Communist nations which do not fit into the topic of Dreyer's paper.

First, central planners are faced with the task of fitting foreign trade into their overall plans. From an administrative standpoint, this is done most "conveniently" by means of trade agreements with other nations that specify the total exports and imports to be traded during the year. In intra-COMECON trade, each pair of nations holds a gigantic barter session each year in which most of its mutual trade is specified in detail and sealed by contracts. The Communist nations would like to have such arrangements with capitalist nations—but the latter cannot commit their exporters and importers. However, under trade agreements, many Western capitalist countries have brought their traders into similar meetings and have facilitated deals by various kinds of preferential treatment. From the standpoint of the liberal economic order, large "barter-type" deals of this sort hide many discriminatory purchases and sales that would never have been made in open competition. For example, Alec Nove argued that the reason one sees Italian cars but not British cars in Budapest was probably "because the Italians demanded a quota for cars in their bilateral agreement and the British did not."[4] (He also points out that Polish, Czech, and East German cars outnumber the Italian.)

That such transactions represent deviations from the optimal pattern of trade is clear. If East-West trade amounted to 25 percent of world trade and all of it were conducted under the umbrella of trade agreements as described above, the problem for the West could be serious. However, East-West trade amounts to less than 5 percent of world trade, and most of it is not conducted as described. Further, given the size of the Communist debt to the West, it seems unlikely that East-West trade will grow faster than world trade. It is my feeling, therefore, that, while undesirable, discrimination arising out of East-West trade is not quantitatively a serious problem; it is probably less serious than the analogous phenomenon that characterizes much of the multinational corporation, intrafirm international trade.

Second, in order to consummate sales to the East, many Western exporters have been more or less forced to accept all or part payment in kind—so-called buy-back or countertrade agreements. The acceptance of Soviet vodka for American Pepsi Cola is a well-known case in point. The same has been true of Western investments in the East—repayment has often involved accepting the products produced by these investments or even other products instead of currency. Such reversions to barter clearly represent a retrogressive trend when viewed in terms of Western objectives of achieving a more liberal international economic order. Why do the Communist nations press for buy-back arrangements? Partly because much of their intrabloc trade is handled on such a basis, that is, trade between bloc countries is bilaterally balanced. With the West, it is primarily because of the hard-currency shortage—vodka substitutes for dollars. Since the hard-currency shortage is likely to be a long-run phenomenon, attempts at this kind of barter are probably here to stay.

If buy-back arrangements were caused by a virus that might spread and infect capitalist trade, they might be a cause for concern. They are not and, in fact, many Western exporters even in East-West trade refuse to accept payment in kind. So there does not appear to be much to worry about even if the number of barter deals increases somewhat over time. In fact, one might look at these deals as a kind of second-best solution to a serious disequilibrium situation. That is to say, because of the hard-currency shortage, the Eastern nations have a large repressed demand for Western products. Ability to arrange buy-back deals expands their purchasing power and the level of East-West trade—although not necessarily by the full amount of the barter since some of the Eastern exports-through-barter might have been sold for hard currency anyway. So the Eastern nations gain—and presumably so do the Western enterprises, although perhaps not by as much as if they had been paid in cash. This second-best argument for buy-back is similar to the argument prevalent after World War II that it made sense for the nations of Europe to discriminate against the United States, the cheapest market, and trade with each other, because of the "dollar shortage." By discriminating, they were able to engage in a higher level of trade than would otherwise have been possible.[5]

Third, perhaps the major distortions introduced into the trading practices of the United States and to a lesser extent into those of the Western European nations have resulted from responses to the cold war. The cold war led the Communist nations, under Soviet persuasion, to concentrate their trade among themselves to an extraordinary degree. The implicit equivalent tariffs to their hidden quotas on most Western products, especially in the earlier postwar period, would have made Smoot-Hawley look like a pygmy, I am sure. However, part of the responsibility for COMECON autarky must be laid at the feet of the Western nations, especially the United States, with their rigorous controls over exports to the bloc, not to mention quotas on many imports, controls on credits, and in some cases lack of MFN treatment. The situation at present (1977) is much freer than it was in the past, and in some cases (subsidized export credits, for example) it might be argued that the pendulum has swung too far. My main point here is that the cold war has led this country to distort its trade significantly and to engage in illiberal practices in what I believe to have been a relatively fruitless attempt to deprive the USSR of economic and military gains from trade. U.S. losses in exports have clearly amounted to many billions of dollars in the postwar period. This can be shown by projecting our share of Communist bloc trade and comparing it with the actual trade realized *or* by looking at our market share in general of various industrial products and then comparing that share with our share of Western exports of the same products to the Communist nations. A major reason we failed to hurt the USSR and lost so many billions of dollars in exports was the unwillingness of Western Europe to join fully in our embargo. Another fallacy of our policy was the overestimation of the damage that could be imposed on the USSR, an economy which for most of the postwar period imported only 3 percent or less of its GNP. Several other fallacies of our policy are discussed elsewhere.[6]

Finally, most distressing, to me at least, were the provisions of the Trade Reform Act of 1974 which *explicitly* linked the granting of MFN status to the USSR and Eastern Europe to their emigration policies and also limited Export-Import Bank loans to the USSR to $75 million annually, an amount more appropriate to a nation the size of Luxembourg. These provisions represent an interruption in the gradual U.S. trend of trade liberalization toward the Eastern nations. Like the controls of the 1950s and 1960s, these have already proven ineffective in achieving their goals. Emigration from the Soviet Union, which had reached a peak in

1973, declined almost immediately, and the USSR and Eastern Europe have received enormous amounts of credit from other Western nations since 1974. Furthermore, the USSR was moved by these provisions of the Trade Reform Act to annul the U.S.-USSR Commercial Agreement, so laboriously put together in 1972, and accordingly ceased repayment of its Lend-Lease debt.

Notes

1. General Accounting Office, *The Government's Role in East-West Trade: Problems and Issues,* February 1976.
2. Ibid., p. 66. Quoted from U.S. Department of Commerce, *US-USSR Trade and the Whipsaw Controversy,* August 1977, p. 6, emphasis in original.
3. "Whipsawing" is defined "as the ability of a large buyer to play off potential sellers against one another to obtain maximum price breaks or other contractual concessions." Department of Commerce, *US-USSR Trade,* p. 3.
4. Alec Nove, "East-West Trade," in Paul A. Samuelson, ed., *International Economic Relations* (New York: St. Martin, 1969), p. 111.
5. See Ragnar Frisch, "Forecasting a Multilateral Balance of Payments," *American Economic Review,* vol. 37 (September 1947); Franklyn D. Holzman, "Discrimination in International Trade," *American Economic Review,* vol. 39 (December 1949).
6. Franklyn D. Holzman, "East-West Trade and Investment Policy Issues," in *United States International Economic Policy in an Interdependent World,* Williams Commission Report to the President, July 1971.

Part Three
CONVERTIBILITY AND EXCHANGE RATES

8
CMEA's
Hard Currency Deficits
and Rouble Convertibility[1]

Over the past fifteen years, the CMEA countries[2] have consistently run hard currency deficits in their trade with the West. I will first consider very briefly the extent and causes of these deficits. In Sections II and III, various Eastern convertible-currency proposals, which are related to financing these deficits, will be discussed. The policy issues will be summarised in the final Section. Because of the limitations of space, some of the issues discussed below will be considerably oversimplified.

I. Extent and Causes of CMEA's
Hard-Currency Deficit

According to Western estimates, CMEA's hard-currency indebtedness was in the neighbourhood of $32 billion at the end of 1975.[3] This is considerably above the $22.3 billion estimated for the end of 1974; and the 1974 figure represents an approximate $5 billion increase over 1973.[4] About half of the present debt is attributed to the USSR and Poland. These debts represent something like a 20 percent debt service/export ratio for the USSR and ratios probably of a similar order of magnitude for the rest of Eastern Europe, with the Bulgarian ratio on the high side and those for Czechoslovakia and the GDR on the low side. These are fairly high figures by most Western standards and there is some feeling in both East and West that the CMEA may be beginning to approach a credit ceiling. As early as 1971, an experienced Hungarian economist remarked that 'To maintain East-West trade even at the present

Reprinted with permission of St. Martin's Press, Inc., from *Economic Relations Between East and West*, Nita G. M. Watts, ed. (London: The Macmillan Press Ltd, 1978), pp. 144–163. Copyright © 1978 by the International Economic Association.

level, the unbalanced payments situation must be recognised'. He also observed: 'a deficit balance of the Eastern European nations seems to be a constant phenomenon of these relations'.[5]

Why is it that the CMEA's deficit balance with the West is a 'constant phenomenon?' It is my view, presented at length elsewhere,[6] that these deficits can be attributed largely to (a) the practice of central planning with direct controls and, related to this, (b) excessive tautness in the plans—what some have called 'overfull employment'—and (c) distorted domestic prices.[7] Briefly the arguments are as follows:

(1) Almost three-quarters of the exports of advanced industrial nations are manufactured products (SITC categories 5–8). This is also true of intra-CMEA trade. In trade with the West, however, CMEA's exports of manufactured products are no more than one-third whereas imports are more than four-fifths of the total. This—as it might be called—comparative disadvantage in manufactured products is due, according to Imre Vajda, to lack of innovation and to deficiencies in 'performance, reliability . . . appearance, packing, delivery and credit terms, assembling facilities, after-sale services, advertising . . . selling itself . . .'.[8] These deficiencies, in turn, are due to the relative lack of competition in both domestic and intra-CMEA trade as a result of distribution according to plan, excessive tautness and consequent pervasive sellers' markets, and other well-known deficiencies of the existing systems of success indicators.

(2) Excessive tautness in plans, like inflationary pressures in the West, puts pressure on the balance of payments as excess demand seeks satisfaction both through higher imports and through diverting exportables to domestic use.

(3) Central planning by direct controls results in so-called 'commodity inconvertibility'. Foreign buyers cannot make unplanned purchases because of the disruptive effect this would have on the exporting country's plan. This significantly reduces the competitive ability of CMEA exporters. It also contributes to the inconvertibility of CMEA currencies.

(4) Again to avoid plan disruption, CMEA countries are prevented from rapidly adjusting imports downward to levels which can be supported by exports. Hence the Western recession in 1975, and decline in Western imports, may have resulted in greater deficits for CMEA nations than would have been the case for some comparable capitalist nations.

(5) The distorted domestic prices in CMEA countries[9] necessitate using adjusted world prices in intra-CMEA trade and using world prices unrelated to CMEA domestic prices in East-West trade. This, along with commodity inconvertibility, makes the domestic currencies of the CMEA, and also the transferable rouble (TR), all inconvertible. It also deprives their exchange rates of any real price function. Devaluation, for example, cannot affect East-West trade and can only affect a small percentage of transactions in intra-CMEA trade. Inability to use devaluation as a tool for achieving an equilibrium in the balance of payments is a serious shortcoming and is certainly responsible, in part, for hard-currency problems.

(6) Commodity inconvertibility results in rigidly bilateral trade within CMEA (see below). The use of world currencies and world prices frees East-West trade from this straitjacket.

Having traced briefly the extent and causes of the hard-currency balance-of-payments problems of the Eastern nations, I will now examine two important proposals which have been made regarding convertibility. One is for the CMEA to develop an externally convertible rouble (ECR) which would be used exclusively in East-West trade. The ECR would be a purely financial instrument which could not be used to buy goods within the CMEA but only for exchange into Western currencies. Of course, to the extent that any Western trader holding ECRs was able to use them to purchase goods in other Western countries, there would be no hindrances from the CMEA side. The second proposal, one which has been around for at least a decade, is to make the transferable rouble (TR) a convertible currency. Both of these proposals have implications for the hard-currency problems of the CMEA. Making the TR a convertible currency is a much more difficult and profound change than the establishment of an ECR and in effect would make an ECR unnecessary. It would also have important implications for intra-CMEA trade. Therefore let us consider first the possibilities and implications of establishing an ECR.

II. The Externally Convertible Rouble

To my knowledge, the ECR as such was proposed first by Peter Wiles.[10] More recently (October 1975) at a conference of Eastern and Western international monetary experts held near Athens, the proposal was made by a number of Eastern European bankers. A related proposal—using the TR in East-West trade without solving the commodity convertibility problem—has been advanced by Soviet economists on at least two occasions recently[11] and was also suggested in Section 7, Articles 5 and 12 of the 'Comprehensive Programme' of 1971 (see below).

The idea of an ECR is attractive: if successful, it could provide another financial link between East and West, one upon which more profound monetary relationships might be developed. From the standpoint of the Eastern nations, the proposal must have positive political value since it would give them for the first time representation among world currencies. Still another possible advantage of financial convertibility mentioned by Wiles[12] is that it would enable CMEA countries which joined the IMF to comply technically, if not substantively, with Article VIII which requires members to strive for currency convertibility. Financial convertibility might satisfy this condition, though in a way not envisaged by the Bretton Woods fathers since they never anticipated the existence of financial convertibility without commodity convertibility. On the other hand it might not—unless the CMEA could join the IMF as a group—since the ECR is not identified with individual nations.

A main purpose of the ECR, however, must be that it would provide the CMEA with some economic advantages. What economic advantages might be expected? Gains accruing to a nation which issues currency that is used in international transactions are usually called seignorage. Normally seignorage results when a nation pays a lower rate of interest on outstanding holdings of its currency than it is able to earn, either at home or abroad, on the investments[13] made possible by the fact that foreigners are willing to hold its currency. Related to this is the fact that foreigners, by their willingness to hold others' currencies, in effect extend credit and allow debtor nations to live beyond their means, at least temporarily. In the 1950s and early 1960s, the United States was able to live beyond its means because foreigners were willing to hold dollars, and to hold them at low or zero rates of interest. Seignorage on this score was partly offset, of course, by various constraints and costs which the United States was forced to bear as a result.[14] The question to be raised here is whether the CMEA can expect to get more and cheaper credit if an ECR is created. Other possible gains to the CMEA must also be considered, however. As we have seen, the CMEA nations suffer from other disadvantages in international trade. Therefore it would be worth enquiring whether the use of the ECR would ameliorate these problems—inability to devalue the currency, commodity inconvertibility, and excessive bilateralism in trade.

It is simple enough to create ECRs. The member nations of CMEA must make deposits in their International Bank for Economic Cooperation (IBEC) or some other financial institution against which they can draw ECRs with which to pay hard-currency debts to Western nations. Some portion of these deposits must be in convertible currencies and/or gold so that the bank can convert upon request outstanding ECRs held by foreigners. This means that the CMEA members as a group must hold larger hard-currency reserves than before, because now they are needed not only to satisfy transactions demands but also to guarantee ECR convertibility. If Westerners are willing to hold more ECRs than the additional value of hard-currency reserves necessarily impounded, an increase in CMEA ability to buy Western products results. The extent of the increase in available credit will depend in part on the percentage of hard-currency reserves to foreign-held ECRs that it is deemed necessary to hold.

What are the determinants of, and what is likely to be, the demand by foreigners for ECRs? Will there be an intrinsic demand for the ECR as there is for gold and dollars or will the CMEA have to pay foreigners a high rate of return to prevent them from converting? Whether or not positive seignorage results from issuing ECRs will largely depend on the answer to this question.

There are at least four reasons why foreign currencies are demanded and held:

(1) for intervention purposes—to buy or sell against one's own currency, usually in order to maintain a fixed exchange rate;
(2) as a vehicle currency—that is, as a third currency in which two nations' traders denominate and conduct their trade;
(3) for transactions purposes—when a nation's traders use their own currency in trade;
(4) as a store of value.

The demand for currencies used for intervention and as vehicle currencies is, of course, much greater than the demand for currencies for other purposes and only the major currencies fall into these first categories. An intervention currency is bound to be one which is widely used and relatively stable in value; it is, in effect, a standard of value against which other currencies are measured and this puts it in a class by itself. There are also strong economic reasons for transacting trade in a few major vehicle currencies rather than in the more than 100 national currencies. First, vehicle currencies are usually those which over the long-run have been relatively stable in value; and their wide use is partly attributable to low exchange-rate risk. Secondly, use of vehicle currencies enables a nation both to conserve reserves and to reduce transaction costs. To understand this, we must note that a nation's transactions-demand for currencies depends to a considerable extent on the country composition of its trade and the currencies in which trade is denominated.[15] If there is any uncertainty at all regarding the amount and direction of trade, then obviously the amount of foreign exchange reserves which a nation needs to hold is reduced if trade is transacted in vehicle currencies acceptable to all nations rather than in dozens of national currencies. Use of one or a few vehicle currencies also reduces the amount of money-changing which takes place and thereby reduces transactions costs. However, despite these advantages of using vehicle currencies, any two nations which trade a lot with each other will undoubtedly find it convenient and inexpensive to conduct some part of their trade in their national currencies.

Now, with these factors in mind, compare the qualifications of the proposed ECR with those of the dollar and other world currencies. The dollar currently serves as the main world intervention and vehicle currency. In 1973, with world exports totalling a little more than $500 billion, the United States exported over $70 billion worth of goods, considerably more than any other country. Further, the USA had more investments in other countries, and more countries had investments in the USA, than is true of any other nation. Other factors also contribute to the universality of the dollar. Existence within the borders of the USA of the largest financial market in the world guarantees a relative stability in the face of possible internationally generated financial shocks. Confidence is also generated by the size and variety of US output—a foreigner with dollars can always find things to buy at reasonable prices within the United States. Finally, the dollar has demonstrated as high a degree of stability of value as any currency over the past thirty years.

The British pound and French franc also play fairly important roles as vehicle currencies, and to some extent also as intervention currencies. For one thing, the British and French are among the world's largest five trading and investing (abroad) nations; for another, they have had close political and economic relationships for a century with many smaller nations which use their currencies as reserves and as units of account. The West German Mark is also used quite heavily in world trade and as a reserve asset. This is explained by the facts that West Germany's trade is second only to that of the United States and that the Mark has been possibly the strongest currency in the world over the past decade, with very large foreign exchange reserves to back it.

What about the trade of the CMEA nations? Their truly mul-tilateral hard-currency trade with the West in 1973 was less than $15 billion and may not have exceeded $10 billion—approximately the level of Sweden's trade and less than half that of Italy or the Netherlands, for example. Further, their investments in the West are negligible and local financial markets nonexistent. It seems highly unlikely, in light of these facts, that there would in the foreseeable future be a demand for

ECRs either for purposes of intervention or as a vehicle currency. This would imply a sharp limit to the value of ECRs which foreigners (private or official) might demand or be willing to hold, all other things being equal, which would, in turn, reduce the probability of substantial seignorage resulting from the issuance of ECRs. It is indeed sobering to consider that even the British receive little or no seignorage from the very wide use of pounds sterling in world trade.[16] It is even more sobering to consider that on balance even the United States may not have derived a net gain from the almost universal use of the dollar by the rest of the world in the postwar period.[17]

Under these circumstances, what is the likelihood of the ECR replacing Western vehicle currencies in East-West transactions? Arguments against this occurring on a wide scale are stated in the previous paragraph; what we have perceived as the advantages of vehicle currencies are disadvantages of the ECR. Use of the ECR would increase both the transaction costs and amount of reserves Western trading partners would have to hold. While these costs would not loom large, because East-West trade is such a small part of Western trade, they might loom relatively large in terms of the value of the trade (East-West) in connection with which they would be incurred. Another obstacle to the use of the ECR as a transactions currency, at least initially, would be the artificiality of drawing up contracts in ECRs, particularly when prices in ECRs would really be world prices mechanically translated into roubles. Further, Western traders are used to their own currencies and to the vehicle currencies in which they usually transact business. These factors present psychological obstacles that might significantly impede the introduction of ECRs or, alternatively, raise the costs of introducing them; admittedly, these impediments might be overcome in time.

Two further impediments to the use of the ECR as a transactions currency are the facts that it would be a currency without a country and that like all Eastern currencies, including the transferable Rouble, it would have very low if not zero commodity convertibility. That there would be low or zero commodity convertibility is attested by the very name of the proposed currency—it is only 'externally convertible'; commodity inconvertibility would appear to be compounded by the fact that the ECR has no real referent in a specific country.[18] It is a fairly obvious historical fact that the currencies which have been used the most in the world, with the exception of gold which has a unique mythology, have been currencies of the major trading countries which provide, in fact, a maximum of commodity convertibility. It is all well and good to guarantee 'financial convertibility'; but it must also be recognized that a currency with financial convertibility not backed up by commodity convertibility will have a lower value to prospective holders than one with commodity convertibility. When Western currencies have been financially inconvertible, as after the Second World War, the values of these currencies always fell. But there was always a limit to the loss of value as a result of the fact that one could always convert the currencies into a wide range of commodities, admittedly a second-best solution. The value of an ECR must be almost exclusively based on financial convertibility, since its commodity convertibility would be much more limited if not zero.

The upshot of this discussion is that there is nothing inherently attractive about ECRs to encourage Western traders, banks, or treasuries to hold them. This suggests that if the ECRs are to be launched successfully, they will have to be endowed with special features which will create a demand for them, essentially as a store of value. By special features I mean both the terms of convertibility and the interest to be paid on ECR deposits.

Wiles proposed that in a period of world inflation, like the present one, ECR deposits be indexed to the US dollar price level.[19] There certainly would be a demand for any asset which proved to be relatively inflation-proof—so long as inflation persists. In periods of rapid inflation, the implicit interest rate on such balances could be very high; but should prices once more become stable, demand for new ECRs on this account would undoubtedly collapse. Wiles thinks that it would be a real coup for CMEA to introduce ECRs on this basis. He seems to forget that it could be costly to redeem such a currency if prices had been rising rapidly.[20]

The ECRs could also be guaranteed against devaluation. Presumably the CMEA could guarantee holders of ECRs the exchange rates which prevailed on a particular date around the time of issuance. On the assumption that inflation continues, that most exchange rates are pegged, and that adjustments between other currencies are made more by devaluations than by revaluations,[21] the ECR would gradually become worth more and more in terms of all other currencies. This would make it a fairly attractive asset with an implicit interest rate equal to the average rate of devaluation of world currencies—perhaps approximating the rate of world inflation.

The ECR might also be tied to the SDR and thereby to an average of major exchange rates. Like a share of stock in a mutual fund, an ECR so denominated would eliminate some of the exchange-rate risk attached to holding foreign currencies, retaining its value better than those currencies which depreciate the most, but not as well as those which depreciate less than the average or even appreciate. The implicit rate of return on ECRs held under these terms would not be high.

Other possible convertibility terms can be conjectured of course, but this is not necessary for our purposes. To the extent that the terms of convertibility yield an implicitly high rate of return to those holding ECR deposits, explicit interest payments may not be necessary. On the other hand, under less favourable convertibility terms—like tieing the ECR to the SDR—it may be necessary to pay interest on deposits if creditors are to be cajoled into holding ECRs.

The question to be asked is: given the need to overcome depositor reluctance, what possibility is there that positive seignorage would be realised on the use of ECRs? Normally, seignorage would be measured by comparing the interest costs on deposits with the returns from investments which are made by banks with their free resources. In this case, the interest costs are those, both implicit and explicit, on ECRs held by Westerners; and the returns on investment are properly viewed as the rate of return on, or profitability of, imports financed by the ECRs. In comparing interest costs on liabilities with returns on assets (i.e. imports), it is necessary to take account of the fact that some assets must be held as reserves in liquid form to insure convertibility.[22] The returns on these reserves are likely to be relatively low and on gold and cash, of course, zero. The possibility of profitably using ECRs to finance imports will vary inversely with the percentage of liquid reserves to total assets which it seems prudent to hold and with the gap between the rate of return on imports and rate of interest paid on deposits. If it is profitable to issue ECRs, then CMEA's ability to import Western products is expanded beyond the value of its hard-currency reserves by an amount which depends on the ratio of reserves to ECRs that must be maintained. How large must this reserve ratio be?

Let me answer this question by considering a crude diagrammatic representation of the static relationship between the interest rate on currency deposits (or near-moneys) held by foreigners and the ratio of hard-currency reserves to the value of these foreign-held deposits. As implied above, the relationship will be inverse—the lower the percentage of reserve backing, the higher the interest rate required to induce foreigners to hold the currency.

In Figure 1 the three lines reflect this trade-off; and the relative distances of the lines from the axes reflect the various factors mentioned above. Line $aa'd$ may be taken to represent an intervention currency (say, the dollar) which is held interest-free or at a very low rate until the reserve/deposit ratio falls to a', after which a small interest payment is required. Line $bb'd$ could be taken to represent a slightly weaker currency—say, a vehicle currency like the pound sterling. It should be noted that a very low reserve/deposit ratio (say, oe) probably reflects a serious balance-of-payments problem, in which case any but one of the

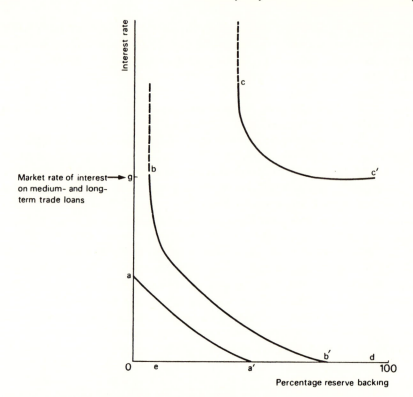

Fig. 1. Relationship between the percentage of reserve backing and the interest rate on currency deposits held by foreigners.

most traditional vehicle currencies would probably cease to serve as such, and the whole curve would shift to the north-east. Finally, line cc' is taken to represent a hypothetical ECR. It is my belief, for reasons set out below (and above), that even with large reserves to back the ECRs, interest on ECR deposits held by foreigners would have to approximate the market rate on foreign trade loans (og) if deposits are to be maintained; and that if reserve ratios were to be lowered, the required interest rate would rapidly become prohibitive.

Let me now return to the main line of argument.[23]

To complete the framework it is also essential to consider alternative ways of financing deficits. Is there any reason to believe, for example, that the interest rate which CMEA nations would have to pay on ECRs would be any lower than that which would be necessary to raise funds in the Eurodollar or other private financial markets or to get additional official credit from, say, the French Government?[24] In a perfect financial market, there should be no difference between interest rates; and if there is no difference, it might be possible for the CMEA to make its resources go further by borrowing directly than by issuing ECRs. This is because, unlike raising credits, the issuance of ECRs would require the CMEA to hold additional hard-currency reserves to ensure ECR convertibility, thereby immobilising resources which could otherwise have been spent in the West. How likely is it that there will be little difference in interest rates between credits and ECRs? Probably much more likely than in the West. This is because in the East the borrower and issuer of currency are one and the same economic unit—a government or group of governments—whereas in the West borrowers may be governments and their institutions, private businesses, private banks or some combination of these. This leads us to conclude that the CMEA nations can probably do as well or better by borrowing in world credit markets than by issuing ECRs.

To sum up so far: there would appear to be little or no reason for ECRs to be demanded as vehicle currencies or for transactions purposes. Given a high enough rate of interest (explicit or implicit) on ECR deposits, they would be held by foreigners as a store of value. Under these circumstances, of course, there would be no positive, but probably negative, seignorage on ECRs. The fact, noted above, that the pound sterling earns little or no seignorage would lead one to predict negative seignorage for ECRs. This fits with the current theory[25] that seignorage results only when the currency-issuing nation is possessed of monopolistic powers in world money markets, which would not be the case for the issuer of ECRs any more than it is for most other nations.

Even if a case could be made, in general, for ECRs, this would be a poor time to introduce them. The debt-service/export ratios of all the CMEA nations are at present high. As noted, over the past year (1975), very large deficits were sustained because of the Western recession and the disastrous Soviet grain crop. Large deficits were predicted for 1976. Imagine how holders of ECRs would have felt in 1975 when the news of the disastrous Soviet grain crop was announced or when, as the impact of the recession reduced CMEA exports, reports of rapidly rising deficits were made public. Surely, demands for conversion would have created serious problems, if not a convertibility crisis!

Before leaving the ECR, it is worth questioning briefly whether its use would help to resolve other major difficulties which have beset CMEA foreign trade—bilateralism, commodity inconvertibility, and inability to use devaluation as an instrument for achieving trade balance. While bilateralism is a serious problem in intra-CMEA trade, it is absent from East-West trade. East-West trade is conducted largely in Western vehicle currencies. Since there is at present general convertibility in the West, CMEA nations can spend their export earnings wherever they wish. The trade data show that earnings are spent relatively multilaterally, not bilaterally. Since the ECR is proposed for East-West trade, it can contribute nothing to solving the problems of intra-CMEA bilateralism.

Unlike bilateralism, commodity inconvertibility and inability to devalue are problems which do affect East-West trade. However, both of these problems are intimately connected with central planning by direct controls as it is practised in Eastern Europe today; their amelioration requires, in my opinion, nothing more and nothing less than a significant decentralisation of planning and pricing, as discussed below.

III. Convertibility of the
Transferable Rouble (TR)

Before 1963, trade between CMEA countries was conducted bilaterally and each pair of countries attempted to achieve a balance as close to perfect as possible. Occasional deviations occurred as a result of specially planned trilateral arrangements, planned credits, and failures of plans to be fulfilled. Because of the heterogeneity of distorted price structures which existed among the Eastern countries, negotiations were based on adjusted world prices and usually held stable for at least five years. Domestic prices and currencies of the CMEA countries played no role whatsoever in this process. While each country reported its trade in its own currency, this represented simply a mechanical translation from adjusted world prices at some exchange rate (often an unrealistic one) and the domestic-currency values reported implied prices in fact quite unrelated to the actual domestic price structure. No currency needed to be exchanged since trade was balanced. In fact, trade was balanced because of the desire of each country to avoid holding the currencies of other CMEA countries—a consequence of commodity inconvertibility and distorted prices.[26]

In 1963, the International Bank for Economic Cooperation (IBEC) was formed. A major purpose of IBEC was to free intra-CMEA trade from the shackles of rigid bilateralism. Toward this end a transferable rouble was created. All intra-CMEA trade was to be transacted in TRs and members were encouraged to trade with each other multilaterally, settling their imbalances in TRs. But rigid bilateralism remained despite the use of TRs. In particular, the CMEA countries which 'tended' to be in overall surplus insisted on balancing their trade with those which tended to be in overall deficit. With commodity inconvertibility, it mattered not whether countries held zlotys, roubles and other national currencies *or* TRs—none of them could be spent freely.

So the search for a multilateral settlement system has continued. Section 7 of the well-known CMEA *Comprehensive Programme* of 1971 was devoted to 'Improvement of Currency-Financial Relations'. Measures were to be developed and implemented by 1973 which would expand the use of the TR for multilateral settlements (Article 9). The TR is to be used, like other currencies, for settlements with third countries (Articles 5 and 12). Mutual convertibility of the TR and other CMEA currencies is envisaged (Article 15). Conditions for this mutual convertibility are to be worked out by 1973 (Article 18). IBEC is to be used to secure convertibility of the TR (Article 26).

The year 1973 has come and gone and so far as I am aware, nothing has been accomplished to *significantly* reduce bilateralism or achieve convertibility. Some insight into the causes of this lack of progress is gained by considering in traditional theoretical terms, what attributes of money the TR has. V. F. Garbuzov, Soviet Minister of Finance, states a view which can be found in several Soviet writings about the TR. He argues that experience demonstrates that 'the transferable rouble performs all of the basic functions of an international socialist currency: measure of value, means of payment, means of accumulation'.[27] It seems doubtful to me that this view can be as widespread among Eastern economists as the printed word suggests. I say this because, in my opinion, the TR embodies less 'moneyness' than almost any other currency presently in use and I totally disagree with the Garbuzov view cited above.

Is the TR a measure of value? Only in the most trivial sense of the term. This can easily be seen by asking first how prices in TRs are set? Prices in intra-CMEA trade are 'fixed on the basis of world prices freed of the harmful influence exerted by the interplay of speculative forces on the capitalist market which ensures its stability and excludes all influence on it by the crisis-like phenomena inherent in the capitalist currency system'.[28] In other works the relative values of products are based on capitalist relative values as expressed in world markets at some point in time, then adjusted (as noted above) and maintained fixed, usually for a period of five years. At this point, these capitalist prices are transformed into TRs at an arbitrary rate of exchange, based on the fact that a TR is declared to be worth 0.987412 grams of gold. The point is that the TR has nothing to do with the relationships among prices; these 'measures of value' flow basically out of the capitalist market. For purposes of CMEA trade, it wouldn't matter whether they remained in dollars, or were translated into TRs, Dutch guilders, Mongolian tugriks or, for that matter, into (American) Indian wampum.

Another problem arises regarding the validity of the TR as a measure of value when one considers that both the TR and the Soviet rouble are declared to be worth 0.987412 grams of gold yet (1) since the TR was established, world prices (hence prices in TRs) and Soviet internal prices have changed at different rates[29] and (2) relative prices in the USSR have often been quite different from those used in CMEA expressed in TRs.[30] In fact, a Soviet economist, Iu. Ivanov, published in 1968 an article demonstrating how to translate exports and imports in foreign trade prices into domestic prices.[31] Can the rouble (zloty, lev, etc.) and the TR both be valid measures of value when they attribute different relative and absolute values to the same pairs of commodities?

Is the TR a 'means of payment' or, as Western textbooks say, a medium of exchange? Again, only in a trivial sense of the meaning of the term. The power of a currency as a medium of exchange is related to the degree of option that one has in spending it. An American citizen with a dollar can spend it in literally thousands of different ways. The same is true of a Soviet citizen with roubles or a Polish citizen with zlotys. The possessor of a TR is in no such fortunate position. As a result of commodity inconvertibility, he can only spend it on a particular product in accordance with advance plans. Each TR is like a ration card—it is designated in advance to buy a particular product. No one to my knowledge has ever called a ration card 'money'. Money is, after all, generalised purchasing power.

There are at least two ways to interpret bilateral exchanges of goods valued in TRs between two CMEA countries. On the one hand, one might say that each country has thousands of ration cards denominated in TRs, each for the purchase of a separate product. On the other hand, since a planned balance of total trade is usually the immediate goal of each pair of trading partners, it could be argued that the TR does not even serve the function of a ration card. To the extent that trade is balanced, as planned, one might view the trade process as an instance of a gigantic barter. The fact that the products are denominated in TRs relates to the measure of value, or unit of account, function discussed above rather than to the medium of exchange. Only the imbalances, in this interpretation, could qualify for status as medium of exchange and this would represent a tiny fraction of total intra-CMEA trade. Further, it would be subject to the commodity inconvertibility qualification already mentioned.

Is the TR a 'means of accumulation' (store of value). It is a means of accumulation but, certainly, not a desirable means of accumulation. If it were a desirable means of accumulation, the various CMEA countries would not strive so hard to balance their payments with each other so as to avoid accumulating TRs. Not only is the very low rate of interest paid to holders of TRs undoubtedly far below the social rate of return on investment in all of the CMEA countries, but the existence of commodity inconvertibility and distorted domestic price structures creates great uncertainty regarding the true value which might be realised on each particular TR that one might hold.[32] A 'Store of value' at the time of its realisation becomes a 'medium of exchange'.

The Eastern literature does not ascribe to the TR a role as a 'standard of deferred payment', typically one of the characteristics of money listed by Western economists. In fact, it would seem to me that the TR, particularly in times of inflation like the present, is a better standard of deferred payment than most capitalist currencies.

We have argued so far that the TR serves very poorly the major functions of money. Not having strong characteristics as 'money', it is easy to understand why the introduction of the TR was of no assistance in reducing intra-CMEA bilateralism. So long as the CMEA does not have a truly convertible currency, CMEA nations will continue to have to trade on a largely bilateral basis.

Would convertibility of the TR be difficult to achieve? Some observers are optimistic. At a Conference in Venice in 1975, Yuri Ivanov, President of the Soviet Foreign Trade Bank, is reported to have said that the CMEA is considering introducing convertibility of the TR, particularly in relation to Western industrial countries, and that this could 'easily' be done.[33] I would be much less optimistic. The TR is inconvertible for the same reasons that national CMEA currencies are inconvertible—commodity inconvertibility and price structures which are distorted in the sense described earlier and which, therefore, are unrelated to world prices. What would it take to eliminate commodity inconvertibility and arbitrary prices? In my opinion, this can only be achieved by radical economic reforms which substitute decentralised planning for the central planning with direct controls which dominates the CMEA at present (Hungary being a partial exception). The establishment of free internal markets and free prices in which both domestic and foreign buyers and sellers can operate, subject only to indirect state controls, would lead eventually to an organic connection between internal and external markets and price structures, as is the case among Western countries. This would create necessary conditions for the convertibility of CMEA currencies. It would not be sufficient, however: it would also be essential that each country get itself into approximate balance-of-payments equilibrium, thereby establishing the conditions for 'currency' as well as 'commodity' convertibility.

The elimination of commodity inconvertibility and arbitrary pricing and the achievement of payments equilibrium would permit each country to make its currency convertible and would eliminate the need for bilateral balancing of trade. Each currency would then serve in the international market as a measure of value, medium of exchange, and store of value. What about the TR? There would, in fact, be no need for a TR if national currencies became convertible. (There would also be no need for an ECR, of course.) What probably would happen is that trade would be conducted in one of the vehicle currencies, say dollars, or if the USSR continued to be the major trading partner of most other CMEA countries (which it might not be under the assumed conditions set out below), then the Soviet rouble might assume the role of vehicle currency for the Eastern group of nations.

So far, I have discussed the impact of radical reforms primarily on bilateralism in intra-CMEA trade, not the subject of this Conference. However, such reforms would also have a profound impact on East-West trade relations. Most important, such reforms might serve to reduce the Eastern balance-of-payments pressures in trade with the West, although there might be a medium-term transition period before beneficial effects were experienced in which the reverse was true. An end to allocation according to plan and excessive tautness in planning, along with greater Western competition in the domestic markets of the CMEA countries, should gradually raise the quality and saleability in the West of CMEA manufactured products. Competition should also improve incentives to innovate and to diffuse innovation. The combination of these factors should eventually reduce CMEA demand for Western manufactured products and technology and increase the amount they can profitably sell to the West. Ability to sell to the West would also be strongly enhanced by commodity convertibility. There seems little doubt that if Western importers were able to compete freely for currently produced Eastern products and were not faced with the delays and uncertainties connected with having to get desired products into the 'planned export' category, more exports to the West would result. Still another advantage of radical internal reforms and convertibility would be that CMEA nations which were encountering hard-currency balance-of-payments problems would have available to them the possibility of devaluing their currencies in order to get into equilibrium. It is my belief, discussed elsewhere,[34] that inability to devalue is an important factor behind the CMEA's persistent deficits with the West.

To sum up: I see no possibility of making the TR convertible in either intra-CMEA or East-West trade so long as present methods of central planning with direct controls dominate CMEA practice. Radical economic reforms would make possible a convertible TR but would also render it unnecessary, since the reforms required for TR convertibility would also lead to convertibility of the national currencies of the Eastern nations. Such reforms would also make the ECR unnecessary. Finally, radical reforms would remove some of the problems that have led to CMEA's persistent hard-currency deficit with the West and by this token reduce the demand for credit.

IV. What Policy for CMEA?

Faced with persistent hard-currency deficits in East-West trade and with persistent bilateralism in intra-CMEA trade, CMEA policy-makers and economists have been casting about for solutions, some of which relate to creating convertible supranational currencies. I have argued that these efforts are misguided, and that the way to mitigate or eliminate these foreign trade problems is by introducing radical economic reforms in which planning is decentralised. The question is: should CMEA introduce radical economic reforms in order to eliminate its foreign trade problems, not to mention other (internal) problems attributable to central planning with direct controls?

This question cannot be answered in strictly economic terms but is more properly a question of political economy and of politics. While radical reforms might result in improvements in foreign trade performance, for the reasons noted above, they might well conflict with other CMEA goals. For example, CMEA constitutes the most tightly knit trading group in the world. Intra-CMEA trade is at present probably in the neighbourhood of 55–60 per cent of the total trade of the CMEA countries, or about three times the degree of concentration of trade among them in the pre-war period. The introduction of decentralised planning and freer trade would certainly lead to a much sharper reduction in intra-CMEA trade than would otherwise be likely to occur. The leaders of the Eastern nations may consider this an undesirable result.[35]

The Eastern leaders may also have a political or ideological preference for planning with direct controls rather than for allowing their economies to experience some of the so-called anarchy of the market. They are, of course, entitled to such a preference. In the West, the preference is for the anarchy of the market. In the pre-war period, market anarchy in the West led to the Great Depression and, in the past ten to fifteen years, it has led to stagflation. Great Depressions of the magnitude of that experienced in the 1930s are probably a thing of the past; but stagflation, with the socio-economic disruption it involves, is an unsolved problem. Stagflation could be wiped out by the introduction of planning and controls. However, the preference of most Western economists and political leaders is to stick with the market and to try to find a market solution to stagflation—although the prospects at the moment are not bright.

Convertibility and freer trade would do violence to other accepted goals of the socialist nations. Dedication to full employment, job stability and stable prices, particularly of consumers' goods, is much more absolute in the East than it is in the West. Radical economic reforms, convertibility and so forth, would open the economies of the CMEA nations to much of the relative instability that characterises Western capitalist countries. Would any Eastern country allow itself to import the Western inflation of the past ten years? As Professor Csikós-Nagy says, 'The importation of inflation is incompatible with the economic policy of the socialist countries.'[36] Or would Eastern authorities allow foreign exporters freely to outcompete some domestic industries, all of which are nationalised? (In the West, after all, governments do not always allow foreign exporters to outcompete even their private industries!) It seems unlikely, in my opinion, without a total transformation of values and goals. As Janos Fekete, Deputy President of the National Bank of Hungary has put it, 'Convertibility in the Western sense would introduce such spontaneous elements into our planned economies which we cannot undertake.'[37]

There is no need to expand this list of examples further. Both the planned and market economies have their problems and both prefer to try to solve them in ways which are consistent with political and ideological predilections. Radical changes under either system will be delayed while there is still a chance that conservative solutions will work and while economic performance, if not entirely satisfactory, is still adequate.

In light of the above, I feel that radical reforms to solve foreign trade problems are not likely to be undertaken by the CMEA in the near future. As indicated earlier, I feel that an attempt to establish an ECR for East-West trade would be misguided. The CMEA nations have received large amounts of Western credits and are unlikely to enlarge their imports significantly and at reasonable cost through ECRs. Further, the use of Western currencies ensures multilateral East-West trade and so there is nothing to be gained on this score. Even more misguided are those who talk of making the TR a convertible currency. Given the inconvertibility of TRs, and unwillingness to adopt radical economic reforms, there is in my opinion no first-best solution to the problem of intra-CMEA bilateralism. The goals for convertibility set in Section 7 of the *Comprehensive Programme* of 1971 will not be implemented, given central planning with direct controls.

On the other hand, some multilateralism may be achieved through the planning for integration on a multilateral basis which is envisaged in other sections of the *Comprehensive Programme*. This is, of course, a much less effective way of achieving multilateralism even if it can be so achieved.[38] Any multilateralism so achieved should not be attributed to the TR, as some Eastern economists have done. As K. Nazarkin, President of IBEC has admitted, multilateral balancing which is planned in advance is not 'real transferability'.[39] When Iu. Konstantinov, head of the Currency-Financial Division of the Secretariat of CMEA says 'The planned organisation of commodity flows is essentially the factor that assures the effectiveness of the "work" of the transferable rouble, its actual convertibility into commodities, and real utilisation of assets in the collective currency,'[40] he is partly echoing Nazarkin's insights; but he is also confusing the issue in suggesting that the TR is doing any work at all: it is not.

A few other possibilities of ameliorating intra-bloc bilateralism do exist and were proposed by this writer in 1964.[41] One is to establish a market for national CMEA currencies in which interest rates on outstanding balances would be allowed to reflect flexibly the relative desirability of each currency. Growing deficits would be accompanied by rising rates of interest sufficient to attract holders. Such market prices on outstanding currency balances would facilitate multilateral currency and trade exchanges and would also give the deficit-prone nations an incentive to balance their accounts. Another possibility would be to introduce commodity convertibility in consumers' goods. This would be much less disruptive of planning than commodity convertibility in producers' goods and other intermediate products.[42] I am not sure how feasible either of these proposals is. My third proposal was for the CMEA nations to accumulate hard-currency balances and to use these to multilaterialise their payments. More recently it has been proposed that the process be started by requiring small percentages of any imbalance to be paid in hard currency and that this percentage gradually be increased until all imbalances are settled in hard currency. In 1964 I felt that this was an impractical proposal and that is still my opinion. The reason is the very great shortage of, and therefore premium on, hard-currency balances in CMEA. With all CMEA nations short of hard currency, no nation will willingly accept a creditor position in trade when only, say, 10–30 per cent of the balance is payable in hard currency. On the other hand, as the percentage of deficit payable in hard currency rises, the debtors will gradually become more and more reluctant to incur deficits with CMEA partners. So, until CMEA is in some kind of hard-currency equilibrium with the West it would not seem possible to use hard currencies to multilateralise intra-CMEA trade since at least one partner will always insist on a bilateral balance. Such multilateralisation as might take place would, in any case, not affect the basic inconvertibility of the TR. It would not, therefore, affect CMEA's position in East-West trade.

[*Professor Holzman has asked, since the conclusion of the Conference, for the following note to be added to his paper* (N. Watts, ed.).]

Since this paper was completed, it has been reported that the IBEC Council decided in October 1976 to allow traders and banks of noncommunist nations to accept and hold TRs in payment for exports and to use them in settlement of accounts (Moscow Narodny Bank, *Press Bulletin*, 8 December 1976, pp. 14–18; *Financial Times*, 17 December 1976). Apparently importers cannot use TRs directly for purchases in CMEA countries and banks holding TRs must have the prior agreement of the governments involved. This may be inferred from the statement in the *Press Bulletin* (p. 14) that 'The requirement of agreement between competent organs of the interested countries on purchase/sale of goods or services under settlement in transferable roubles remains in force.' The interest rate on TR accounts opened with the IBEC remains, as before, at 1 per cent per annum. Careful reading of the *Press Bulletin* suggests that once having accepted TRs, instead of convertible currencies, the Western exporter or bank cannot exchange the TRs into convertible currencies (unlike the envisaged ECRs) but can only use them in settling accounts within its own country or purchasing imports from CMEA countries; and this despite the fact that Western banks receiving credits in TRs from the IBEC are allowed to repay in either TRs or convertible currencies!

The new regulation thus appears to be an attempt, on the lines of the ECR proposal, to secure cheap credit. For the reasons noted above in connection with the ECR, it seems doomed to failure. It seems very unlikely that a Western exporter would agree to accept in payment for goods more than a token amount of TRs. Not only is the 1 per cent interest rate non-competitive, but the TR deposit appears to be inconvertible into Western currencies. Further, the IBEC requirement that the use of these deposits to pay for imports from a CMEA country requires an intergovernmental agreement underlines their commodity inconvertibility.

Notes

1. This paper has benefited from discussions with Charles Kindleberger, Rachel McCulloch, Robert Tarr and Gordon Weil. I also gratefully acknowledge support from the Bureau of East-West Trade of the US Department of Commerce, Contract 6-362-42, in writing this paper.

2. We will be concerned with the Eastern European (including the USSR) members of the CMEA.

3. L. Brainard, 'CMEA: Rising Deficits', *East-West Markets* (12 January 1976), p. 10.

4. L. Brainard, 'Financing Eastern Europe's Trade Gap, the Euromarket Connection', *Euromoney* (January 1976), p. 16; International Monetary Fund, *International Financial News* (Washington, D.C., 15 March 1976), p. 91.

5. B. Csikós-Nagy, 'Foreign Trade and Monetary Policy in Eastern European Countries' in *Foreign Trade and Monetary Policy* (CESES Milan, 1974), p. 207.

6. Franklyn D. Holzman, *Foreign Trade under Central Planning* (Cambridge, USA, 1974), pp. 225–9; Chapter 1 of this book, 'Some Theories of the Hard Currency Shortages of Centrally Planned Economies.'

7. The analysis presented immediately below is less relevant to Hungary than to other CMEA countries because of Hungary's relatively radical economic reforms.

8. Imre Vajda, 'External Equilibrium and Economic Reform', in I. Vajda and M. Simai, *Foreign Trade in a Planned Economy* (Cambridge, 1971).

9. In the words of three Polish economists: 'Because of the autonomous system of domestic prices in each country, an automatic and purely internal character of the monetary system and arbitrary official rates of exchange which do not reflect relative values of currencies, it is impossible to compare prices and costs of production and particular commodities in different countries. . . .' (cited by Z. Fallenbuchl [from a Polish source], 'East European Integration: Comecon,' in Joint Economic Committee, Congress of the United States, *Reorientation and Commercial Relations of the Economies of Eastern Europe* [Washington 1974]).

10. Peter Wiles, 'On Purely Financial Convertibility', in Y. Laulan (ed.), *Banking, Money and Credit in Eastern Europe* (NATO Colloquim: Brussels, 1973).

11. K. Miroshnichenko, 'International Collective Currencies', *International Affairs* (March 1973); K. Nazarkin 'IBEC and the Monetary System of the Socialist Community', *International Affairs* (March 1974).

12. As in Note 10, p. 124.

13. Actually, earnings on investments also have to cover the costs of bank services and a normal profit before seignorage results.

14. R. Z. Aliber, 'The Costs and Benefits of the US Role as a Reserve Country', *Quarterly Journal of Economics* (August 1964).

15. A. Swoboda, *The Euro-Dollar Market: An Interpretation,* Essays in International Finance, No. 64 (Princeton, 1968).

16. B. J. Cohen, 'The Seignorage Gains of an International Currency', *Quarterly Journal of Economics* (August 1971).

17. As in Note 14.

18. Some reluctance has been observed even with respect to the SDR, and also the European Unit of Account (EUA) and the European Currency Unit (ECU) (Cf. *The Economist,* 14 February 1976, p. 13).

19. As in Note 10, p. 123.

20. Actually, Wiles's proposal is quite arbitrary. A more flexible approach would be to view the ECR deposit as equivalent to a kind of short-term interest-bearing security and to let the interest rate on it be set (determined) with reference to competitive money market instruments.

21. In a world of universal float, adjustments would probably be made roughly equally by devaluation and revaluation and, presumably, the ECR would also float.

22. The return on imports is not much affected by inflation since their values rise with other prices. On the other hand, to the extent that Western currencies are held as reserves, CMEA runs a devaluation risk.

23. This is not the place to discuss in detail the factors determining the shapes and positions of the curves in Figure 1, including the possibilities of shifts in position over time.

24. We abstract here from the important fact that ECRs would be backed and used by CMEA as a group whereas securing credits is on an individual-country basis. Clearly, under an ECR system, the financially weaker CMEA nations would benefit relatively to the financially stronger, who actually might lose.

25. H. Grubel, 'The Distribution of Seignorage from International Liquidity Creation', in R. Mundell and A. K. Swoboda (eds), *Monetary Problems of the International Economy* (Chicago, 1968); Ronald I. McKinnon, *Private and Official International Money: The Case for the Dollar,* Essays in International Finance No. 74 (Princeton, 1969).

26. It is probably more correct to say that the country suffered from commodity inconvertibility than that commodity inconvertibility was a characteristic of the currency—for even holders of gold and dollars could not freely purchase products, particularly intermediate products, in CMEA countries, because of the havoc this would wreak on the central plans.

27. V. F. Garbuzov, 'The Development of Currency and Financial Relations of Comecon Member Nations', in *Soviet and East European Foreign Trade* (Summer 1973), translated from *Ekonomicheskaia gazeta,* No. 7 (1973), pp. 76–7.

28. *Comprehensive Programme for the Further Extension and Improvement of Cooperation and the Development of Socialist Economic Integration by the CMEA Member Countries,* Section 7, Article 3 (CMEA Secretariat, Moscow, 1971).

29. At this point, it should be noted that, at least until the recent rapid increase in world prices, the 'adjusted world prices' used by CMEA were substantially higher than real world prices.

30. Holzman (1974) as in Note 6, Chapters 10, 13, 14.

31. Iu. Ivanov, 'Matrichnoe opisanie sistemy natsional'nykh schetov i balansa narodnogo khoziaistva', *Vestnik Statistiki* No. 5 (1968), pp. 51–60.

32. By extension of the above logic, it can be argued that any multilateralism introduced into CMEA trade by IBEC credits in TRs should not be attributed to the inherent qualities of the TRs.

33. *East-West Trade News* (15 May 1975), p. 4.

34. Holzman (1974) as in Note 6, pp. 687–8; Chapter 1 of this book.

35. The smaller CMEA nations, with their higher trade participation ratios, are likely to be influenced relatively more by economic than by political factors in their preferences regarding foreign trade policies.

36. As in Note 5, p. 206.

37. Janos Fekete, *Some Reflections on International Monetary Problems and East-West Economic Relations* (Budapest, 1975).

38. Mme Lavigne says that coordination has been largely bilateral thus far (Marie Lavigne, *The Socialist Economies of the Soviet Union and Europe* [White Plains, New York, 1970]).

39. Nazarkin, as in Note 11, p. 47.

40. Iu. Konstantinov, 'Increasing the Role of the Transferable Ruble', *Problems of Economics*, translated from *Economicheskaia gazeta* (1975): 8.

41. Reprinted in Holzman (1974), as in Note 6, Chapter 6.

42. Mme Lavigne says that this proposal seems to be currently under consideration (*op. cit.*, pp. 315–316).

Part Four
INTRABLOC TRADE

9

Comecon:
A "Trade-Destroying"
Customs Union?

Introduction

The great advance in static customs-union theory since World War II was the demonstration by Viner that the formation of a customs union could lead not only to trade creation but to trade diversion as well. Trade creation occurs when the lowering of trade barriers between partners enables one partner to supply the other partner with products it previously produced for itself. Trade diversion refers to the increase in trade between partners at the expense of third nations, which nations, though the lowest-cost producers, lose their markets as a result of tariff discrimination. In this paper, we introduce a third category, trade destruction, to be described below.

Nations are motivated to form customs unions by both political and economic factors. In some instances, the former dominate, in others the latter. Where economic factors are dominant, one would expect to find more trade creation and less trade diversion; where political factors dominate, the probability is greater that the balance would lie in the other direction. This should not be taken to exclude the possibility, of course, that two nations with the most to gain economically (politically) to form a customs union may also be very strongly motivated by political (economic) considerations.

The trade-creation–trade-diversion dichotomy is based on a view of the world in which there is a reasonable trade-off spectrum between political and economic factors within the relevant range and which does not usually envisage extreme situations in which political factors are so strong as to lead to a customs union in which the static economic effects

Reprinted with permission from *Journal of Comparative Economics* 9 (December 1985): 410–423. Copyright © 1985 by the Academic Press, Inc.

are extremely negative. Within the traditional framework, of course, the overall economic effects would be negative if the gains from trade creation are smaller than the losses from trade diversion. In terms of this analysis, the limiting case is that of pure trade diversion with no trade creation. In this paper,[1] it is argued that, in the case of Comecon (or CMEA), economic opportunities for trade were so poor that there may have been no trade creation and that, in the case of Eastern Europe, trade may in fact have been reduced. This could happen under two possible circumstances (for reasons that are noted below): the nation finds either that it is cheaper to produce some products at home than to import them from its partner or that the price of some products is so high and income so much reduced within the union that consumption (imports) declines.

The effects noted above are demonstrated diagrammatically, using both partial and general equilibrium representations. In each instance, we consider two cases, one that assumes the use of tariffs or tariff equivalents, the other that does not, a more realistic view of Comecon practice, in my opinion.

1. The Model

According to the usual conventions, S_d and D_m represent the home nation's supply and demand curves for importables; A and B are the supply curves of exports of third nation A and partner B, respectively, and are drawn to reflect the assumption that the home nation is a price taker on imports (see Fig. 1). A_t and B_t are the same supply curves including uniform tariffs which are totally removed from B's exports after the customs union is formed. Since we assume partial equilibrium, changes in trade policy do not affect S_d and D_m. Welfare is measured by areas under S_d and D_m from which the cost of imports (to the nation, not to the consumer) must be subtracted.

Before the customs union is formed, the price to the consumer is OA_t, and MN is imported from A at a cost OA to the nation. Formation of the union lowers the consumer price, OA_t to OB, increases imports to RS, and raises the import cost price to the nation to OB. This involves a gain through trade creation of $\frac{1}{2}BA_t(RM + NS)$ and a loss through trade diversion of $MN \times AB$. The traditional limiting case occurs if B's supply curve is B', infinitesimally below A_t. Under these circumstances there would be no change in the volume of trade with the formation of the customs union and therefore no trade creation; the loss from trade diversion would be $MN \times AB'$.

It's a simple and logical step to carry the analysis further by postulating a partner with supply curve B'', higher than A_t.[2] Under the

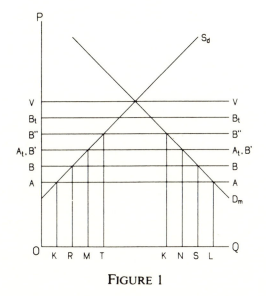

FIGURE 1

usual assumptions, the formation of a customs union would lead to no change in trade since, even with tariff, A's goods enter the importing nation's market at a lower price than B's goods without tariff. But suppose the importing nation, at the same time that it forms a customs union with B (removing the tariff on imports from B), either raises its tariff on A's goods so that A_t is now higher than B'', or, alternatively, excludes A's goods by use of quotas or other such controls. In this case, not only would there be trade diversion, there would also be trade destruction—a decline in the volume of trade to TK. In effect, the importing nation finds that some commodities (MT) which it had formerly imported from A can now be produced at home at a lower cost than if purchased from partner B; other imports (KN) cost so much to purchase from B or produce at home that they are no longer consumed. The losses from trade diversion and destruction, respectively, are $TK \times AB''$ and $(AA_t + \frac{1}{2}A_tB'')(MT + KN)$. It is also worth noting that the losses per unit of trade from trade diversion increase when the conditions favoring trade destruction prevail.

The analysis so far is taken to apply to the Eastern European nations after World War II, all of which experienced a reduction in trade relative to the prewar period. The Soviet Union, however, experienced an increase in trade once it began to trade with the nations of Eastern Europe after World War II. It could be argued, therefore, that the formation of Comecon led to trade creation in the case of the USSR. This would have given the USSR some economic motivation toward forming a customs union with Eastern Europe after the War whereas Eastern Europe had no such motivation, of course.

The existence of trade creation in the Soviet case was due to very special circumstances, namely, that, before World War II, the Soviets were almost completely autarkic. The ratio of imports to GNP had reached a peak of approximately 4–5% of GNP in the early thirties then declining to approximately 0.5% in the late 1930s. Such extreme protectionism involved, in effect, an enormous amount of trade destruction. If Eastern Europe is to be viewed as shifting its imports under Comecon from A_t to B'', the USSR may be viewed as follows. In the early thirties they traded with the world at A_t. Then they increased their protective-tariff equivalent to A'_t (not shown) which fell, say, between B'' and B_t and which reduced trade to less than TK. Formation of Comecon shifted the foreign supply of imports from A'_t to B'' increasing the trade to TK. Had the Soviets traded normally with the world at, say, A_t in the prewar period, forming a customs union with Eastern Europe would have involved for them also trade destruction rather than trade creation. Trading with Eastern Europe at B'' in preference to trading with the West at A_t (or at A—see below) was, as we shall see, most disadvantageous to the USSR, probably resulting in a near maximum of trade diversion and a minimum of trade creation.

The preceding analysis implicitly assumes that when CMEA was formed, its member nations operated like market economies. It further assumes that all had tariffs on imports both from each other and from non-CMEA nations or that they had quotas that had an impact on internal prices equal to that of tariffs which provided equivalent protection. Introducing a quota will usually lead to a rise in domestic price equal to that of an equivalent tariff to the consumer but not necessarily to an equivalent rise in cost to the country. Should foreign suppliers have direct access to final consumers, they may well be able to raise their prices to the full extent that excess demand dictates, thereby making excess profits and raising the costs of importing to the country levying the quota. If, on the other hand, the importing is assigned to a few favored licensees, they may be able to bargain for part or all of the excess profits created by the quota, thereby lessening or eliminating the adverse shift in the importer's terms of trade.

The case of the centrally planned economy (CPE), in my opinion, is one in which the terms of trade do not shift against the importing nation. CPEs do not levy tariffs or impose explicit quotas—these techniques for controlling imports are unnecessary since government foreign trade organizations (FTOs) handle all trade in accordance with government economic plans, which can be viewed as embodying implicit quotas. Now, when a CPE decides to reduce such a quota, while this may reduce the available supply of the product relative to the final demand for the product, it does not usually have an impact on the terms of trade. Internal and external markets are completely separated from one another. In the foreign-trade negotiations, the FTO offers to buy less. This appears to the exporter as a decline in demand by the importer. Unless the supply curve is infinitely elastic, the result may be improvement rather than deterioration in terms of trade. Furthermore, there is rarely any connection between internal and foreign-trade prices—changes in quantities of imports rarely affect internal prices, especially in the USSR.[3] In fact, the relationships between quantities and prices rarely conform to supply and demand forces because of the widespread prevalence of both repressed inflation and structural disequilibria in CPE internal commodity markets. Finally, even if internal prices sometimes were changed with changes in quantities imported and were different from the prices at which products were imported, planners' decisions regarding imports would be based on the costs to them of the imports, not on the internal prices.

At the time that trade among the future CMEA nations began to increase, it is not absolutely clear, except in the case of the USSR, whether the market model with tariffs and tariff equivalents or the CPE model more accurately described foreign-trade behavior. By February 1948, when Czechoslovakia entered the fold, all of the Eastern nations had become politically part of the Communist bloc. And, from what I've been able to gather, by the end of 1948, they had all nationalized much of their economies and were conducting foreign trade as sketched in the preceding paragraph. Certainly, within another year or two—and thereafter—all vestiges of the market model must have disappeared.

To represent more accurately the CPE model, assume in Fig. 1, as before, that *A* and *B* represent the export supply curves of third nation A and partner B, respectively. Assume the importing nation trades with the cheaper source, country A, to the full extent dictated by profits. In this case, *KL* would be imported at price *OA* to the home country. Formation of a customs union with B would be implemented by quotas against A's products; profitable trade, at home country price *OB*, would be reduced to *RS*. This would involve trade diversion of *AB* × *RS*, trade destruction of $\frac{1}{2}AB(KR + SL)$, and no trade creation. Without removal or reduction of tariffs from the partner's supply curve, there can be no positive consumption (trade creation) effects.

This is not, of course, a totally realistic scenario because, from the very outset, trade would probably have been subject to a quota less than *KL*. This would probably not have affected the home country cost of imports, however, which would be *OA*. The formation of a customs union with B would raise the purchase price to *OB* reflecting the higher

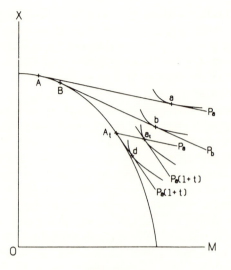

FIGURE 2

real costs of imports. Quotas would continue to control imports with B but would undoubtedly be smaller than quotas with A, reflecting the higher costs of importing.

Both sets of results presented above can also be demonstrated on a general equilibrium production-possibilities diagram. Since this type of diagram allows the income effects of the worsened terms of trade that result from the formation of the customs union, trade tends to be reduced even more rapidly than in the previous cases. Examine first the market-tariff model in Fig. 2. Before the customs union is formed, the home country produces at A_t because of the tariff and through trade with A at external prices, P_a, reaches a_t. Formation of a customs union with B worsens the home country's external terms of trade (from P_a to P_b), but due to the shift in the internal terms of trade from P_a $(1 + t)$ to P_b, domestic output and exports of X are increased. Simultaneously, consumption effects of the lower price of imports leads to an increase in imports and in consumption of M. The nation moves from point a_t to point b as trade creation dominates trade diversion.

To the extent that country B is a less appropriate trading partner with which to form a union than diagrammed in Fig. 2, P_b would be represented by a steeper slope. Should P_b be steep enough that point b falls somewhat to the left of point a_t, then consumption and eventually imports of M will be less than in the pre-customs-union situation and imports will have been "destroyed." In comparison with the Fig. 1 analysis, this will have been due to the inclusion of terms-of-trade income effects. As P_b becomes still steeper, production and exports of X decline, imports of M decline and output of M rises. By the time P_b is as steep as P_a $(1 + t)$ (the point at which trade destruction begins in Fig. 1), trade will be at point d with considerable trade destruction relative to point a_t which is due to the rising output of M along with declining consumption and imports of M due to the price and income effects of poorer terms of trade.

Assume now, as in the second part of the discussion relating to Fig. 1, that trade is regulated by explicit quotas and is transacted at prices exclusive of tariffs or tariff-equivalent prices. In the absence of a customs union, the home country would trade with A at point a if trade were carried to its profitable limits. If the decision were made to form a customs union with B, then trade would shift from point a to point b. This would represent a reduction (destruction) in trade of both X and M; more M is produced at home and less is imported. Admitting that trade would not be carried to its profitable limits in either case, the presumption is that quotas on imports would be reduced because of lower profitability as the shift was made from trading with A to trading with B and, as before, quotas would not affect terms of trade.[4]

To sum up, the conditions outlined above, which make trade destruction possible, do not usually arise when Western customs unions are formed. Minor exceptions may occur for individual nations when members adopt a common average tariff against nonmembers but these exceptions are not likely to amount to much. The formation and existence of CMEA, on the other hand, is a case that, in my opinion, may have resulted in considerable trade destruction especially for Eastern Europe and certainly resulted, in the very least, in much greater trade diversion than trade creation.[5] While it is not possible to demonstrate these assertions rigorously we briefly provide some evidence in their support in Sections 3 and 4 below. Two kinds of evidence are adduced: changes in the country structure of Eastern trade[6] and changes in Eastern trade-participation ratios.

2. Further Comments on the Model

Before turning to the evidence, some related issues need to be considered. First, in conformity with the usual practice, the preceding analysis assumes implicitly that international trade is an exchange of goods purchased by final users but not of intermediate products, machinery and equipment, or other products which enter into the production processes in the importing nations. To the extent that intermediate products, etc., are imported, then a possible impact of a customs union is to be seen not just through the changes in welfare that result from changes in the terms of trade—but also in the shape and magnitude of the production-possibilities curve itself. So, the formation of a highly trade-diverting and trade-destroying customs union would lead to a reduction in potential GNP, i.e., would lead to a shrinking of the production-possibilities curve as well as a showing up of its growth over time, as a result of losses of imports important in the production process as well as from the lower quality and technology of imports still available through diversion. These losses, it should be noted, would fall more heavily on the smaller CMEA nations because of their greater dependence on foreign trade, and least heavily on the Soviet Union.[7]

Second, the diagrams and related discussion in Section 1 have been assumed to apply equally to all of the CMEA nations. It has also been assumed that trade with Western nations took place at world prices. These assumptions are not in accordance with the facts. From the formation of CMEA until at least the difficulties in 1956 in Hungary and Poland, the Soviet Union exercised political power to trade with the Eastern European nations at very favorable terms of trade to itself. In fact, the ex-enemy Eastern nations were exploited ruthlessly (and this includes exploitation via deliveries of reparations). This means that the losses from CMEA trade diversion fell much more heavily on Eastern Europe in this period than they did on the Soviet Union. On the other hand, the losses from trade diversion experienced by the USSR and Eastern Europe alike were reduced by the fact that they were unable to trade with Western nations at world prices but were, in fact, discriminated against (see Holzman, 1962 and 1965) once they became part of the Soviet bloc. Discrimination took many forms, which affected the costs of trade, including lack of MFN status with regard to tariffs and quotas, special Western discriminatory licensing arrangements, bureaucratic delays, treatment as marginal suppliers and customers, and so forth. Since as members of the Soviet bloc, trade with the West had become less profitable, the losses from trade diversion were also lower.

The situation has been different since the late fifties and early sixties and much different since 1973. Apparently in the late fifties, the Soviet Union stopped using political power to extract extra gains from trade with Eastern Europe which caused the losses from trade diversion to be less than before for Eastern Europe and even more so for the USSR. Then, as time passed, and as détente replaced cold war, Western discrimination against the CMEA nations was gradually reduced, increasing the terms-of-trade losses from diversion for all Eastern nations. At the same time, however, in reaction to this fact and to the changes in the political climate that caused it, trade with the West increased sharply, in effect reducing the quantity of trade diversion. Since 1973, Soviet terms of trade with Eastern Europe have improved but terms of trade with the West have improved much more sharply, which resulted in Soviet terms-of-trade losses from having to trade with other CMEA members (i.e., trade diversion), losses which represent gains to the other CMEA members.[8]

A final point on trade destruction as well as on high levels of trade diversion is that nations that form customs unions involving these two categories of change are likely to be in a relatively polarized political situation. That is to say, nations are unlikely to undertake a union that involves significant economic losses in the absence of strong political motivations. Such motivations certainly characterized the Soviet Union after World War II and, of course, the new Eastern satellites had little choice but to go along with Soviet policy. While intra-CMEA trade still, no doubt, involves considerable trade diversion (e.g., buying more of each other's machinery than of Western machinery), it seems doubtful that much, if any, trade destruction remains. CMEA nations now have little hesitation about buying commodities from the West that are unavailable in the bloc. The major exceptions to this are security-related. For example, it could be argued that the Soviet Union might produce less grain and import more if a member of CMEA could meet its needs. In light of its internal difficulties in agriculture, the huge Soviet investment in that sector betrays an unwillingness to be any more dependent on imports of feed from the West than is necessary (see Holzman, 1984).

3. Change in the Structure of Trade

A major proposition of customs-union theory is that the greater the percentage of trade between nations before the formation of the union, the lower probability that a union will lead to trade diversion (Lipsey, 1968). This proposition is easy to understand if one thinks of a union between two nations conducting 90% of their trade with each other beforehand: if there is to be a significant increase in trade between partners, it would have to come about through trade creation since there is very little to divert. On the other hand, if one envisages a union between nations that conduct 5% of their trade with each other, even a doubling of trade with each other through 100% trade creation would only increase total trade by 5% and leave the percentage of trade with each other at 9½%! Any substantial increase in intraunion trade is bound to involve trade diversion. Presumably, the two nations are not naturally suited to conduct much trade with each other and so they import most products they need from third nations. Formation of a union is more likely to divert goods from third nations than to create new trade between such obviously ill-suited partners.

Trade among CMEA nations would appear to fall into the latter category: they traded very little with each other before World War II

TABLE 1

SOVIET AND EAST EUROPEAN IMPORTS: 1928, 1938, 1950, 1953
(PERCENTAGE OF TOTAL IMPORTS)

	1928	1938	1950	1953
Eastern European imports from Eastern Europe	18.7	15.7	31.1	30.7
Eastern European imports from USSR	2.1	1.6	33.9	41.2
Total Eastern European Imports from CMEA	20.8	17.3	65.0	71.9
Soviet imports from Eastern Europe	11.8	5.5	59.1	61.0

Source. Holzman (1976, p. 70). (Figures for 1928 were not included in Holzman's book but were available from the same sources.)

as the estimates in Table 1 indicate. Eastern European imports from each other approximately double in relative importance almost overnight as the Soviet Bloc is formed; Eastern European trade with the USSR increases its relative importance by from 10- to 20-fold (depending on which year is used as a base). In contrast, the EEC started out in 1959 with an intratrade percentage of roughly 35 and reached approximately 70 in the 1970s at which time barriers had been virtually eliminated. Obviously, the economic basis for the union in the case of the EEC was much stronger to begin with than that for the CMEA. It is significant that the percentage of intra-CMEA trade has declined since the 1953 peak and at present is about 50, still far higher than before World War II.

On the basis of the above data, one can reasonably infer that in the early years, at least, the tremendous increase in percentage of intra-CMEA trade must have involved primarily diversion from trade with the West rather than trade creation. And, in fact, Wilczynski (1969, p. 54) estimates that socialist nations' trade with the nonsocialist world fell from 73.8% of its total trade in 1938 to 14% in 1953—evidence of enormous diversion. These figures are consistent with those presented in Table 1.

These conclusions are supported inferentially in a study published by Hewett (1976). He constructed a so-called gravity model using 1970 trade flows between 19 nations including the 7 CMEA nations and 12 advanced Western nations, all members of either EEC or EFTA. Trade flows were made a function of GNPs, populations, and distances between nations with dummy variables for each communist country plus dummy variables to capture the effects of the three preferential trade systems:

CMEA, EEC, and EFTA. He found that the trade of the CMEA nations with EEC-EFTA was far below what one would normally expect, ranging from 11 to 30% of "typical" trade. On the other hand, trade among CMEA nations tended to be higher than trade between "similar western countries if they were not members of a western customs union." (Hewett, p. 9). However, with some exceptions, intra-CMEA trade was lower than trade between similar Western nations after taking the impact on member trade of EEC and EFTA into account.

The relatively high (for CMEA) levels of trade with each other among the Eastern nations is attributed by Hewett to CMEA's preferential arrangements. He finds that, whereas intra-EEC and intra-EFTA trade were 1.42 and 2.35 times greater, respectively, than they would have been in the absence of preferential arrangements, intra-CMEA trade was almost 20 times greater than it would have been.[9] Hewett suggests that the CMEA coefficient is biased upward by the fact that it measures the intensity of intra-CMEA trade in comparison with the very depressed trade of its members with EEC and EFTA. If one allowed for this so-called bias, the CMEA effect would still be high—in the neighborhood of 4. However, if CMEA preferential treatment involves not only reducing or eliminating barriers to intra-CMEA trade but also raising barriers to East-West trade (as I argued earlier), then a coefficient of 20 for CMEA might truly reflect its relative intensity (subject to qualifications elaborated below). That is, the depressed trade of CMEA with EEC-EFTA is not something that "biases" the results but is in itself in part a result of CMEA's raised barriers to trade with the West. Significantly, Hewett's results are for 1970 after East-West European trade had moved a good way toward normalization.

4. Changes in Trade Participation Ratios (TPRs)

Pure trade diversion would leave TPRs unchanged and trade creation would increase them; by the same logic, net trade destruction would decrease them. All other things being equal, calculation of TPRs would seem to be the most direct method available of determining what kind of "customs union" CMEA is. There are, however, several problems with this approach. First, the year 1928 is the last "normal" year for which data are available for the Eastern countries for comparison with the early postwar period. This is a long period, indeed. Second, there are no reliable TPRs for these years.[10] Third, the lowness of Eastern TPRs right after World War II partly reflects disruption from the war. Fourth, the Soviet Union barely traded at all before World War II. In a sense, one could almost say that, relative to the late 1930s, any trade engaged in by the USSR was trade creation. What we assume here is that the USSR had, right after the war and ever since, opportunities, despite Western export controls, to expand trade with the West which were not taken and which were, in effect, either diverted toward Eastern Europe or "destroyed."

As a substitute for reliable trade-participation ratios, there are available two suggestive studies by Pryor and the above-cited paper by Hewett. In his first study, Pryor (1963, p. 27) concluded that, in 1955, the trade of each Eastern nation, including the USSR, was below its "potential" level by 50% or more. "Potential" level was based (1) on a regression of Chenery's (1960) which related trade per capita to per capita national income and to population for 60 nations and (2) on another regression by Pryor himself which related per capita trade to per capita industrial production and population for 8 comparable West European nations. In a later study (Pryor, 1968) which included the 7 CMEA nations and 21 developed West European and North American nations, Pryor made trade a function of GNP, population, and a dummy variable standing for Western Europe for the years 1928, 1956, and 1962. The results showed no statistically significant difference between East and West for 1928, whereas for the postwar years, trade of the Eastern nations was 50–60% of that of comparable Western nations.

Hewett's (1976) calculations for 1970 are consistent with Pryor's. He found that "typical eastern foreign trade is, ceteris paribus, much lower than typical western trade. . . ." (p. 8).

5. Some Caveats

It could be argued that the high percentage of intra-CMEA trade has been due not to barriers imposed by CMEA but at least in part to East-West trade barriers imposed by the Western industrial nations. There is certainly merit to this argument and there is no question but that Western controls have led to greater intra-CMEA trade than would otherwise have taken place. Several pieces of evidence lend support, however, to the position taken in this note that CMEA as well as Western controls have been responsible for the low level of East-West trade. Wilczynski (1969, p. 46) has calculated intrasocialist[11] trade figures for 1948, a year before Western controls (except for those of the United States) were in effect to any extent. He found that intrasocialist trade increased from 12.8% of total in 1938 to 44.4% in 1948 (and to 79.6% in 1953). Most of this increase must have been due to Eastern (Soviet), not Western, controls.[12] Further evidence is provided by the fact that in 1947, the USSR, Poland, and Czechoslovakia were offered the opportunity of participating in the U.S. financed Marshall Plan aid, an offer that was eventually rejected by all three as a result of Soviet pressure. Nevertheless, the projections made by Marshall Plan participants assumed "substantial and steady resumption of the flow of the principal goods from the East, reaching prewar levels in some important categories by 1952" (Dieboldt, 1948, p. 715). At the same time, however:

> The chief special factor affecting the trade of Eastern European countries is the Soviet Union's great need for goods of all kinds for reconstruction. Partly as reparations, partly as ordinary commercial exchange, partly as politically dictated trade, much larger quantities of Eastern European goods are going to the Soviet Union than before the War . . . increased trade among themselves were already parts of the economic plans of all the Eastern countries before the Marshall Plan was announced. (Dieboldt, 1948, pp. 711–712)

It could also be argued that the evidence of low trade-participation ratios presented above results not from trade destruction but from trade aversion which is generally believed to be a by-product of central planning with direct controls. This is undoubtedly partly true—but so far no one has been able to demonstrate convincingly which of several possible causes is most important in having kept Communist trade for at least two decades much below optimum levels. The data are, at least, consistent with the hypothesis of trade destruction, if they do not provide unambiguous support for it.

Notes

1. I am indebted to Drusilla Brown and Padma Desai for helpful suggestions in writing this paper. The basic ideas of this paper were first presented in the spring of 1966 at Professor Henri Chambre's seminar at the Ecole Pratique des Hautes Etudes of the Sorbonne. Several years later, all drafts were lost (along with several other manuscripts) when my office at Tufts University was destroyed in a fire. The paper was not rewritten until a few years ago.

2. A less extreme assumption would have sufficed had we let AA and BB be rising supply curves.

3. Evidence on this is presented in Holzman (1970).

4. For convenience of exposition, the preceding analysis based on Fig. 2 has made implicit assumptions that price lines are tangent to the production possibility frontier and to collective indifference curves. This is not true of market economies and, a fortiori, of centrally planned economies. The results would not likely be changed significantly, in my opinion, by attempting to diagram the trade according to more realistic assumptions. That this would be the case is, I hope, suggested by the evidence presented in Sections 3 and 4.

5. CMEA is not ordinarily thought of as a customs union since trade among its members is not governed by usual market mechanisms and because implicit quantitative controls rather than tariffs are the sole Eastern barriers that keep trade with the West at low levels. Nevertheless, in terms of its results, as well as for purely analytical purposes, it is useful to think of CMEA in customs-union terms. It is also worth noting that while CMEA is referred to here as the agency that orchestrates Soviet bloc trade, it functioned little if at all until at least the mid 1950s. Until that time, the Soviet Union largely dictated the trade policies of CMEA members directly and, when we refer to CMEA's activities in this early period, it is with this in mind.

Finally, while reference here is primarily to the period in which CMEA was formed, the analysis is meant to apply, although to a lesser extent, to later periods when intra-CMEA trade had expanded significantly. We can say, in effect, that if CMEA members were to eliminate all discriminatory practices in trade and this led to a shift in trade toward the West as well as to an increase in total trade (i.e., trade creation), then it could be inferred that the failure to dismantle discriminating trade controls implies that these controls result in trade destruction.

6. Change in country structure of trade cannot provide direct evidence of trade destruction. However, if one views the effects of a normal customs union as falling along a spectrum that ranges from all trade creation to all trade diversion, the more (less) the evidence of conditions that might lead to trade diversion in CMEA, the greater (lesser) probability that net trade destruction might also have resulted.

7. These points were first made in Holzman, 1962, p. 146. See also Holzman, 1976, p. 86.

8. These are the so-called Marrese-Vanous (1983) studies. For discussions of the nature of these subsidies, see Brada (1985), Holzman (1984), and Chapters 10 and 11 below.

9. Hewett notes (p. 8) that normally one would expect the EEC effect to be greater than that of EFTA. He suggests several possible explanations for this counterintuitive result.

10. Ernst (1966, p. 900) provides calculations for Eastern Europe of import/GNP ratios for six East European nations. Estimates are presented for prewar (1936–1939), 1950, 1955, 1960, and 1964. A major problem with these estimates is that all are based on "constant 1963 dollars" and it is not clear what impact on the ratios such a valuation procedure has. For what they are worth, the ratios in 1950 and 1955 are equal to or slightly higher than prewar. However, it is well known that trade-participation ratios in the late 1930s were no more than one-half those in the late 1920s before the depression. In light of this, it is safe to conclude that Ernst's data show trade-participation ratios not achieving "normal" prewar levels until at least 1960. Moreover, since trade-participation ratios of virtually all Western nations have increased in the postwar period, one might well have achieved much higher trade-participation ratios by the 1960s than in 1928.

11. Including the Asian as well as European socialist nations.

Comecon: A "Trade-Destroying" Customs Union?

185

12. Wilczynski (1969, pp. 47–50). This was also Abram Bergson's opinion in 1964 (as cited by Adler-Karlsson, 1968, p. 162). In his final published volume, Joseph Stalin ([1952]1972, pp. 30, 31) says that "the single all-embracing world market disintegrated, so that we now have two parallel world markets . . . confronting one another." While he admits that the Western blockade is partly responsible, he attributes much credit to "the fact that since the war these [eastern] countries have joined together economically and established economic cooperation and mutual assistance."

References

Adler-Karlsson, Gunnar, *Western Economic Warfare, 1947–1967.* Stockholm, 1968.
Ausch, Sandor, *The Theory and Practice of CMEA Cooperation.* Budapest, 1972.
Brada, Josef C., "Soviet Subsidization of Eastern Europe: The Primacy of Economics over Politics." *J. Comp. Econ.* 9:80–92, Mar. 1985.
Chenery, Hollis, "Patterns of Industrial Growth." *Amer. Econ. Rev.* 50:624–654, Sept. 1960.
Desai, Padma, "Is the Soviet Union Subsidizing Eastern Europe?" *Europ. Econ. Rev.,* 29 (1985):107–116.
Dieboldt, William, "East–West Trade and the Marshall Plan." *Foreign Aff.* 26:704–722, July 1948.
Ernst, Maurice, "Postwar Economic Growth in Eastern Europe." In *New Directions in the Soviet Economy,* pp. 873–916. Papers, Joint Econ. Comm., U.S. Congress. Washington, D.C.: U.S. Govt. Printing Office, 1966.
Hewett, Edward, "A Gravity Model of CMEA Trade." In Josef C. Brada, ed., *Quantitative and Analytical Studies in East–West Economic Relations,* pp. 1–16. Bloomington, Ind.: Int. Dev. Res. Center, Indiana Univ., 1976.
Holzman, Franklyn D., "Soviet Foreign Trade Pricing and the Question of Discrimination: A Customs Union Approach. *Rev. Econ. Statist.* 134–147, May 1962.
Holzman, Franklyn D., "More on Soviet Discrimination." *Sov. Stud.* 44–65, July 1965.
Holzman, Franklyn D., "On the Technique of Comparing Trade Barriers of Products Imported by Capitalist and Communist Nations." *Europ. Econ. Rev.* 2:3–22, Fall 1970.
Holzman, Franklyn D., *International Trade under Communism: Politics and Economics.* New York: Basic Books, 1976.
Holzman, Franklyn D., "The Burden of Soviet Security: Military Spending, Agricultural Self-Sufficiency, and Trade Diversion in CMEA." Mimeo, 1984.
Lipsey, R. G., "The Theory of Customs Unions: A General Survey." In Richard Caves and H. Johnson, eds., *Readings in International Economics* (AEA), pp. 261–280. Homewood, Ill.: Irwin, 1968.
Marrese, Michael, and Vanous, Jan, *Soviet Subsidization of Trade with Eastern Europe.* Berkeley: Univ. of Calif. Press, 1983.
Pryor, Frederic L., *The Communist Foreign Trade System.* Cambridge, Mass: MIT Press, 1963.

Pryor, Frederic L., "Discussion." In Alan Brown and E. Neuberger, eds., *International Trade and Central Planning*. Berkeley: Univ. of Calif. Press, 1968.
Stalin, J. V., *Economic Problems of Socialism*. (Reprint of 1952 Soviet English edition.) Peking: For. Lang. Press, 1972.
Wilczynski, Josef, *The Economics and Politics of East–West Trade*. London: Macmillan, 1969.

10

The Significance
of Soviet Subsidies
to Eastern Europe

It is generally accepted that for about two decades there have been implicit transfers from the USSR to Eastern Europe in intrabloc trade. These result from differences in terms of trade among product groups in intrabloc and East-West trade, respectively. That is to say, the USSR exports petroleum and other raw materials to Eastern Europe at less than world prices and buys machinery and other manufactured products from Eastern Europe at higher than world prices. Marrese and Vanous (1983) interpret these transfers as implicit subsidy payments by the USSR to Eastern Europe in return for the military and political cooperation supplied by the latter. While few have questioned the existence of such transfers (but see Marer, 1984), questions have been raised by several writers regarding their magnitude and interpretation. I shall be concerned here only with interpretation. In part I, on the assumption that Marrese and Vanous are correct that the USSR has been transferring subsidies to other CMEA members, I propose two alternative reasons for the subsidies. In part II, it is argued that what appear to be subsidies are not such and that the statistical results that Marrese and Vanous measure are reflections of the fact that CMEA has many of the characteristics of a highly autarkic customs union. Evidence is presented to support the customs union interpretation over that of subsidies. In section III, a method is proposed by which it should be possible to test conclusively whether the subsidy or the customs union hypothesis is the correct explanation of the data.

Reprinted with permission from *Comparative Economic Studies* 28, 1 (Spring 1986): 54–65.

I. Other Possible Purposes of the "Subsidies"

If Marrese and Vanous (hereafter M-V) are right in arguing that the transfers are a subsidy payment for "something," I would like to propose two candidates in addition to Bloc military and political cooperation. First are the losses that all of the CMEA nations suffer from overtrading with each other and undertrading with the rest of the world, especially with the leading western industrial nations. Some of these losses are the kind that are identified as due to the trade diversion which results when nations not well-suited to trade with each other form a customs union. In the case of CMEA, the East European nations were forced by the USSR, in the late 1940s, to divert their trade away from their customary western European channels and to substitute trade with each other and especially with the USSR. The burden of trade diversion fell much more heavily on Eastern Europe than on the USSR because of the so much larger trade participation ratios of the nations of Eastern Europe (Holzman, 1962, p. 146).

It has been argued elsewhere (Holzman, 1985) that the CMEA nations were so unsuited to trade with each other and applied such restrictive controls over trade with the West that there were, in addition to losses from trade diversion, losses from trade destruction. That is, not only were imports more costly as a result of trade diversion, there were also many instances in which customary imports either had to be produced at home at still higher costs or consumption had to be foregone because the products were totally unavailable in CMEA or available only at prohibitive prices.

Losses from trade diversion and trade destruction are likely to be viewed and measured statically but they do in fact cause dynamic losses as well. To the extent that nations are unable to import intermediate products at all or intermediate products of as high quality as before, future output is reduced. Further, the unavailability in CMEA of many products including numerous high quality machinery and equipment inputs has made it necessary for each CMEA nation to change its output and export structure to conform to the needs of other CMEA nations. This has often been difficult and costly to accomplish and has resulted in every nation getting lower quality goods through trade. Moreover, since production for export, particularly in the machinery and equipment area, is geared to lower quality markets than would otherwise be the case, and to lesser competitive pressures, there is little incentive to quality improvement.[1]

I think it could be argued that if the M-V terms of trade transfers can, in fact, be interpreted as subsidies, they may represent, in part at least, compensation for economic losses imposed on Eastern Europe by forced participation in CMEA.

Second, I believe that the substantial increase in subsidies that resulted from the natural resource (mainly oil) price increases after 1973 and again after 1979 are due to entirely different factors from those mentioned above. M-V recognize this fact now and refer to the increases as "unplanned" subsidies. They were unplanned and resulted from the fact that when oil and other raw material prices were raised sharply in the world markets, the CMEA prices did not rise at first because of the nature of CMEA pricing formulas. This conferred windfall gains on other CMEA members at the expense of the USSR. As is well-known, the windfall losses experienced by the USSR were viewed as sufficiently large that a new pricing formula was adopted with the apparent purpose of gradually, but more rapidly than before, phasing out the "unplanned" subsidies. The question which must be asked is why in 1974, the USSR did not demand a pricing formula which would have resulted in the immediate elimination of the so-called unplanned subsidies. I think the answer relates to the fact that had the whole burden of the price increases been shifted immediately onto Eastern Europe, the economies of some of these nations might have been sufficiently hurt as to have caused serious economic and internal political problems. In my opinion, it was this factor that led to the CMEA decision to change over gradually via a five-year moving average of prices.[2] The Soviets were in a good position to be generous in the short run and accept a gradual changeover because their windfall profits on oil and other energy exports to the West were so large, not to mention analogous profits from the rising price of gold and from increased sales of arms for hard currency to the Middle East. In effect, then, I feel that it is accurate to view these so-called unplanned subsidies as a form of non-repayable aid to help the other CMEA nations to weather both the severe adverse changes in terms of trade as well as the drop in hard currency exports that they were experiencing due to the 1970s recessions and slowed economic growth rates in the western industrialized nations.

The 1979 price rise put an additional strain on Eastern Europe and, in fact, several of the East European nations were, as a result, unable to balance their trade with the USSR. In consequence, the USSR was forced to grant credits to Eastern Europe, which show as trade surpluses and which amounted to over $10 billion from 1979 to 1982 (*Vnesh, Torg.*, various years). These loans are quite exceptional in CMEA experience, may not be repaid for a long time, if ever, and may represent a form of aid to Eastern Europe not unlike the below-world prices of petroleum, etc., imported from the USSR after 1973. Had the Soviets put more of the burden of higher oil and other raw material prices immediately on other CMEA countries, undoubtedly they would have had to extend to those nations still larger credits as a substitute.

II. A Customs Union Explanation

There is another possible interpretation particularly of pre-1973 M-V subsidies which is based on an argument made by this writer in 1962 in connection with allegations by Horst Mendershausen (1959, 1960) that the Soviet Union was exploiting Eastern Europe in their mutual trade relations, just the reverse of claims being made at present by M-V. Among other things, it was argued at that time (Holzman, 1962) that relative prices in intrabloc trade differed from world prices, and also from East-West trade prices because CMEA was, in that period, a relatively autarkic customs union with different scales of economic values from those in the West and whose prices did not tend to get equalized with world prices as is the case under free trade. IntraCMEA terms of trade have been and are, at present, quite consistent with such an interpretation. Marrese and Vanous have demonstrated that in intraCMEA trade machinery and equipment prices are higher and raw materials prices are lower than in world trade (see Table 1). Intuitively, it seems quite obvious that this could be due to the relatively large supply of raw materials in the Bloc (especially the USSR) and the relatively shorter supply of and lower efficiency in producing machinery and equipment and other sophisticated manufactured products. It could be argued, then, that the USSR has not been subsidizing CMEA but that the prices in intraCMEA trade simply reflect, among other things, the different economic conditions which prevail there.[3] Further, it is simply a coincidence that the Soviets happen to be net exporters of the products (raw materials) in which CMEA has a comparative advantage and net importers of the products in which CMEA has a comparative disadvantage and thereby loses on both counts.[4]

The only place, to my knowledge, that M-V explicitly consider the customs union effect is in a brief discussion of Holzman (1962) in their monograph (pp. 24–25). Here they dismiss, once and for all, the CU model. They argue, briefly, that conditions have changed since the 1950s and that the CU effect, if it ever existed, had become less important in the period covered by their analysis (1960–1980). This would have resulted from the relatively greater amount of East-West trade and corresponding reduced percentage of intraCMEA trade that developed in the latter period. While CMEA was (is) less insulated from world markets than it had been in the 1950s, it was (is) still insulated to a considerable extent in my opinion.

M-V attempt to belittle the CU effect in several different ways, all of which are wrong but only one of which need be discussed in this section. They claim that ". . . the custom-union effect formalized the common knowledge of that time—namely, even if *wmps* (world market prices) are applied to intraCMEA trade, it is only after they have been adjusted for undesirable elements such as temporary *wmp* fluctuations, monopoly effects, and other characteristics deemed 'unfair'" (p. 25). I agree that this was the common knowledge of that time—the statement was included in most Soviet textbooks on foreign trade. What sort of CU effect M-V had in mind is not clear, for on the face of it there is nothing in their summary of the "common knowledge" that suggests such an effect. My own interpretation at that time was that a world price would have been deemed "unfair" (or "unjust" as other writers put it) if that price were relatively much lower or higher for some commodity, relative to other commodities, than a price dictated by economic conditions within the Bloc. This interpretation was suggested to me originally by a United Nations source (p. 156) which paraphrased an argument that appeared in the Bulgarian foreign trade journal *Vnsha Torgovia*, 1956, #10: ". . . there was a tendency to base prices in trade among centrally planned economies on world prices adjusted to cost levels of the exporting country and to conditions in importing countries. . . ." I interpreted "conditions" to mean, in this context, "costs," "reservations prices," "values," and the like. What else could it have meant? This interpretation is consistent with a Czechoslovak source quoted by Smirnov (Liubimov, p. 331) to the effect that world prices must be adjusted so that intrabloc trade is "mutually profitable." So, for example, one could not expect a CMEA exporter to supply high technology equipment or quality TV sets to other CMEA countries at low American or Japanese prices.

The fact is, of course, that even absence of mention in CMEA sources of the existence of CU effects is, in any event, no reason to doubt their existence and their impact on CMEA pricing. As Brada put it: ". . . if the resource endowment of the integrating countries differs from the endowment of the rest of the world, then relative prices within the union will differ from relative prices on the world market . . ." (1985, p. 87).

Let us return now to the current argument. As noted above, data provided by M-V (p. 124), a sample of which is summarized in Table 1, indicate dramatically for the period 1960–1978 that prices were consistent with the customs union interpretation just presented. M-V argue, of course, that these data are consistent with their subsidy interpretation. While superficially this appears to be the case, in fact there are several grounds for questioning.

Table 1. Soviet Relative Foreign Trade Prices:
P_{CMEA}/P_{WEST}; Selected Years

	1967 Exports	1967 Imports	1972 Exports	1972 Imports	1977 Exports	1977 Imports
Machinery and equipment	1.65	1.37	1.68	1.27	2.17	1.27
Industrial consumer goods	1.19	1.17	1.82	1.13	2.51	1.11
All goods — average	1.00	1.00	1.00	1.00	1.00	1.00
Fuels	0.94	0.82	0.76	0.73	0.66	0.66
Non-food raw materials	0.84	0.64	0.84	0.70	0.90	0.64
Food and raw mat'ls for food	0.74	0.57	0.75	0.64	0.86	0.73

Source: Calculated from M-V, p. 124.

Note: Since the Soviets export to CMEA fewer high priced goods and more low priced goods than they import, the average import ratio, P_{CMEA}/P_{WEST} is higher than that for exports, a fact not obvious from the above figures since both average ratios have been set at 1.00. Nevertheless, this causes the import ratios for the five categories of goods listed above to be biased downward relative to the export ratios.

First, if one were to subscribe to the M-V subsidy argument, one would expect the Soviets to pay more for imports of machinery, etc., from and to receive less for exports of fuel, etc., to CMEA than to the West. But one would hardly expect offsetting subsidies to the USSR from CMEA for Soviet exports of machinery, etc., and imports of fuels and raw materials, etc. Nevertheless, this is exactly what the data in Table 1 show. Prices of machinery, etc., are higher than world prices whether the Soviets are importing or exporting them; and prices of fuels, etc., are lower than world prices whether the Soviets are exporting or importing them.

Moreover, these offsetting subsidies are not trivial. For example, in 1979, Soviet imports of machinery and equipment from socialist countries totaled 45.8 percent of total trade with these nations whereas the comparable export figure was 24.2 percent. In the case of "ores, concentrates, metals and their products" in 1979, the export proportion was 13.5 percent and the import proportion 5.6 percent. The balance is much more lopsided, of course, in fuels and electric energy and in industrial consumer goods, the Soviets having much larger export surpluses in the former and import surpluses in the latter. In total, Soviet gross subsidies to other CMEA may well have been reduced by a third or a fourth as a result of "subsidies" flowing in the other direction. Even more dramatic, the offsetting subsidies from Bulgaria and Romania to the USSR are larger during the pre-1973 period than Soviet subsidies to those nations; that is, by M-V measurement, these two nations subsidize the Soviet Union rather than vice versa. The implications of this fact are explored in our third point below.

This two-directional flow picture is more consistent with a customs union interpretation than with the M-V subsidy interpretation. Machinery is high-priced within CMEA, fuels and raw materials low-priced, regardless of who are the exporters and importers. If the subsidy theory were correct, it would be necessary to include in the rationale not just the net flow of subsidies as M-V do, but the gross flows in each direction as well. Certainly, the neat simplicity of the M-V theory is ruffled by recognition of the fact that so-called subsidies flow in both directions.

Second, as noted earlier, the Soviet subsidies are viewed as implicit payments for non-market, non-economic benefits received from the other CMEA nations in the form of military-political support. The greater the amount of support rendered, the larger the subsidies, so goes the argument. In the 1970–73 period, for example, per capita subsidies in constant 1970 dollars were estimated as follows (M-V, Table 7, page 50):[5]

Bulgaria	Czechosl.	E. Germ.	Hungary	Poland	Romania
2.4	11.2	24.8	14.2	5.2	1.0

By this measure, East Germany was the most cooperative nation and Romania least cooperative. Subsidies to East Germany, which were large, were accomplished by large Soviet net imports of machinery and equipment and industrial consumer goods and by large Soviet exports of fuels and raw materials (M-V, p. 174). On the other hand, the Soviets had an export (rather than import) surplus with Romania of machinery and equipment, no net fuel exports and only small net imports of industrial consumer goods and net exports of non-food raw materials.

This raises an interesting problem with which to confront M-V's implicit subsidy mechanism. Suppose that Romania were the most cooperative, and East Germany the least cooperative nation in the Warsaw Pact, how would the appropriate subsidies be implemented? Actually, there are two possible ways of implementing subsidies. One is by changing prices of exports and imports, the other by changing quantities. Let us look first at prices.

Table 2. Soviet Relative Foreign
Trade Prices, 1972:
$$P_{CMEA}/P_{WEST}$$

	Machinery & equipment	Industrial consumer goods	Fuels	Foods & raw mat'l for food	Non-food raw mat'l
Exports to:					
All CMEA	1.68	1.82	0.76	0.75	0.84
Bulgaria	1.70	1.78	0.70 (3)	—	0.81 (2)
Czechosl.	1.60	1.94	0.80 (4)	0.78 (2)	0.92 (6)
E. Germany	1.69	1.80	0.69 (2)	0.73 (1)	0.76 (1)
Hungary	1.76	1.72	0.92 (6)	0.78 (2)	0.87 (4)
Poland	1.66	1.86	0.80 (4)	—	0.80 (2)
Romania	1.59	1.91	0.57 (1)	—	0.90 (5)
Imports from:					
All CMEA	1.27	1.13	0.73	0.64	0.70
Bulgaria	1.46 (2)	1.27 (2)	—	0.63	0.66
Czechosl.	1.14 (6)	0.95 (6)	—	0.64	0.71
E. Germany	1.21 (5)	1.03 (5)	0.90	—	0.71
Hungary	1.40 (3)	1.24 (3)	—	0.68	0.71
Poland	1.30 (4)	1.17 (4)	0.69	0.64	0.75
Romania	1.62 (1)	1.38 (1)	1.13	0.65	0.68

Sources: All CMEA — Table 1. All other derived from M-V, Tables A-7 to A-12, A26-31.

Numbers in parentheses represent the rankings of price ratios from the most favorable (1) to least favorable (6).

The Note to Table 1 applies to this table also.

Relative foreign trade prices for 1972 are disaggregated by country in Table 2. The differences in prices between countries are much less than the differences between per capita subsidies suggesting that differential quantities, rather than prices, were the major means of implementing the subsidies in this period. This inference is fortified by the fact that, by simple unweighted ranking, the two lowest per capita subsidy recipients, Romania and Bulgaria, receive the most favorable price treatment.[6]

Implementing the subsidies by changing quantities would have involved very substantial changes in patterns of trade. To have increased the subsidies with Romania, the Soviet Union would have had to import rather than export large amounts of machinery and would also probably have had to import much larger amounts of industrial consumer goods than it already did. It would also probably have had to export to Romania large amounts of fuel and raw materials, which exports were in this period very slight. With the GDR, the Soviet Union would have had to stop importing machinery, etc., and also stop exporting fuels and raw materials.

Would these have been reasonable or even feasible adjustments for nations which are all, in effect, in a customs union, with much higher relative levels of intra-trade than would be found under any other institutional arrangement that now exists in the world? It seems highly unlikely. Changing trade to implement such a subsidy pattern would have involved enormous trade distortions. Since intrabloc trade is relatively very large and since a large part of that trade carries implicit subsidies, the whole basis of the profitability of Bloc trade with the USSR would have been jeopardized. The cost to the Soviet Union, especially, from the distortions in trade that would result from a lack of correspondence of what appear to be natural trade patterns with the desired pattern of subsidies would be far greater than the costs represented by the so-called subsidies themselves and might well be viewed as prohibitive.

Looking at the subsidy hypothesis from this standpoint suggests that if it is valid, then it must be viewed as an extraordinary coincidence that the profitable patterns of Soviet-CMEA trade were such that raising the CMEA prices of machinery, etc., above world prices and lowering below world prices the CMEA prices of fuels and raw materials resulted in an appropriate pattern of implicit subsidies. The more likely explanation is, in my opinion, that the transfers are not subsidies but represent profits and losses generated implicitly by trading in an autarkic, trade-diverting customs union.

Third, and related to the two preceding points, it seems quite clear that even in the pre-1973 period, the pattern of implicit subsidies to the CMEA nations did not fully conform to the non-market benefits received by the USSR (as viewed by M-V) as indicated in Table 3. The major deviation was in the case of Bulgaria which ranked third highest after the GDR and Czechoslovakia (M-V, p. 85) in rendering non-market services and nevertheless was taxed (received *negative* subsidies) by the USSR from 1960 until 1972, except for 1970. It was not until the "unplanned" subsidies began in 1973 that Bulgaria began to benefit along the lines envisaged by M-V and then it received huge subsidies. M-V mention the fact that Bulgaria subsidized the USSR in all but one year between 1960 and 1972 but provide no explanation of this "dramatic" exception to their model. "Dramatic" because Bulgaria's per capita taxes exceeded the subsidies to every nation but the GDR.[7]

Table 3. Soviet Implicit Trade
Subsidies to CMEA Six

Total subsidies in constant 1970 dollars (millions)	1960-64	1965-69
Bulgaria	-438.9	-415.8
Czechoslovakia	268.8	673.4
East Germany	994.4	1497.4
Hungary	243.2	375.8
Poland	133.3	428.7
Romania	-239.6	-114.2
TOTAL	961.1	2445.3
Per capita average annual subsidies (1970 dollars)	1960-64	1965-69
Bulgaria	- 10.3	- 9.8
Czechoslovakia	3.8	11.7
East Germany	11.7	17.6
Hungary	4.9	7.5
Poland	0.8	2.6
Romania	- 2.4	- 1.1
TOTAL	1.9	4.7

Sources: M-V: Totals — Table 5, p. 48. Per capita — Table 7, p. 50.

Romania was also taxed, rather than subsidized, throughout the 1960s. M-V's explanation is that taxes and subsidies between the USSR and Romania were inconsequential ". . . because we are convinced that unconventional gains from trade do not characterize Soviet trade relations with Romania . . ." (p. 69). It would be hard not to agree with M-V that Romania was and is the least cooperative member of the Warsaw Treaty Organization. Nevertheless, it is unfair of M-V to say that Romania was of no political or ideological value to the USSR. Just by remaining a member of CMEA and the WTO, by supporting the USSR in the UN, and so forth, it did cooperate and should have been eligible for some subsidy, if much less than that received by other CMEA members. At the very least, one would not expect it to be taxed by a per capita magnitude almost equal to the subsidies received by Poland (see Table 3).

We must conclude that if an implicit subsidy policy were implemented in intraCMEA trade either by the USSR or bilaterally negotiated by the USSR and each CMEA partner, then one would expect that somehow subsidies to these two nations rather than taxes would have been implemented early on. On the other hand, taxes from, rather than subsidies to, Bulgaria and Romania are easily understandable in terms of customs union effects. In the 1960s, at least, Bulgaria and Romania, like the USSR, had greater advantages as raw material producers and lesser advantages as producers of machinery and manufactured products than the other CMEA nations. Therefore they, like the USSR, stood to lose (relatively) rather than gain by trading within the Bloc rather than with the West. In fact, as the M-V data show, they even stood to lose by the M-V criterion, in trade with the USSR. In terms of the reverse subsidy flow argument made earlier in this section, Bulgaria and Romania were nations in which reverse subsidy flows to the USSR exceeded the conventional subsidy flows from the USSR.

III. Subsidies vs. Customs Union Effects: A Test

As noted, the M-V approach is to examine the terms of trade of the USSR with other CEMA nations and in comparison with terms of trade with the rest of the world. This is analogous with Mendershausen's procedure in documenting alleged Soviet exploitation of the other CMEA nations. It was possible to test Mendershausen's allegation by performing, with Bulgarian and Polish trade data, the same operations that he performed with Soviet data. In effect, Bulgarian and Polish data appeared to show Bulgarian and Polish exploitation of all other CMEA nations including the USSR, thereby refuting Mendershausen's hypothesis that Soviet political and economic power had led to exploitation of other CMEA.

An analogous test would seem in order in the M-V subsidy case. Let us suppose that M-V are correct and that the same procedures are applied to, say, Polish data as M-V applied to Soviet data. What would the results show? Presumably, Polish trade with the USSR would reflect, as gains to Poland, the same subsidies that analysis of Soviet data revealed. What about Poland's trade with the other CMEA nations? Presumably, Poland's terms of trade with other-CMEA would show no subsidies at all. Price in intrabloc trade relative to prices in trade with the West (as in Tables 1 and 2), should be approximately equal for all commodity groups. This is because the differential terms of trade for different commodity groups are ascribable in the M-V model exclusively to Soviet purchases of non-market, non-economic benefits from other CMEA. So, for example, in a Table 1 based on Polish data, the terms of trade for machinery, etc., with non-Soviet CMEA would not be above the average of all traded goods nor would the terms of trade for fuel and raw materials be below the average.

Let us suppose now that custom union effects are responsible for the pricing patterns shown in Table 1. In this event, each CMEA nation's trade data would show positive or negative gross "subsidies" with almost every other CMEA nation. The net incidence of "subsidies," positive or negative, would depend on which products, and how much of each, each nation exported or imported. Net exporters of fuels, raw materials, etc., would be subsidy-givers; net exporters of machinery, equipment, and manufactured products would be subsidy-receivers. The "subsidies" would not be subsidies, however, but simply the "opportunity" gains or losses of the different nations which result from trading in a relatively autarkic customs union with different scarcity relationships and relative prices than in world markets, rather than trading with the West.

If this scenario turns out to be correct, and ten transferable rubles says that it is, then the M-V hypothesis would be wrong unless M-V can adduce convincing explanations of the many additional positive or negative transfer relationships that result. I would hazard a guess that, in the 1960s at least, Bulgaria and Romania, who were net subsidy-givers to the USSR, were also subsidy-givers to other CMEA along with the USSR.[8]

IV. Final Remarks

Having been a student of intraCMEA relations since the late 1950s, I find the subsidy interpretation harder to accept than those who arrived on the scene in more recent years. As the Mendershausen exploitation hypothesis lost currency, it quickly came to be realized that the Soviet Union's terms of trade with CMEA were not very favorable. News reports from CMEA meetings often highlighted the Soviet Union's dissatisfaction with the terms of trade, particularly with the low prices it was receiving for its fuels and other raw materials. In fact, in the mid-sixties, it was reported that as *quid pro quo* for these low prices, the major importers of these products agreed (had to agree?) to help finance Soviet investment in the extractive industries (Kaser, p. 185). The negative Soviet feelings toward intraCMEA prices, as expressed on these matters, do not seem to fit into a scenario in which subsidies are being voluntarily offered for services performed. This seems especially the case in light of the fact that in the first half of the 1960s, the annual transfers amounted only to around $600 million in 1980 prices and in the second half, to just about double that amount. Moreover, if these were voluntary subsidies for services performed, it certainly would have been within the USSR's power to have reduced them.

On the other hand, such complaints are more consonant with the spirit of a nation railing against the fate of having to trade, largely for political reasons, with a group of nations with which the terms of trade are, as a result of economic conditions, relatively unfavorable. Differential relative prices exist all over the world because of differences in factor proportions and the absence of enough free trade or factor flows to equalize prices. To the extent that trade is restricted, these differentials are even less likely to be reduced. CMEA represents the most restrictive, autarkic trading group in recent history and it would be very surprising if its relative prices were equalized with those of the rest of the world.

After 1973, the sharp increase in transfers, whether subsidies or losses from a customs union effect, take on the character of aid. Clearly, Soviet losses had become so extreme that pricing arrangements were fairly quickly changed with the purpose of restoring, in part, the pre-1973 status quo. That the restoration was gradual rather than immediate suggests that this was to reduce the negative impact of higher fuel and raw material costs on Eastern European economies; that Soviet loans to Eastern Europe accompanied the 1979 oil price increases strengthens this interpretation.

To conclude, there is a difference of opinion about whether the CMEA/West price differentials, especially before 1973, are due to Soviet "subsidies" or to customs union effects. Therefore, it behooves M-V, or someone else, to put the question to test by seeing whether or not implicit subsidies show up in non-Soviet intraCMEA trade before 1973.

Notes

1. Some of these CMEA problems are discussed by Köves (1983).
2. At one point (p. 78), M-V concede that the new pricing formula was designed to shield the CMEA nations from the ". . . oil and raw materials price shock. . . ."
3. Anyone who has traveled in the Soviet Union or Eastern Europe is aware of how different relative prices are from those in the industrialized west, especially the United States.
4. This general approach has also been used by Brada (1985) and Desai (1985) to criticize M-V although the routes by which the analyses are developed are somewhat different from those presented here.
5. I use a pre-1974 period here because of the admittedly unplanned nature of the price changes after the 1973 oil crisis.
6. There is a high probability, of course, that the difference among price ratios in Table 2 reflect, simply, differences among the nations in the product-mixes in the various categories traded and is therefore purely coincidental.

7. M-V's only statement in explanation is: "... it is apparent that the Soviet-Bulgarian relationship is more complicated ... because both the Bulgarian government and the Bulgarian people seem to approve of the Soviet Union's dominance of CMEA and the WP. At first glance, this would suggest that the Soviet Union had no need to subsidize Bulgaria. ..." (p. 82). M-V provide no "second glances" except to note that large Soviet subsidies to Bulgaria developed beginning in 1973. In effect, M-V hint that the size of a subsidy may vary not only directly with the amount of political-ideological-etc. support rendered but may vary inversely with the spirit in which the support is offered. By this type of reasoning, one would expect Romania's subsidy to be relatively large.

8. After this was originally drafted, I became aware of Brada's statement (1985) that the Romanians were "subsidizing other bloc members and it was these adverse terms of trade that led them to shift some of their trade away from CMEA and toward the West." Apparently the basis of this statement is impressionistic and not the result of careful study.

References

Brada, Josef C., "Soviet Subsidization of Eastern Europe: The Primacy of Economics Over Politics?" *Journal of Comparative Economics*, March 1985.

Desai, Padma, "Is the Soviet Union Subsidizing Eastern Europe?" *European Economic Review*, 29 (1985).

Hewett, Edward A., "A Gravity Model of CMEA Trade," in *Quantitative and Analytical Studies in East-West Relations*, ed. by Josef C. Brada, Bloomington, Ind., 1976.

Holzman, Franklyn D., "Comecon: A 'Trade Destroying' Customs Union?" *Journal of Comparative Economics*, December 1985.

Holzman, Franklyn D., "Soviet Foreign Trade Pricing and the Question of Discrimination: A Customs Union Approach," *Review of Economics and Statistics*, May 1962.

Holzman, Franklyn D., "More on Soviet Bloc Trade Discrimination," *Soviet Studies*, July 1965, pp. 44–65.

Kaser, Michael, *Comecon*. London: Oxford University Press, 1967 (2nd ed.).

Köves, A., "'Implicit Subsidies' and Some Issues of Economic Relations Within the CMEA," *Acta Oeconomica*, vol. 31 (1–2), 1983.

Liubimov, N. N. (ed.), *Mezhdunarodnye Economicheskie Otnosheniia*, Moscow 1957.

Marer, Paul, "The Political Economy of Soviet Relations with Eastern Europe," in *Soviet Policy in Eastern Europe*, ed. by Sarah Terry. New Haven: Yale University Press, 1984.

Marrese, Michael and Jan Vanous, *Soviet Subsidization of Trade with Eastern Europe*. Berkeley: University of California Institute of International Studies, 1983.

Mendershausen, Horst, "Terms of Trade Between the Soviet Union and Smaller Communist Countries," *Review of Economics and Statistics*, May 1959, pp. 106–118.

Mendershausen, Horst, "The Terms of Soviet Satellite Trade," *Review of Economics and Statistics*, May 1960, pp. 152–163.

United Nations, *World Economic Survey, 1958*, Geneva 1959.

Vneshniaia torgovlia SSSR (Foreign Trade of the USSR), annual statistical handbook.

11
Further Thoughts on the Significance of Soviet Subsidies to Eastern Europe

"Hard" and "Soft" Goods Balancing and Customs Union Effects

In the course of a discussion with Ed Hewett, I became aware that my article "The Significance of Soviet Studies to Eastern Europe" (1986) neglected to allow for the well-known fact that the Eastern European nations tend not only to bilaterally balance overall trade with one another but to also bilaterally balance trade in *hard* goods and *soft* goods, respectively. Hard goods are those with lower prices in CMEA nations than in the West; they can be sold easily for hard currency. Petroleum is an example. Soft goods tend to have higher prices (and poorer quality) than similar products made in the West and are not easily marketed in Europe, the United States, or Japan—for example, advanced machinery. The function of separate balancing for hard and soft goods rather than aggregate balancing is to reduce or eliminate the gains and losses from implicit subsidies of the sort that result from Soviet-CMEA trade. This was Hewett's point.[1]

In the article I theorized that the Soviet subsidies were due to customs union effects and were not payments by the USSR for military and political cooperation, so-called noneconomic services, as Marrese and Vanous (M-V) (1983) argued. I predicted that such customs union effects that, in my opinion, caused Soviet–Eastern European trade prices to differ from world prices would do the same to intra–Eastern European trade prices and would lead to apparent "subsidies" by some eastern nations to others. If true, this would be strong evidence against the M-V hypothesis. However, the existence of hard and soft goods balancing

Reprinted, with changes, from *Comparative Economic Studies* 28 (Fall 1986): 59–63, by permission of the publisher.

obviously reduces the extent of such subsidies, and a different test is needed to distinguish between the two hypotheses. That test is to examine directly intra–Eastern European prices of hard and soft goods to see if the former are below, and the latter above, world prices as they are in Soviet–Eastern European trade. If yes, the customs union explanation is validated; if no, the M-V explanation is correct.

In fact, the existence per se of hard and soft goods balancing in Eastern European trade is evidence in support of the customs union effect as the cause of subsidies. Balancing by commodity groups substantially reduces the gains from intrabloc trade by *reducing* and distorting trade flows relative to what they would have been if intra-CMEA and world prices were equalized. If differential prices were due, as Marrese and Vanous argued, to Soviet payments for noneconomic services, certainly such differentials would not be necessary, nor would they be tolerated, in Eastern European trade. On the other hand, if world prices do not reflect the relative values of goods in Eastern Europe, then one would expect these nations to conduct trade with one another at their own, rather than at world, prices even though this happens to involve commodity group balancing with all its disadvantages, including *reduction* of intra-CMEA trade.

When commodity group balancing is analyzed in terms of customs union theory, balancing may be interpreted either as a limit to "trade diversion" or as an example of "trade destruction." Let me explain. Typically, the nations forming customs unions experience trade creation (an increase in trade at the expense of domestic production—involving gains) and/or trade diversion (the diversion of trade away from lower cost nonunion nations to higher cost union members—involving losses to importing member nations). CMEA nations have also experienced trade destruction, defined as a situation in which union members produce, at such a high cost, commodities that had formerly been imported from nonmembers that the importer ceases trade in that product—i.e., trade is destroyed (Holzman, 1985). This would be the correct interpretation of commodity balancing if the intra-CMEA trade destroyed by commodity balancing were not recreated in East-West trade. If, on the other hand, hard goods not sold to, and soft goods not purchased from, other CMEA nations are sold to or bought from the West, the commodity balancing could be viewed as a limit to the possibilities of trade diversion imposed by its high costs.

To complete the argument that hard and soft goods balancing by Eastern European nations is evidence of the customs union effect, it is necessary to explain, without invoking M-V subsidies, why the Soviet Union does not balance trade in hard and soft goods categories to avoid making transfers to Eastern Europe.[2] My view is that the losses experienced by the USSR simply represent trade diversion plus its export equivalent.[3] These losses happen to be fairly large because the decision to form a preferential trading group was primarily politically, not economically, motivated. If the Soviets had balanced trade by commodity groups to cut their losses, trade with Eastern Europe would certainly have shrunk well below actual levels. However, such a result would have been counter to the long-term avowed Soviet economic and political policies of trying to increase the integration of CMEA, particularly of the Eastern European nations with itself. Under these circumstances, the transfers—i.e., Soviet losses from trade diversion—would be viewed as a general cost of Soviet international economic and political policies and not as a technique to dispense differential subsidies to Eastern European nations as quid pro quo for noneconomic services rendered. Instead, as I argued in my earlier article (Holzman, 1986), the differentials have resulted from factors related to the comparative advantages of the different CMEA nations and to the relative prices of different products in the East and West, respectively (as is the case whenever customs unions are formed).

Saudi Arabia, as the leading member of OPEC, plays an analogous role to that of the USSR in CMEA, although in a cartel rather than a customs union framework. The Saudis bear the financial burden of trying to maintain the profitability of the cartel. The gains to the other members of the cartel are distributed differentially, *not by Saudi design* but by other factors, the most important of which is probably the members' differential levels of exportable output. The U.S. Marshall Plan was another instance in which the lead nation bore some of the economic costs of supporting its political allies. However, in contrast with CMEA and OPEC, sizes of the subsidies to the different Marshall Plan nations were largely determined by the United States, although not without constraints.

It is important to note that although the Soviets have at times complained about their intra-CMEA terms of trade, the costs of the transfers to them were relatively small and easy to bear before 1973, averaging less than $200 million a year in 1960–1964, less than $500 million in 1965–1969, and $870 million in 1970–1972 (Marrese and Vanous, p. 43). This was undoubtedly due to the very small trade participation ratio of the USSR in those periods. The post-1973 period is, of course, an entirely different story, and the transfers take on a quite different character and magnitude (Holzman, 1986).

Another Test of the Two Hypotheses

Another way to test which theory—the "subsidy" or the "customs union" effects—is the better explanation of the price phenomena measured by Marrese and Vanous would be to bypass the relationships between

Table 1
Bulgarian and Polish Exports to and Imports from the USSR at Ratios of
Average Bloc Prices to Actual Prices

	Prices					
	Exports (bloc/actual)			Imports (actual/bloc)		
	1958	1959	1960	1958	1959	1960
Bulgaria	107*	100*	—	101	103	—
Poland	—	101.9	101.6	—	101.8	106.3

*These figures exclude Bulgarian exports of tobacco to the USSR. The figures
including tobacco read 122 and 123, respectively. Tobacco was excluded because
of very convincing evidence, presented in Holzman (1962), that the USSR has
always (at least since 1939) imported very low quality tobacco from Bulgaria.
Also, there is evidence that because the USSR is such a large importer of this
tobacco, the low price paid may also reflect quantity discounts.

A final note: The usefulness of this test is reduced by the fact that the data
include very few machinery and industrial consumers-goods items for lack of
homogeneity of these products.

East-West and intrabloc prices and concentrate on the latter, because
they are the prices that, presumably, are distorted by the subsidies. The
argument in terms of intrabloc prices, per se, is as follows.

If the Soviet Union is subsidizing the bloc, as argued by Marrese
and Vanous, then the Soviets will have been exporting (say) oil at low
prices and importing (say) machinery at high prices from Eastern Europe.
However, the export and import prices of these products between other
Eastern European nations should not reflect these subsidies and should
therefore differ from Soviet–Eastern European trade prices. If, on the
other hand, the customs union effect is responsible for Marrese and
Vanous's results, Soviet–Eastern European prices for different products
should be roughly similar to intra–Eastern European prices for those
same products.

Some calculations made many years ago (Holzman, 1962, 1965)
using Bulgarian trade data for 1958–1959 and Polish data for 1959–
1960 can be used for the purpose just described. These calculations
compare, in the aggregate, the actual prices at which Bulgaria and Poland
exported to and imported from the USSR with the average prices of
those products in intrabloc trade, including trade with the USSR.[4] The
results are presented in Table 1.

The figures presented in Table 1 show that Bulgaria would have
gained 7 percent in 1958 but nothing in 1959, and Poland would have
gained 1.9 percent in 1959 and 1.6 percent in 1960, from having

exported to the USSR at all bloc prices. The comparable unrealized gains from having imported from the USSR at all bloc prices would have been, for Bulgaria, 1 and 3 percent, and for Poland, 1.8 and 6.3 percent. Two comments are in order. First, these figures represent losses, not gains (subsidies), from trading with the USSR rather than with Eastern Europe. Second, and more important, the losses are small, and it would appear that prices in trade with the USSR are not very much different from intra–Eastern European trade prices. In fact, the deviations from equality (100) are so small that they probably represent nothing more than differences in quality, product-mix, and other such "noise."

* * *

To conclude, the above figures support the customs union rather than the subsidy explanation. However, they are no substitute for new studies involving larger samples and data from more recent years than were available to me.

Notes

1. It should be borne in mind that the bilateral balancing of manufactures implies the existence of a subsidy from the country with a smaller quality discount on its exports to the West in favor of the country with a larger quality discount.

2. Even if my explanation is not convincing, the M-V subsidy explanation would not be valid if it turns out, as I predicted, that intra–Eastern European trade prices and Soviet–Eastern European trade prices differ in similar ways from Soviet-West trade prices.

3. Among market economies, losses from trade diversion are only experienced by importers because the constraints on trade are imposed almost exclusively by the levy of tariffs or quotas on imports. No comparable constraints are applied to exports. In fact, customs unions exporters benefit from having trade diverted toward them. In the CPE equivalent of a customs union, there are not only implicit import quotas that divert imports away from lower cost nonmember sources toward members, there can also be implicit constraints that force exporters to divert products away from more profitable nonmember markets and toward members. To the extent that this imposes losses on the exporters, they are equivalent to importer losses from trade diversion. In CMEA, the USSR loses both from having to import machinery from CMEA at high prices and from having to sell so much in the way of raw materials to CMEA at below world prices. Eastern Europe now reduces these losses by commodity balancing.

4. It would have been better to have calculated average bloc prices without Soviet trade. Unfortunately, most of my files were lost in an office fire in 1970, and recalculations are no longer possible.

References

Holzman, Franklyn D. "Soviet Foreign Trade Pricing and the Question of Discrimination: A Customs Union Approach." *Review of Economics and Statistics* 44(2) (May 1962): 134–147.

———. "More on Soviet Bloc Trade Discrimination." *Soviet Studies* 17(1) (July 1965): 44–65.

———. "Comecon: A Trade-Destroying Customs Union?" *Journal of Comparative Economics* 9 (December 1985): 410–423.

———. "The Significance of Soviet Subsidies to Eastern Europe." *Comparative Economic Studies* 28(1) (Spring 1986): 54–65.

Marrese, Michael, and Jan Vanous. *Soviet Subsidization of Trade with Eastern Europe*. Berkeley: University of California Institute of International Studies, 1983.

Index